MARXISM AND THE THEORY OF PRAXIS

Marxism and the Theory of Praxis

of Praxis

A critique of some new versions
of old fallacies

by

John Hoffman

INTERNATIONAL PUBLISHERS

NEW YORK

Library of Congress Cataloging in Publication Data

Hoffman, John, 1944-
  Marxism and the theory of praxis.

  Includes index.
  . Dialectical materialism.   2. Marx, Karl, 1818-
1883.   I. Title.
B809.8.H564   1975   335.4'11   75-7186
ISBN 0-7178-0428-3
ISBN 0-7178-0472-0 (paperback)

CONTENTS

1

THE PROMISE OF PRAXIS—AN END TO POSITIVISM?

(i) *"Non-Practical Thinking" in Contemporary Positivism*

Theory and practice: the two must unite! This cry of protest is to be heard everywhere today by those who find their interest in philosophy and society sabotaged and sidetracked by the scholasticism and "academicism" of much of official philosophical thought and by many of the attitudes and postures adopted in the social sciences.

Some even regard the term "science" as a dirty word, for "science" today is often taken to mean theory without practice, facts without values, technical knowledge without human consideration. Science, we are told, can only be concerned with "means": what actually happens to knowledge is somebody else's concern. Indeed so extreme has this "agnosticism" become, that Marx's famous dictum has been explicitly turned on to its head so that one social scientist has written that "the function of science is to understand and interpret the world, not to change it".[1] It is scarcely surprising, then, that much academic social science seems pointless and trivial—a body of work more concerned with methodological technique than with serious social criticism.

A leading U.S. sociologist once described his "conceptual framework" as "non-practical theory" and, ironically, he had a point: for learned works on "pure theory" are unlikely to assist in solving social problems, while the professional desire to be "value-free" often means in practice robbing work of its *value* for society. The attempt to keep value judgments out of social science is simply a back-handed way of supporting the *status quo*.

Fewer and fewer people today take seriously the claim that it is possible to be "impartial" (i.e. *indifferent*) towards the class-divided society in which we live. Indeed, it was precisely this cloak of "neutrality" which thousands of natural and social scientists in the U.S. used to try to conceal their complicity in the slaughter, bombing and defoliation which the Americans and their South Vietnamese puppets practised in Vietnam. Radicals like Noam Chomsky have courageously

[1] Heinz Eulau, *The Behavioral Persuasion in Politics* (New York, 1963), p. 9.

exposed this ideological fraud, and it is significant that it was a former "behavioural scientist", Daniel Ellsberg, who lifted the curtain on some of the lies and fabrications which have served U.S. foreign policy in the name of "science". Nor is it only in the United States that sham "impartiality" has played a reactionary role. In Britain, for example, it has become fashionable to preach racism in "scientific" quarters, as in the case of Hans Eysenck, a well-known psychologist who purports to prove that black people and the Irish are intellectually inferior to Anglo-Saxon whites.[2] Of course, Professor Eysenck insists that his "discoveries" are value-free, and are, as a matter of fact, a source of personal regret to him. But the idea that it is possible for scientific theory to be value-free and above the world of practice, should fool nobody, and it certainly did not fool the students at the University of Leeds who demanded recently that the authorities withdraw the honorary doctorate which they had offered to an American professor, because of the professor's "scientific" arguments that people of low IQ should be voluntarily sterilised. Of course, Professor Shockley protested that his theories were only intended as a "thinking exercise": they were not intended to be put into practice. The students, however, saw through the nonsense of "a theory without practice" and as a result of their pressure, the honour was withdrawn. Not of course without provoking a storm of protest from the "value-free" philosophers who argued, like Antony Flew, that to "confuse" genetic theories about intelligence with racism was a serious "muddle", the result of an inability to separate out value from fact![3]

What is this philosophy then, which purports to separate theory and practice, fact and value, in this drastic and self-defeating way? Although it appears with many labels and in a variety of forms, we can describe it broadly speaking, as positivism.

I will have a good deal more to say about this doctrine of positivism later (and particularly in Chapter 9), but for the moment it is worth stressing the following features. Positivism as a philosophical approach begins with the essentially correct and scientific premise that things in the external world are knowable to us only through *observation*. The problem arises, however, what do we mean by observation? And it is here that positivism, as a way of understanding the world, ceases to be "positive" and goes completely off the rails; for the positivists treat observation as though it was an essentially *passive* process, an act of

---

[2] See, as a recent example of his position, his remarkable letter in *New Statesman*, 27.4.1973.
[3] *Times Higher Educational Supplement*, 4.5.1973.

merely "contemplating" the world rather than one of actually finding out. As a result, the errors flow thick and fast.

(i) The act of knowing things, seen as a process which is passive and contemplative, becomes hopelessly mixed up with the objects about which we want to find out. The term "sense data", which the positivist uses to describe his discoveries, smudges together the activity of our cognitive senses and the object world which these senses reflect.

(ii) Because of this confusion, the distinction between things as they *appear* (the impressions made upon our senses from the world around us) and things as they *really* are (the objective world itself) dissolves into thin air, and we are left pondering the absurd and anti-materialist conclusion (to which all positivism is driven) that the objective world outside our senses is an unknowable thing-in-itself, which may not even exist.

(iii) Taken to its logical conclusion, this attitude would make all science and scientific judgment a practical impossibility, for positivism leaves us uncertain as to whether the "causes" and "laws of development" which make reality intelligible to us, do in fact exist. Since everything ultimately rests with each observer's private world of "sense data" (which the positivist misleadingly considers the "facts"), nobody can really say what is true or false or right or wrong about the world outside. "There is nothing good or bad but thinking makes it so."

(iv) Predictably an extremely contemptuous attitude towards people and society follows on. After all, if we cannot condemn or praise what is happening around us since these critical activities involve us making forbidden "value judgments", we will inevitably look upon the world with a cynical disdain, for even people themselves are the mere "sense data" of our own making. Flaubert, the French novelist of the nineteenth century, expressed the positivist creed to perfection, when he declared that "one must regard people in the same way that one regards mastadons or crocodiles. Can one possibly get worked up over the horns of the former or the jaws of the latter? Display them, stuff them, pickle them in spirits—that is all. But do not pass moral judgments on them." For that would mean admitting, of course, that outside of one's own "observing ego" there was an objective material world.

(v) It is clear, then, that the consequence of this form of scepticism is the destruction of science and reason. For in the last analysis, positivism leaves us simply to "manufacture" our own "reality" as we please; and anyone who wants to pass moral judgments, should turn to his priest or witch-doctor for help.

It is scarcely surprising that a philosophy which in the work of David Hume (1711–1776) began with "raising doubts", has ended up in well nigh total paralysis, and instead of getting to grips with practical problems (as Hume intended), positivism has increasingly withdrawn itself from the real world and become absorbed in rather trivial problems, often linguistic or semantic, of its own making. As Maurice Cornforth pointed out just after the war, positivism "concentrates within itself all the most negative features of bourgeois philosophy" and "at the same time it carries to the furthest pitch the narrow specialisation of philosophy, scholastic phrasemongering and barren abstraction".[4] The critique was also taken up by Barrows Dunham in a very fine book, Man Against Myth, in which he ridiculed the cowardice and triviality of philosophical empiricism, describing its "profound" propositions that "thinking makes it so", "all problems are merely verbal", etc., as nothing more than a "source of paralysis", "a frightened and self-defeated theory" which led straight to solipsism, that infantile belief that the world exists only in the individual's mind.[5] It is most revealing that even philosophers like Bertrand Russell (or for that matter Karl Popper) who defend empiricism, have become alarmed at the escalating subjectivism which this sceptical creed has unleashed, while Enst Gellner in a useful critique of "linguistic philosophy"—avant garde positivism—has commented acidly:

> It is the story of Plato over again—only this time it is the philosopher's job to lead us back into the cave.[6]

It is true of course that these currents of "arid mysticism", as Russell calls them, are by no means unrelated to the general uncertainty and insecurity of the post-war world, for the only response which some philosophers have to the growing social chaos, rising unemployment, runaway inflation and international currency crises in the West is to scuttle into an analytical world of their own and firmly bury their heads in the sand. But by no means all philosophers are prepared to retreat in this way and there is an increasing recognition that

---

[4] In Defence of Philosophy (Lawrence and Wishart, 1950), pp. xiii–xiv.
[5] Man Against Myth (Boston, 1947), p. 240; p. 255.
[6] Words and Things (Pelican, 1968), p. 117.

positivism, whatever its guise, has become bankrupt and has nothing more to offer. This is how a newly formed "Radical Philosophy Group" sees the situation:

> Contemporary British philosophy is at a dead end. . . . Its academic practitioners have all but abandoned the attempt to understand the world, let alone change it. They have made philosophy into a narrow and specialised subject of little relevance to anyone outside the small circle of professional philosophers.[7]

A philosophy which considers itself to be "pure theory" is no use to anyone, and the Group pledges itself to break down the barriers between philosophy and the social sciences, students and teachers, and the institutions of higher education and the rest of society. Philosophy must be transformed into an instrument of practical social change.

Now this critical reaction against the post-war "retreat" with its mole-like empiricism and warren of scholastic rabbit-holes is welcome indeed, for it promises to tackle a problem which goes right back to the origins of philosophy and the division of society into mutually antagonistic classes. As Marx and Engels write in *The German Ideology*,

> division of labour only becomes truly such from the moment when a division of material and mental labour appears. From this moment onwards consciousness *can* really flatter itself that it is something other than consciousness of existing practice, that it *really* represents something without representing something real.[8] (stress in original).

In other words, the sharp division between theory and practice, which contemporary positivists take to absurd extremes, reflects a division, at a much more basic level, between mental and manual labour and this division lies at the heart of every exploiting society. To question abstract philosophy, a pure theory which flatters itself that it is something other than the consciousness of existing practice, is to throw into doubt the very structure of class society itself. And there is certainly plenty of evidence to show that the development of abstract philosophy ("above" the mundane world of practice) was itself the product of the division of society into warring classes.

Take Plato's *Republic*, for example. Here we are presented in the "preliminaries" with the picture of a kind of natural community (Glaucon rudely calls it "a community of pigs") where there are no slaves, no wars, no luxuries, and limited trade, and most revealingly of

---

[7] *Radical Philosophy*, Summer 1972: inside cover.
[8] *The German Ideology* (Moscow, 1964), p. 43.

all, no philosophers. Plato explains why. In a society without serious defects and deep divisions, a society where everybody leads "a peaceful and healthy life",[9] no philosophical "healing" is called for to put things right. But what happens with the onset of "civilisation" (i.e. an exploiting society)? Passions run riot, sensuality threatens "reason", war breaks out, and civil disorder is inevitable. The world of social practice seems to dissolve (when viewed from the standpoint of the landed aristocrat) into mere "chaos", a realm of shifting, bewildering "appearances", which the philosopher must somehow mystically transcend if he is to discover Order, Truth and the Good Life. A "higher" world of divine-like abstractions where there is no change. Of course the "good life" turns out to be an unrealisable utopia, for the real causes of "chaos", "excess" and bewildering "appearances" remain intact, and the irreconcilability between philosophical principles and practical change reveals itself not simply as a theoretical problem, but as a problem rooted in the character of social exploitation itself. The metaphysical nonsense of a "pure theory" is a sure sign that society is divided into those who "think" and those who work—an exploitative relation which creates antagonisms which are essentially irreconcilable.[10] No wonder, at the philosophical level, that theory and practice are thought to inhabit separate worlds.

It is of course perfectly true that some of the ancient Greek philosophers were materialists in that they accepted that a real world existed outside the mind, but like Plato, they came unstuck on the problem of trying to make the world of change, of "practice", theoretically intelligible. Atomism, for example, substituted for God the famous "brick of the universe", a kind of "primeval" unit, itself exempt from actual change. Theory still yearned for a world of timelessness. Even the theorists of the Renaissance, who accepted change as a fact of life and, like Machiavelli, despised those who justified practical idleness in the name of "contemplation", nevertheless professed to see beneath all the comings and goings "an order which remains ever the same".[11] One form of metaphysics was replaced by another, and the reason why even the greatest of the philosophers of the Renaissance and the later Enlightenment failed to resolve the divide

---

[9] *The Republic* (Penguin, 1955), p. 105.

[10] The same philosophical disdain for practice can be found in Aristotle, as for example in a passage in *Politics* where he puzzles over the problem of educating a "gentleman" to enjoy music without, at the same time, being degraded by the "manual labour" of playing a musical instrument.

[11] Machiavelli, *Discourses* (Pelican, 1970), I.II.

between theory and practice is not difficult to see: for all of them, whether we think of Bacon or Hobbes, Hume or Kant, took it for granted that society would be divided into warring classes—that *fundamental* change, a transformation of the exploitative basis of "civilisation" itself, could not come about. They either accepted empiricism—that truth is simply relative to the way we order the "appearances" of the world as they impress themselves upon our minds—or they resorted to a "higher metaphysics" which furnished absolute truths in a realm "above experience". Rousseau, for example, bitterly castigated the "celebrated philosophers" for their futile relativism, but was forced to "scan the heavens" for the principles of Justice and Equality so dear to his heart. Either reality was a figment of the imagination or it was an objective creation of God: but in neither cases could a *theory* of the universe be reconciled with the *practice* of historical change, the "only immutable thing"—*"mors immortalis"*.[12]

The present predicament of contemporary positivism, its inability to relate philosophical thought to the practical problems of society, has roots therefore which go right back to the origins of "civilisation" itself. No exploiting class can accept the view that the very foundation of society including human nature is *itself* in a continual process of change, and hence the philosophers who have consciously or unconsciously spoken on behalf of this class have invariably placed the world of Absolute Truth above history, so that what changes cannot really be true. What is and what ought to be, the world of facts and the world of values, theory on the one hand, and practice on the other, the absolute and the relative, each of these dichotomous pairs have been thought of as polar opposites, mutually exclusive and irreconcilably apart. As antagonistic to one another as the "doers" and "thinkers", the exploiters and exploited in the real world.

This means of course, if we accept and emphasise the "relativist" side of the equation, as positivism does, that we end up arguing, with Karl Popper, that history in itself has no real meaning and that, instead of the rational understanding of a real world, we have mere "hypotheses", interpretations, "conjectures". Instead of an objective truth, we are confined to the uncertain probabilities of the world of appearances. It is one thing to be open-minded; quite another to postulate in all seriousness that the real world does not, in fact, exist. How much worse is it then to put forward this credo of mere scepticism, as Popper does, in the sacred name of "rigorous science"!

For the problem is this. Although positivist philosophers talk a good

[12] Marx's words in the *Poverty of Philosophy* (Lawrence and Wishart, 1936), p. 93.

deal about basing knowledge in "experience", what they mean by experience is not activity in any real practical sense, but simply the "act" of passively observing a kaleidoscopic world of events with no logic or order of its own. This implies that we cannot really be sure whether the "patterns" we witness are actually real in themselves or merely "sense data" perspectives of our own mind; for the mind, as Locke puts it,

> in all its thoughts and reasonings, hath no other immediate object but its own ideas, which it alone does and can contemplate. . . .[13]

In other words, "experience", as construed by the positivists, does not enable us to actually get to grips with the real world, but in fact acts as a barrier beyond which the mind, entrapped in its own "thoughts and reasonings", cannot go. It is scarcely surprising therefore that this sort of "science" is quite compatible with any kind of mysticism we care to imagine, for if everything is an "empirical appearance", then how can truth and delusion be possibly separated out? As Frederick Engels pointed out in his witty (yet scathing) critique of empiricism in the *Dialectics of Nature*, even eminent natural scientists like Alfred Russell Wallace and William Crookes could believe in "spirits", on the deceptively plausible grounds that what was "physically verifiable" really did exist.[14] In an amusing passage, Engels describes, as an example of "scientific" mysticism, his encounter with a Mr. Spencer Hall in Manchester in 1843–44,

> a very mediocre charlatan, who travelled the country under the patronage of some parsons and undertook magnetico-phrenological performances with a young woman in order to prove thereby the existence of God, the immortality of the soul, and the incorrectness of the materialism that was being preached at that time by the Owenites in all big towns. The lady was sent into a magnetic sleep and then, as soon as the operator touched any part of the skull corresponding to one of Gall's organs,[15] she gave a bountiful display of theatrical, demonstrative gestures . . . right at the top of the skull he had discovered an organ of veneration, on touching which his hypnotic miss sank on to her knees, folded her hands in prayer, and depicted to the astonished, philistine audience an angel wrapt in veneration. That was the

---

[13] *Selections* (Everyman), p. xliii.

[14] See the fragment "Natural Science in the Spirit World", *Dialectics of Nature* (Moscow, 1964), pp. 51–62.

[15] Gall was an Austrian physician in the early 19th century who claimed that every mental faculty of man had an organ of its own, located in a specific section of the cerebrum.

climax and conclusion of the exhibition. The existence of God had been proved.[16]

Of course not all the attacks on materialism are as childish as the antics of Mr. Spencer Hall, nor are all the "charlatans" involved necessarily so "mediocre", but our central point remains. Positivism tries to restrict science to the world of "appearances" and thus leaves it vulnerable to fetishism of every kind. The truth of a phenomenon is only intelligible when we really *understand* it, when we can begin to explain it, relate it, dig out its causes, in short, reason about it. This is why Engels warned that

> we should hardly err in looking for the most extreme degree of fantasy, credulity, and superstition, not in that trend of natural science which, like the German philosophy of nature, tries to force the objective world into the framework of its subjective thought, but rather in the opposite trend, which, exalting mere experience, treats thought with sovereign disdain and really has gone to the furthest extreme in emptiness of thought.[17]

Positivism provides a philosophy which can readily be used to support any claim, allegedly based on "experience" and experiment, about "the power of mind over matter". More to the point nowadays, its "arid mysticism" likewise provides apparent respectability to "scientific discoveries" which preach racism and class rule in the name of varying "genetic endowments". At the top of the IQ scale are, it goes without saying, top civil servants, professors, research scientists—in Eysenck's version—and at the bottom, "labourers; gardeners; upholsterers; farm hands; factory packers and sorters; and miners".[18] It is the "phrenology" of Engels' Mr. Spencer Hall brought up to date. For located in the brain, in the reticular and cortex arousal system, lie those heredity traits which make us introverts or extroverts, neurotics and criminals, slaves or masters for the rest of our lives.[19] This *must* be true, for there are "experiments" with identical twins and statistical analyses of extensive IQ testing to show this is so: in Engels' time, there were batteries and magnetic needles to reveal the existence of otherworldly spirits—now there are doses of glutamic acid to be used on unfortunate children in order to explore the possibility of

[16] *Dialectics of Nature*, op. cit., p. 53.
[17] Ibid., p. 51.
[18] See Tony Agathangelou's article, "Some Strange 'Facts'", *Morning Star*, 11.12.1973.
[19] H. Eysenck, *The Inequality of Man*, Woodcock lecture, University of Leicester, 25.11.1971.

"conditioning" the immutable gene . . . and the basis of both forms of pernicious obscurantism? The same empiricist lie that reality is no more than an assortment of mutilated appearances: if people of different classes or "races" look different, behave differently, think differently, then this is somehow "empirical proof" that class and "race" can only be explained in physiological terms. The historical forces which make people what they are, which shape them and mould them, giving them a specific appearance at a specific point in time—these are simply ignored—and the momentary form is ossified into a timeless reality. No real change is possible: all that remains is for charlatans and mystics to carry out their fascist-type experiments in order to coerce the "defective" and the "aberrant" to "genetically adjust" to a capitalist status quo.

Positivism with its dogmas of socially irresponsible (allegedly "value-free") science, of a theory without practice, brings to an ugly head the age-old philosophical activity of trying to freeze historical development into timeless "verities", mental abstractions, which leave the world as it is. Sacrificing objective reality for its empirical fragments, positivism strikes viciously at the roots of reason, our ability to control the world around us, and defends instead a religion of passivity and helplessness in the name of "science": we are all victims of circumstance, genetic inheritance, accident, instinctual impulses which nobody can control, and the only bit of philosophy we have to guide us through life is to follow the will of those who know better.

Such is the present state of contemporary positivist thought. Such is the dismal cultural backcloth to what we can call

(ii) The Challenge of Praxis

What exactly is "praxis"? It is the Greek (and German) word for practice. And it is of course the world of social practice, movement and change that contemporary positivism shuns like the plague. In demanding that practice should be focused at the centre of our scientific concerns, the champions of praxis insist that we are a part of the world we study and cannot possibly be expected to theorise in some kind of detached, neutral manner. Where positivism preaches resignation and acceptance, praxis demands commitment and change: for conformity, it puts criticism, for passivity, it demands action, and hence instead of theorising in the abstract, it calls for concrete practice. It rejects therefore—in its manifesto of protest—all the self-defeating antitheses which are the hallmark of positivism, the supposed "gulf" between Ideal and real, concrete and abstract, fact and value, the world of is and the world of ought. Thinking is a *praxical* activity, it insists, and its role is not to contemplate the universe, but to transform it.

But why the substitution of a foreign word, *praxis*, for the English one? Because *praxis* is taken to mean a good deal more than "practice" in the everyday sense of the term. Listen to what Kenneth Megill has to say in his *New Democratic Theory* on this matter:

> praxis, unlike practice, is revolutionary in form. The man of praxis is revolutionary; the practical man takes the given social order as permanent. ... To learn from praxis is to develop a revolutionary doctrine which will enable one to understand the basic forces in history and the possibilities for developing a revolutionary movement so that men may gain control over their lives.[20]

Whereas positivist philosophers stress principles in the place of reality, the theorists of revolutionary praxis insist on the necessity of change. Gayo Petrovic, a leading Yugoslav philosopher and editor of the journal *Praxis*, declares that "man is society, freedom, history and the future",[21] a *creative* being who is neither the helpless plaything of external forces nor a slave to sinful appetites, but a being *who makes himself.* One whose human nature is actually created in the course of praxis: a being who is in a continual process of change.

Since a man does not contemplate the world but creates it, the abstract theories which he has are at the same time concrete truths: theory and practice, ideals and reality are inseparably *fused*. Where positivism postulates a sharp division, praxis forges a basic unity, so that man and nature, the individual and the universe are blended together as an integral whole. Human activity is *reciprocal* and it is, as a praxis writer in Britain recently put it,

> the *reciprocal* action of all aspects of human activity [which] reveals man as producing the conditions that produce him. Human ideas modify, through praxis, the very existential substratum of ideas themselves; history is the unfolding of man shaping his world.[22]

Theory, that is to say, must be grasped as a practical force and it is quite wrong to picture ideas as though they somehow existed in a world outside reality. Consciousness, Alfred Schmidt writes, always enters as an "active spirit into the reality reproduced by it", hence it must be remembered that *facts* are produced by men, they are the product, not

[20] New York, 1970, pp. 57–58.
[21] *Marx in the Mid-Twentieth Century* (New York, 1967), p. 23.
[22] J. Coulter, "Marxism and the Engels Paradox", *Socialist Register*, 1971, p. 134.

of gazing passively at an external universe, but of actually making it.[23]
Getting to know the world is an essentially creative process.

This means of course that if, as Antonio Gramsci puts it, the "only
'philosophy' is history in action, life itself",[24] what is needed are fewer
abstract dissertations on the "nature of Truth" and many more
practical sorties into the real world, intent on social and political
change. Indeed, can we not say that philosophy *as such* with its
traditional penchant for the abstract and the lifeless should be *done away
with*, so that theoretical argument gives way to actual practice? What is
the point of epistemology, for example, that branch of philosophy
customarily concerned with the theory of knowledge, if what is true
and what is false can only actually be demonstrated in the course of
praxis itself? The revelation of a situation, writes Jean-Paul Sartre, "is
effected in and through the praxis which changes it",[25] so that it
follows that action, in the course of its accomplishment, "provides its
own clarification". Henri Lefebvre, another French writer, summarily
states the praxis case against philosophy when he argues that

> abstract logical consistency, theory divorced from social activity and
> practical verification, have no value whatever.

The essence of man is social and the essence of society is praxis:
abstracted from praxis, theory can only become bogged down in
mysticism and mystification.[26]

The theory of praxis, in other words, sets its sights on demolishing
the positivist dogma *on every front*. In practical terms, praxis theory
rejects positivism's uncritical acceptance of the capitalist system and
looks instead to a society in which people can control their own lives,
unhampered in their freedom by exploitation or repression. On the
theoretical level, praxis demolishes all antitheses, conceptual
expressions of practical antagonisms, between subject and object, facts
and values, which make critical activity impossible, and conceives man
as a being who is creatively united with the world around him.
Particularly important as a work which seeks to forge unity in the
praxis position on all fronts is George Lukacs', *History and Class
Consciousness*—a book which gives pride of place (as Lukacs himself
later reminds us) to praxis as a concept which resolves simultaneously
problems of a practical and philosophical kind. Man, writes Lukacs, is

[23] *The Concept of Nature in Marx* (New Left Books, 1971), p. 196.
[24] *The Modern Prince and other Writings* (New York, 1967), p. 81.
[25] *Search for a Method*, trans. Barnes (New York, 1963), p. 32.
[26] *The Sociology of Marx* (Penguin, 1972), p. 33.

"a perfected whole", one whose external freedom mirrors the fact that he is in the process of overcoming the dichotomies of theory and practice, reason and the senses, form and content, a being for whom, indeed, "freedom and necessity are identical".[27] What Lukacs describes as *alienation*, the loss of self-identity and control, cannot be overcome in practice unless it is also overcome in theory, and for this reason the praxis concept is vital. It unifies both dimensions: subjective freedom realises its identity in an objective world, a world which is therefore not outside this subjectivity, but is itself the *objectification* of creative freedom. In Lefebvre's words,

> through praxis, thought is reunited with being, consciousness with sensuous or physical nature, the mind with spontaneity.[28]

In place of positivist division, there is praxical unity: instead of pessimistic doubt, there seems to be the optimistic reassertion of man's creative abilities, the real possibility of "the widening and enriching of humanity":[29] in short, a thorough-going commitment to radical change.

What a contrast to positivism! What a welcome development in a post-war world where cynicism and superficiality have veritably polluted the intellectual atmosphere, allowing racism and class prejudice, metaphysics and triviality to become scientifically respectable as "academic points of view"! Values have been dismissed as mere "prejudices" and facts distorted out of all recognition in the name of methodological sophistication and "pure science". Activity and commitment are darkly denounced as "unprofessional". It is no wonder that this stifling cultural climate has provoked a radical reaction, an increasingly powerful protest which demands from science, relevance, commitment and change, that a growing number of philosophers and social scientists have come to demand that the problems of practice be brought to the fore and that praxis itself should be the only kind of theory we ought to develop.

[27] *History and Class Consciousness* (Merlin Press, 1970), p. 136.
[28] Lefebvre, op. cit., p. 58.
[29] Petrovic, op. cit., p. 125.

2

PRAXIS AND MARXIST THEORY

There is no doubt about it: on first appearance, the theory of praxis·
seems impressive indeed as an authentic alternative to positivism.
Abstracting from the various differences of detail which divide the
particular theorists I want to consider, I have tried so far to present the
praxis concept as it first strikes the reader. A concept which appears
highly critical, thoroughly radical and passionately concerned with the
question of social change.

But of course we cannot allow ourselves simply to be content with
"appearances". The famous Monkey King of the 14th-century
philosopher, Wu Ch'êng-ên, warns us repeatedly in the course of his
adventures, to be wary of appearances—not to be fooled by things as
they *seem*, but to have a good prod beneath the surface and find out
what they *really* are. It is good advice, particularly when trying to assess
the validity of a theory which lays so much stress upon being practical
and concrete. For how can one be sure that praxis theory does in fact
practise what it preaches?

A first step must be to examine the relation of the praxis concept to
other theories, those which it claims to support and those which it
rejects, looking carefully not merely at proclaimed principles, but also
at the hidden philosophical basis upon which these principles rest.
Having done this, we will then be in a position to take account of how
praxis theory actually works out when put into the context of political
programmes and movements for social change in the real world: the
acid test itself.

I hope, broadly speaking, to carry out these two tasks in the course of
this work. For what is the theory which seems closest of all to the
praxis concept? It is obviously Marxism, and the similarity between the
praxis critique and the theory of Marxism seems striking indeed. Not
surprisingly praxis writers frequently cite Marx in defence of their
theses and in some cases (in the writing of Alfred Schmidt or Shlomo
Avineri, for example), present praxis theory as an interpretation of
Marx's work itself. In fact, praxis writers sometimes go further and
argue that the concept of praxis provides us with a theoretical *key* to
understanding Marxism, indeed Marxism's authentic core. Without a
grasp of *praxis*, Marxism itself cannot really be understood: the

question is one of central importance to praxis theory and thus forms the main theme of this book.

Marxism of course has always regarded practice as the essential dimension of all human activity, and its insistence that theory must prove itself in practice results from a materialist rejection of any idea of "pure theory" *as such*. Men are producing beings who produce ideas as part of the process of practical production: there are no eternal truths which are not an intrinsic part of the historical world which they reflect, there is no "human nature" which cannot change. Kenneth Megill quotes Marx's words in *Capital*:

> man opposes himself to Nature as one of her own forces, setting in motion arms and legs, head and hands, the natural forces of his body, in order to appropriate Nature's productions in a form adapted to his own wants. By thus acting on the external world and changing it, he at the same time changes his own nature.[1]

Marx then not only considered man to be an essentially practical being—one who makes even his own nature—but stressed therefore as a consequence of this, that theoretical problems could not be resolved in a world of their own. "The question of whether objective truth can be attributed to human thinking", wrote Marx, "is not a question of theory but is a *practical* question",[2] and there are a number of well-known passages in the *Paris Manuscripts of 1844* (at which we shall look later in more detail) where Marx argues that the "strife" between man and man reflects itself in *theoretical* antitheses which can only be resolved in a practical way, "by virtue of the practical energy of men".[3] In short, as he puts it in the second thesis on Feuerbach:

> the dispute over the reality or non-reality of thinking that is isolated from practice is a purely *scholastic* question,[4]

a scholasticism which, as we noted in the previous chapter, becomes so remote from the real world that it threatens to even choke our practical ability to think.

Clearly then the Marxist concept of practice appears "praxical" to its core, and so it seems quite natural to see Megill, for example, describing "democratic Marxism" as "a philosophy of praxis",[5] or

[1] *Capital*, I (Lawrence and Wishart, 1970), p. 177.
[2] "Theses on Feuerbach" (No. 2), in *German Ideology*, p. 651.
[3] *Economic and Philosophical Manuscripts* (Progress Publ., 1959), p. 102.
[4] "Theses on Feuerbach", op. cit.
[5] Megill, *New Democratic Theory*, p. 58.

Gayo Petrovic defining praxis as "universal-creative, self-creative activity, activity by which man transforms and creates his world", with the comment that

exactly such an interpretation prevails in Karl Marx.[6]

And yet, if it appears perfectly logical for praxis writers to present their theory as authentically Marxist, the matter is not quite as cut and dried as it seems. If we look a little more closely at what praxis theorists actually say about Marxism, a rather curious fact emerges which we must now consider.

(i) The Theory of Praxis and the "Marxism of Karl Marx"

It has long been customary for Marxists to speak of their world-outlook as *scientific* on the grounds that Marxism is not some sort of "revealed truth", but is rather a theory which is grounded in "the concrete study of concrete conditions", a theory which continues therefore to develop and grow as it comes into contact with new natural and social facts and must continually adjust itself to a changing historical world. Basic principles ceaselessly enrich their content and strengthen their form as life moves on. Marxism is thus not only the theory of Karl Marx, but it is the theory of Marx steeled and tempered, enriched and developed, by decades and decades of vital historical experience. To juxtapose Marx to Marxism, the original teachings to the developments which have come out of them, is as meaningless and futile as the attempt to separate the flow of a river from its actual source. For Marxism *is* the theory of Karl Marx as it has developed over the last hundred years of history.

And yet it is this simple point which praxis writers reject. Marx, they argue, has been betrayed, not developed, vulgarised not enriched, by the theoretical contributions of his collaborators and disciples, and nowhere is this great "betrayal" more apparent than in the concept of praxis itself. Praxis is a notion worked out by Marx *alone*: those who saw themselves as following in his footsteps have simply created a dismal trail of confusions and deformations, vulgarisations and dogmatisms, a series of theoretical positions which stand in sharp contrast to the actual position of Marx himself. Marx, in other words, must be rescued from the damage done by his followers—the millions of people the world over who are busy constructing new societies in

[6] *Marx in the Mid-Twentieth Century*, p. 78.

the light of what they see as Marxist principles—if the theory of praxis is to be placed in its proper perspective.

Who precisely are the "dogmatists" and "vulgarisers" to which praxis theory refers? Plekhanov, whose theoretical work Lenin highly praised, is one; and Lenin himself, regarded the world over as Marx's greatest and most gifted disciple, is another. In Shlomo Avineri's opinion, Lenin and Plekhanov were not dialectical but mechanistic thinkers,[7] while Lucien Goldmann, another praxis writer, singles out Lenin's famous *Materialism and Empirio-Criticism* as a target for special abuse, describing it as "one of the most mechanistic and anti-dialectical books there is":[8] Alfred Schmidt feels that Lenin's philosophy owes more to Feuerbach than to Marx, while Sartre describes it bluntly as "idealist". As for Karl Korsch, a dissident writer of the 1920s whose work has aroused some interest in Britain today, Marxism in Russia became "bolshevised" after the revolution, and chiefly responsible for this "degeneration" was, of course, Lenin. Leninism far from enriching Marxist theory, is a wholesale perversion of the praxis concept.

Nor is Lenin the only famous disciple who led Marxism astray. Even Frederick Engels, life-long friend and collaborator of Marx, must accept a good deal of the blame, particularly if one remembers that hundreds of thousands of workers learnt their Marxism from Engels' excellently written and easily assimilable commentaries on the Marxist outlook. It was the view of George Lukacs in his influential *History and Class Consciousness* that Engels never really understood Marx's dialectics and hence applied them in an erroneous and mechanistic manner,[9] and Goldmann contends that it was thanks to Lukacs' "pioneering work" that the sharp differences between the position of Marx and Engels became "clearly visible".[10] Peterovic likewise sees "considerable differences" between the views of Marx and Engels and ascribes many of Lening's "philosophical errors" to Engels' influence. Avineri is harsher still: it is not only "the cruelty and harshness of Bolshevism" which can be blamed on Engels, but "the intellectual wastelands of Social Democracy"—"the ultimate conservatism of the German SPD" can also be laid at Engels' door—an indictment indeed! Engels' politics were as conservative as his philosophy was wrong, and classic theoretical works like *Anti-Dühring* and *Dialectics of Nature* are, it goes

---

[7] *The Social and Political Thought of Karl Marx* (Cambridge Univ., 1968), p. 65.

[8] "Reflections on History and Class Consciousness", in *Aspects of History and Class Consciousness* (Routledge and Kegan Paul, 1971), p. 68.

[9] *History and Class Consciousness*, op. cit., p. 132.

[10] Goldmann, op. cit., p. 65.

without saying, wholly inimical to praxis theory. A "strict differentiation" between the two founders of Marxism must be maintained and the "collective personality projected by partisan propaganda"[11] firmly discarded.

As far as the praxis "school" are concerned, then, "official Marxism", as Lefebvre calls it, is simply a perversion of the authentic Marxism of Marx himself: "official Marxism" fails to get to grips with the nature of praxis, but "takes an empiricist positivist attitude under cover of a philosophical phraseology",[12] and positivism with a Marxist guise is no better than positivism in liberal dress. The "new democratic theory", as Megill calls his version of the praxis concept, is as opposed to the conservative philosophy of the West as it is to the "conservatism" of the East; and "orthodox Marxism", whether we think of the theories of existing socialist societies or those of the Communist Parties which are seeking, broadly speaking, to follow the socialist path, is as much an enemy of praxis as the technocratic positivism which has come under increasing fire, as we noted in Chapter 1, from students of philosophy in Britain today.

It is, however, only fair to point out that praxis theory is not only fiercely critical of Marxist "orthodoxy", it is not always entirely happy with the developed position of Marx himself. Gayo Petrovic, for example, has to concede that some of Marx's own comments, like those in the oft-quoted Preface to the *Critique of Political Economy* are not always easy to square with praxis thinking, and it is a striking feature of the praxis commentary on Marx's work that the early writings (pre-1845) play an important, if not preponderant, part in establishing their case. Avineri comments, as though this were a fact of immense significance, that Lenin wrote his *Materialism and Empirio-Criticism* without having read the Paris manuscripts, and praxis writers naturally reject Lenin's view—one which seems to me to be essentially correct—that "mature Marxism", real scientific Marxism, was only developed by Marx and Engels in the years *following* 1845.[13]

Certainly praxis writers find it necessary to either ignore or simply gloss over statements by Marx in which he explicitly rejects "the true socialism" of his earlier years, and it is amusing to find Jean-Paul Sartre in his *Search for a Method* thoroughly exasperated by Marx's own endorsement of views which praxis theorists disdainfully label as

[11] Avineri, op. cit., p. 3.
[12] Lefebvre, op. cit., p. 36.
[13] *State and Revolution, Collected Works*, 25, p. 401.

"vulgar", "dogmatic", "positivist", etc.[14] Sartre must content himself with the thought that if Marx meant what he said, he was momentarily confused and was only contradicting what he had said about praxis elsewhere in his work.

The problem then is this. Praxis theorists vehemently dissociate their position from what is generally known as Marxism, while insisting at the same time that they speak for the true Marx himself—an argument which is extremely puzzling, partly because the differences alleged between Marx and Engels are so obviously (as we shall see) differences manufactured by praxis theory itself, and partly because it does seem superficially that the praxis concept corresponds broadly with what Marxists have traditionally called "practice" and still do if their tongue is German or Greek!

We must investigate the matter further, looking specifically at the objections of praxis theory to what it calls "official" or "orthodox" Marxism. Is it really true that Marxism has strayed from the path of Karl Marx himself and has become another form of empiricism or positivism despite its stress on practice, revolution and the abolition of the exploitation of man by man? The charges which praxis makes against Marxism are extremely serious and thus deserve our immediate attention. I turn therefore to consider

(ii) *The Praxis Case Against "Orthodox Marxism"*

Broadly speaking, we can present the criticisms and accusations levelled against Marxism by praxis writers under five main heads:

1. *That Marxism cannot itself be a Philosophy*
Engels and Lenin, like other "orthodox" Marxists, have tried to convert Marxism into a philosophy of the universe, thereby ignoring the fact that questions about the nature of truth, reality and consciousness cannot be resolved theoretically in a philosophical manner: they can only be resolved, as Marx himself said, through *praxis*. Indeed, Marx explicitly rejected the need for all "absolute principles" and saw in communism not only the end of practical exploitation, but also the end of the theoretical expression of this exploitation, namely a purely philosophical conception of the universe.

[14] Op. cit., p. 86.

For how, to put the objection at its simplest, can we continue "interpreting" the world when the real need is to change it?

2. That Dialectics cannot exist in Nature

The dialectic of nature is a conception foisted upon Marx which is in fact quite alien to the dialectical character of his own theory. For if at the centre of Marx's theory is *praxis*—free, creative, *human* activity—then how can there be a dialectic outside of society and somehow in nature itself? Just as positivism is guilty of mechanically dividing subject from object, man from nature, so too is the "dialectic of nature" for it seeks to speculatively impose upon the world of nature a dynamic which only makes sense when analysed in human and social terms. Not only are "dialectical" principles about nature scientifically baseless and quite unprovable, but they seriously detract from the emphasis which Marx himself put upon man *as creator*, a being who moulds nature in his own image. Any attempt to place nature "outside" of man leads to metaphysics and a devaluation of the essentially *humanist* content of the revolutionary dialectic.

3. That Consciousness cannot "reflect" Reality

The "theory of reflection", which the orthodox champion, is a purely mechanistic notion borrowed uncritically from 18th-century materialism. Like the dialectic in nature, it is alien to the concept of praxis which ascribes to consciousness an essentially dynamic role. After all, if thinking is an intrinsic part of practice—of changing the world—then how can it be said that consciousness somehow *reflects* reality? Reflection theory relegates ideas to a role of passivity so that consciousness is made to appear as a force which tamely limps along behind reality, rather than playing an active part in transforming society. And in addition to passivity, this notion implies dualism for it inserts a "reflective" wedge between being and consciousness, thought and reality, two dimensions which are in fact not separate at all, but synthetically integrated by the unifying activity of creative praxis. Not only was reflection theory alien to the work of Marx, but even Lenin (who initially supported it) changed his mind when a close reading of Hegel impressed upon him the active, dynamic character of consciousness itself.

4. That the Basis/Superstructure Analysis is a False One

Just as consciousness plays an active role in society, so too does the world of politics and culture. Any attempt to ascribe ideas or politics and culture to an ideological superstructure in contrast to some sort of "material basis"—the latter ultimately determining the former—can only lead to a futile dogmatism which shies away from the facts of social reality. Why should there be a "fixed" relation between say politics, economics and the world of culture? Surely such a relation must vary from time to time. It is of course true enough that under capitalism—*one* type of social system—economic forces do have preponderant importance, for the commodity brings all aspects of social life under its sway; but economic life did not play this crucial determining role in pre-capitalist societies, nor—if the dream of communism is to realised—will it have this importance in the society of the future where people will become full human beings and not remain mere "economic animals". The fact is that the basis/superstructure analysis was not intended by Marx as a "universal theory" but merely to illuminate the fate of man under capitalism.

5. *That Concepts of Determinism can only contradict Human Freedom*

Official Marxism seeks to make man permanently subject to "objective laws" which operate, it is said, independently of his will. And yet if, as Marx himself argued, man is the *maker* of his world, a being of praxis, how can he be the "dupe" of forces outside his control? A deterministic perversion of Marxism can only lead to fatalism and passivity—indeed the same kind of conservatism which prevails in all positivist thinking. It is true enough that men are influenced by their environment: but if they are *products* of their environment, they are also and more essentially the *producers* of their environment. If circumstances make men, it is because men make circumstances, the very point which Marx makes in the "Theses on Feuerbach", and which expresses the kernel of the praxis outlook. All talk about objective laws which determine the fate and destiny of mankind negate Marx's own stress on human *activity* and sacrifice human freedom to a resigned acceptance of forces "outside" our control. Indeed, the very notion of determinism conveniently pin-points all that is erroneous and untenable in "dogmatic", "vulgar" Marxism, and shows how sharply it contrasts with the dynamic humanism of the praxis concept.

Here then is the nub of the praxis critique of Marxism which I have presented under five main heads. Naturally not all the writers I shall draw upon in evaluating this critique would agree with precisely all the criticisms I have enumerated, nor would they necessarily accept the particular way in which I have formulated them. When examining each of the five criticisms in more detail I will of course try as far as possible to let the praxis writers speak for themselves; but it does seem, despite these qualifications, true to say that the points expounded above do *generally* represent the praxis case, the criticisms of a "school" which, I should remind the reader, has been created for the purposes of this argument because of the broad similarities which the group of theorists selected do in fact have in common.

One further point. It soon becomes clear to the reader as he reads through the criticisms which I have summarised in my own words above, that all five are closely interrelated. Even although all the praxis writers might not agree with all of them it does seem to me that each follows on quite logically from the one preceding it, and that together they stand or fall pretty much as a whole. After all, if one denies that Marxism is a philosophy in the sense of being a comprehensive *weltanschauung*—a theory of the universe—(Point 1)—it is because one feels that Marx's theory is or should be applied only to society and not extended to include the sciences of nature (Point 2). Dialectics, strictly speaking, *begins* with human society and hence all talk of the priority of being to consciousness, and thus the reflection of being through consciousness, is just so much metaphysics. For what sense does it make to speak of some sort of reality *in itself* beyond the mind? (Point 3). And if the debate about the priority of matter to mind, nature to spirit is idle and irrelevant, then similarly the re-expression of this argument in specifically *social* terms—in terms of basis vs superstructure—is equally sterile (Point 4). Finally, of course, questions of Marx's theory as a comprehensive philosophy, a theory about society and not nature, a concept which unites rather than divides thought from being through praxis, all these polemical threads come to a head in the pivotal debate of Freedom vs Determinism, and their asserted irreconcilability (Point 5).

The next five chapters will be taken up with examining each of these arguments in greater detail.

3

IS MARXISM A PHILOSOPHY?

There is little question that those who stand accused of "vulgarising" Marx's theory have described Marxism as a *philosophy*. One need look no further than Lenin and his preface to the fiercely argued *Materialism and Empirio-Criticism*, where he observes that a number of "would-be Marxists" have "undertaken a veritable campaign against the philosophy of Marxism", adding that

> all these people could not have been ignorant of the fact that Marx and Engels scores of times termed their philosophical views dialectical materialism. Yet all these people who, despite the sharp divergence of their political views, are united in their hostility towards dialectical materialism, at the same time claim to be Marxists in philosophy.[1]

And in his classic summaries of Marx's teachings, Lenin frequently refers to "the philosophy of Marxism", stressing as always that its "consummate philosophical materialism" has provided mankind and especially the working class with "powerful instruments of knowledge".[2]

Yet, according to the praxis writers, the description of Marxism as a philosophy is a travesty of Marx's views and the concept of praxis. And why? Although, as I have argued, the position taken by praxis theorists is *broadly* similar, in answering this question in detail it is necessary to examine individually some of the arguments raised in the defence of the praxis critique. I begin with

(i) *Henri Lefebvre and the End of Speculative Philosophy*

As far as Lefebvre is concerned, it is only with the rise of "establishment Marxism" that Marx's theory has been expressed as a philosophy, as a set of universal laws which govern both the operation of nature and society: dialectical principles which apply to the world as a whole. Such a philosophy simply contradicts the essentially historical character of Marxist theory, for Marx was concerned not with "absolute truths" about the universe, but with problems of *change*. The

---

[1] *Materialism and Empirio-Criticism* (Lawrence and Wishart, 1964), p. 9.
[2] *Three Sources and Three Component Parts of Marxism* (Progress, 1969), pp. 6–7.

very term "dialectical materialism" as applied to Marxism is, for Lefebvre (although some praxis writers do in fact retain it), a contradiction in terms, for the truth is that

> both materialism and idealism are interpretations of the world and both are untenable in the face of revolutionary praxis.[3]

To continue debating their respective validity, as Lenin does, is simply to overlook the fact that, as far as Marx is concerned, both doctrines have been *superseded*—for Marxism, in its concern with *praxis*, cannot at the same time continue a tradition of speculating about abstract questions, mere "interpretations of life" which, it must be said, "correspond to obsolete stages in the class struggle".[4] The question of what is "truth" is wrongly formulated for, divorced from social activity, it implies a division between thought and reality, consciousness and being, which does not in fact exist. The problem, in other words, arises from a *philosophical* way of looking at things—a speculative tradition whose roots lie in a society in which exploitation and the division of labour have separated theory from practice and placed "absolute principles" above the world of historical change. Once man is seen as *praxis*, then speculative inquiries become irrelevant, and we can concentrate our efforts—as Marx intended—on the practical problem of bringing to fruition human potentialities in a new society.

How valid are Lefebvre's arguments? It is certainly true that as far as Marx was concerned, "pure thought" was the illusory product of the division of labour and a philosophical reflection of exploiting practices. And hence it is also true to say that Marxism is opposed to all speculation *as such*:

> where speculation ends—in real life—there real, positive science begins: the representation of the practical activity, of the practical process of development of men.

And with speculation out of the way, "philosophy as an independent branch of knowledge loses its medium of existence".[5]

But if it is true to say that many of Marx's comments appear to give a measure of authority to some of the things Lefebvre says, in fact they radically refute the main point which he is trying to make, namely that philosophical thought *of any kind* is wholly at odds with Marxist theory. How incredibly silly and superficial Lefebvre's argument is, can be seen if we look again, for example, at Marx's famous 11th thesis

---

[3] *The Sociology of Marx*, p. 30.   [4] Ibid., p. 31.   [5] *The German Ideology*, p. 38.

on Feuerbach, when "interpreting" the world is contrasted with the activity of actually changing it. Is Marx suggesting here that if we want to change the world, then we must *stop* interpreting it? That all theory hampers practice and must be dispensed with? Merely to formulate the question in this way demonstrates its obvious absurdity. For Marx's point is not that we must stop thinking, but that one cannot change the world through thought *alone*: revolutions are made, not in the philosopher's study, but in the real world. This means, therefore, that we do not reject every form of philosophy (i.e. cease thinking), but rather seek to formulate a *new conception of thought* which will consciously set itself the task of transforming the world and not—as philosophers have tended to do in the past—attempt to fossilise it in a reactionary manner. A revolutionary interpretation which leads to action in the place of a conservative interpretation which serves to glorify the time-honoured "activity" of doing nothing. A concrete, practical way of thinking must supplant an abstract, metaphysical one.

Indeed, it occurs even to the highly praxical Lefebvre that practice without theory is likely to be as silly as theory without practice, and he hastens to assure his reader that creative, revolutionary praxis does not, in fact, "exclude the theory it animates and verifies" and comprises both "theoretical decision as well as the decision to act".[6] But what is this supposed to mean? That despite all the praxical sound and fury which has gone before, what is being put before us is merely a *theory* of revolutionary praxis, indeed . . . a *philosophy* of revolutionary praxis! Lefebvre wriggles hard. My emphasis upon praxis, he insists,

sanctions neither the pragmatist interpretation nor the elaboration of a new philosophy, not even a philosophy of praxis.[7]

Naturally the reader is relieved to hear it. But what precisely then does this emphasis upon praxis sanction?

It calls for the analytical study and exposition of praxis itself. This thesis does not relegate philosophy to "the dustbin of history", but situates it in the dialectical movement of consciousness and being, forms and contents.[8]

But I must be forgiven if I treat this clarion call for "analytical study and exposition" with an ounce of scepticism. For it seems to me, in the first place, rather difficult to visualise what precisely is meant by "situating" philosophy in the dialectical movement of consciousness and being, etc. All I see in front of me is the assertion, repeated a number of times over for good measure, that thought and being,

[6] *Sociology of Marx*, p. 54.   [7] Ibid., p. 58.   [8] Ibid., p. 58.

consciousness and reality are united, and if this assertion is not itself a philosophical statement of truth (or falsehood), then I am at a total loss to imagine what it might possibly be. "Man's fundamental relation to nature", Lefebvre adds to strengthen his point, "may legitimately be called 'ontological',"[9] but if ontology is not a philosophical conception, then what is? It is no use saying that "philosophy" cannot restore the unity between thought and being, it is a task for praxis, when this "praxis" is repeatedly expounded in philosophical terms. The argument that praxis constitutes the unity of consciousness and being is an argument about a *principle*, an axiom of the universe (for it is presumed to always hold), an ontological truth which can "situate" itself in any way it likes—it still remains an "interpretation" of the world, a postulate of theory, a philosophical statement. I will argue in a moment that in fact philosophy is far broader, much more comprehensive in its scope than has been traditionally allowed; but Lefebvre's "ontology" stands as a philosophical thesis even in the narrowest and most customary use of the term. Vague talk about "situating" philosophy in dialectical movements does not alter this fact one iota.

Nor does it make any sense to argue that praxis can be "analytically" studied and expounded without at the same time "situating" this analysis on a philosophical basis. Praxis may be action, the dialectical relation between man and nature, a content which creates its own forms, of which revolutionary creative praxis is the "supreme realisation"—but these principles, like all the others, are deemed by Lefebvre to relate themselves to the universe (at least nothing is said to disturb this presumption), and are all formulated in the abstract. Whether they are true or false is beside the point for the moment: what is surely undeniable is that they are philosophical in character, even in the most traditional sense of the term!

Indeed, the concept of praxis has, for Lefebvre, an almost magical quality so that the mere incantation of its name, if made frequently enough, appears to give it immunity from the "outmoded" form of philosophy. All previous principles might be philosophical, but not praxis! And all this in a work which is written at a sustained level of thoroughly abstract conceptual "analysis". If I appear to be labouring the point somewhat, it is only because Lefebvre's position is held (if less boisterously) by most other praxis writers who, while they may describe themselves as philosophers, are anxious to argue that unlike the "dogmatic" Engels or the "mechanistic" Lenin, they have no desire to convert Marxism into a theory of the universe.

[9] Ibid., p. 20.

The truth is that not only is it rather childish to counterpose the *concept* of praxis to a philosophy of praxis, it is in fact *quite impossible*; for in order to expound a theoretical position at all, one must embrace a philosophy of some description with some presumed criterion of truth and falsehood and an idea of what the real world is or is not. There is no way out. When Lefebvre says, for example, that Marx "pointedly refrains" from giving a definition of a human being, but "expects mankind to define itself in praxis",[10] what else is this "expectation" if it is not a "philosophical definition", the view that the character of men depends upon the nature of their practical activities at any given period in history? In fact, Marx's very stress on the universality of practice, his discovery that all thinking is necessarily practical in character and that all activity is necessarily *conscious activity*—a "consciousness of existing practice",[11] points to a conclusion diametrically opposed to the one which Lefebvre draws from Marxist theory, namely the conclusion that *every conscious being is in fact a philosopher*; for whether we like it or not, everything we say only makes sense in the context of *general* ideas about what exists, and what are these general ideas if they are not philosophy? Thought without philosophy is not thought at all.

Let me develop this point further by looking now at the protestations of another praxis theorist on the same matter:

(ii) *Karl Korsch and the "Idealism" of Karl Marx*

In his *Marxism and Philosophy* Korsch argues that Marxism as a science has neither need nor use for a philosophical basis; that as far as Marx and Engels were concerned, all philosophy was *bourgeois* philosophy and an integral part of the class state and its exploiting mechanisms. Scientific socialism, in other words, has transcended philosophy altogether.

Now of course, as with Lefebvre's comments, there appears to be some truth in this view. After all, in his *Critique of the Hegelian Philosophy of Law* Marx spoke of the need to *abolish* philosophy, and in his polemic with Proudhon, significantly entitled *The Poverty of Philosophy*, he ridicules the petty bourgeois economist's reverence for "eternal principles" as the delusion of a philosopher: Proudhon, he says,

holding things upside down like a true philosopher, sees in actual relationships nothing but the incarnation of these principles, of these

[10] *Ibid.*   [11] *German Ideology*, p. 53.

categories, which were slumbering—so M. Proudhon the philosopher tells us—in the bosom of the "impersonal reason of humanity".[12]

But is one to conclude from this, that Marx and Engels regarded all philosophy as irretrievably *bourgeois*? Surely what is meant by "philosophy" in passages like the above is not philosophy as a mere statement of concepts or principles as such, but philosophy *as idealism*, philosophy as it had been traditionally conceived—for we should not forget of course that even traditional materialism was ultimately idealist in the last analysis. What Marx and Engels attacked was not the reality of thinking, but the notion of a thought *above* reality, a belief that "philosophy" could present the "absolute truth" about the universe as a whole so that no new discoveries were possible because the "system" had said the last word on the subject. By ignoring or simply inverting—for obvious class reasons—the real relationship between material production and the production of ideas, philosophers had blinded themselves to the fact that their categories and principles could be no more eternal than the social relations they express: that even ideas are "historical and transitory products"—"the only immutable thing is the abstraction of movement—*mors immortalis*".[13] As Engels explained in his piece on *Ludwig Feuerbach*, it was German idealism and Hegel's work in particular which led philosophy, as traditionally conceived, into a hopeless blind alley so that all further development became impossible. For had not Hegel attempted to present in his philosophy a history of the whole world from "creation" to "realisation", thus seeking to achieve *explicitly* what others before him had sought implicitly, namely an exhaustively documented picture of the absolute truth? By making philosophy unprecedently *concrete*—so that his philosophy of history *was* the history of philosophy, the conscious achievements of civilised man—Hegel brought philosophy to the point where its radical incompatibility with the historical world became dramatically obvious. Hence, as Engels observes,

as soon as we realised—and in the long run no one has helped us to realise it more than Hegel himself—that the task of philosophy thus stated means nothing but the task that a single philosopher should accomplish that which can only be accomplished by the entire human race in its progressive

[12] *Poverty of Philosophy*, p. 92.
[13] Ibid., p. 93.

development—as soon as we realised that, there is an end to all philosophy *in the hitherto accepted sense of the word*.[14] (Stress mine).

This does not mean, therefore, that *all* philosophy, of whatever kind, disappears: it simply means that philosophy as metaphysics, philosophy *as opposed to* science, philosophical thinking *as opposed to* concrete, historical thinking must go, so that

instead one pursues attainable relative truths along the path of the positive sciences and the summation of their results by means of dialectical thinking.[15]

But does not dialectical thinking require philosophical thought? Must not the positive sciences have philosophical bases? Obviously so, and we shall see in a moment that philosophy understood scientifically as a practical instrument of analysis and investigation is of crucial importance to Marx and Engel's theory, and both explicitly acknowledge its pivotal role.

It is true that Marx and Engels called for an end to philosophy "in the hitherto accepted sense of the word", but to conclude from this, as Korsch does, that they rejected *all* philosophy is really a most shallow misreading of the truth. When Marx ridiculed the "true philosopher", his target was not the thinker *per se*, but the over-zealous metaphysician who blithely imagined, as did Proudhon, that the world of reality somehow owed its existence to the immanent presence of timeless principles. Because Hegel and his followers deified Philosophy as a world spirit, a cosmic force which made and unmade an unfolding series of historic civilisations, it was surely appropriate to label this grandiose theorising *Philosophy* and demand an end to it; but it is obvious to anyone who looks to the context of these attacks that it was a specific *kind* of philosophy—abstract, metaphysical philosophy— which was the target Marx and Engels had in mind.

Indeed, Korsch, like Lefebvre, runs into considerable difficulty as soon as he tries to substantiate his claim that Marxism has no place for philosophy as such. It gradually dawns on him that perhaps it would be far better to say that philosophy should be *realised* rather than simply rejected, and that even dialectical materialism, the theory of Marx and Engels, is "by its nature a philosophy through and through".[16] But has

[14] *Ludwig Feuerbach and the End of Classical German Philosophy* (Lawrence and Wishart, 1946), p. 14.
[15] Ibid., p. 14.
[16] *Marxism and Philosophy*, p. 67.

Korsch seen through the error of his earlier formulation that Marx and Engels dismissed philosophy? Not at all: for why has Marxism degenerated at the hands of the theorists of the Second International, on the one hand, and under the influence of Lenin, on the other?

Take the Marxism of the Second International first. Korsch's argument here is that Kautsky and Hilferding, for example, had treated Marxism as "a purely theoretical critique"—simply as a philosophy,[17] so that shorn of its practical consequences it fell prey to reformism. He cites Hilferding's statement in the latter's *Finance Capital* that Marxism is a science "free of value judgments" and therefore with "no implications for practical behaviour".[18] Certainly, this is no Marxist formulation of Marxism. But why then does Korsch, instead of actually rejecting Hilferding's misconception, merely proceed to turn its positivism *inside out*, protesting bitterly that Marxism has been transformed into a "purely theoretical critique"? To argue that the theorists of the Second International deprived Marxism of "practical consequences" is woefully wide of the mark: what in fact happened is that German Social Democracy veered towards subjective idealism and political opportunism, and adopted a "version" of Marxism which led the movement in 1914 into policies of outright betrayal and abject surrender—a consequence of a most catastrophically *practical* kind. Korsch instead of actually examining the *content* of, say, Kautsky's opportunism, satisfies himself with angry protests about its "purely theoretical" *form*, alleging that theory had become separated from political practice. Would this were so! The opportunism of the Second International would not have done the damage it did, if in fact this had been the case.

Ironically Korsch notes that

> the theoreticans of the Second International regarded all questions concerned with general epistemological and methodological bases as an utter waste of time[19]

and this of course is true. But how does this philistine attitude differ from Korsch's own protest that Marxism must be seen, not as a philosophy, but as a way of getting things done? Let me turn briefly to his comments on Lenin.

According to Korsch, Lenin and the Bolsheviks are responsible for turning Marxism into a "philosophical ideology". Lenin, he charges, has led Marxism into sterile abstract paths with extraordinary philosophical arguments about the priority of nature to man, objective

---

[17] Ibid., p. 57.   [18] Cited by Korsch, op. cit., p. 55.   [19] Ibid., p. 31.

reality to consciousness, so that instead "realising" (if not actually rejecting) philosophy, all he has done is to *exchange* an idealist philosophical outlook for a materialist one.[20] But what, one may ask, is wrong with that? Whereas Marx and Engels believed that they could take materialism for granted and concentrated their efforts on stressing its *dialectical* character, Lenin, in a rather different intellectual climate, considered that it was a matter of the greatest practical importance to defend Marxism's *materialist* core. And yet Korsch objects—he offers no substantive critique of Lenin's views, but objects to them solely on the ground that they are expressed as a philosophy. Having bitterly castigated the theorists of the Second International who "regarded all questions concerned with general epistemological and methodological bases as an utter waste of time", he proceeds to follow in their footsteps. Kautsky, notes Korsch, believed that the materialist theory of history was compatible with the theories of Mach and Avernarius and "many other philosophies". But how does this positivist divide between philosophy and politics differ from the one which Korsch himself champions?

For this is the rub. By attacking philosophy *per se*, philosophy in general and not some philosophy in particular, Korsch gets tied up in knots, so that instead of attacking the position he wants to reject, he ends up defending it. He wishes to argue—like others in the praxis school—that the debate between materialism and idealism has been superseded, and that now instead of mere "interpretation" we must have change. But this ultra-revolutionism—like all phrasemongering of its kind—leaves everything as it is; for while we are told that theory without practice is a positivist abomination, practice without theory is the last word in revolutionary truth! It may *sound* fearfully revolutionary to demand one without the other, but idealism has accepted this self-same antithesis between theory and practice for thousands of years. The simple fact is that as long as there is thought there is philosophy; and all the shouting in the world cannot remove this basic truth. If we reject one philosophy, we must replace it with another, for it is no more than a childish delusion to believe that by chanting the magic formula of Praxis—the dialectical unity of thought and being—one can thereby leave the plane of philosophy altogether and batter away at a theoretical adversary from some entirely different realm.

Not only then does Korsch get Marx's and Engels' position on philosophy quite wrong, but he completely misses the really

[20] Ibid., p. 114.

revolutionary point which they do in fact make about the relation between philosophy and practice in a concrete world. It is not surprising, therefore, that Korsch ends up not merely criticising the philosophy of Lenin as idealist, but the theory of Marx himself. For what does Marxism really have to say about philosophy?

The position of Marx and Engels is not simply that "pure theory" is an illusion, but that it is an illusion which arises out of the social practice of men. The fancy that consciousness is really something without being something real is, as we have already seen, an ideological product of the division of labour—so that although it is clearly an *illusion*, it is an illusion which has its roots in the real world. While it is true that theorists may deny the importance of practice, there are good *practical* reasons for making this denial: in other words, the very doctrine of "pure theory" has a practical significance which, by its nature, it is incapable of seeing. Consciousness may *appear* abstract and theoretical: and yet, like other phenomena which have to be *produced* in this world, ideas are in fact, practical and concrete: but if consciousness is *in fact* concrete and practical, why then should it appear abstract and "theoretical"? Precisely because it is produced that way.

The belief that ideas rule the world arises from the division of society into exploiter and exploited, and hence it is an illusion with the utmost practical significance. Plato's doctrine of metaphysical absolutes is precisely what one would expect from a nostalgic landed aristocrat, to whom all historical change is wholly anathema. The fact then that Marxism rejects abstract theorising in the traditional metaphysical manner does *not* mean that it regards the debate between materialism and idealism as "superseded": in fact, exactly the opposite is true. It is because idealism does mean something concrete—a theory whose deeper practical significance it fails to see—that it needs to be rigorously combated; for idealism expresses theoretically *the mentality of the exploiter*, and hence the struggle against metaphysics is part and parcel of the class struggle itself. If metaphysics turns reality upside down, preaching that the real world is produced by the Idea, this is only because the real world is *in fact* upside down, not obviously in the sense that ideas do create reality, but in the sense that a master–servant relationship, the exploitation of one class by another, makes it in fact *appear* that the mind is the master and reality the mere slave.

Idealism, that is to say, is not just "nonsense" (nor is anything else, absolutely speaking), it is nonsense which has to be produced, and this gives it therefore the *appearance* of the truth. It is false because it is only *apparently* true: it reflects the *appearance* of class society and not how things really are. Subjectively considered, idealism may be concerned with the most righteous protest against an unjust world, and idealists may, as often happens, work with other revolutionaries to change it: but the fact remains. Idealism, even when it directs its energies in a progressive direction, can only hamper the direction of those energies. For it is the superficial reflection of a distorted reality, and it is the task of Marxists not simply to reject metaphysics, but to do so by revealing the *concrete* basis of idealist abstractions. Marx and Engels express this point to perfection when they say that

> if in all ideology men and their circumstances appear upside down as in *camera obscura*, this phenomenon arises just as much from their historical life-process as the inversion of objects on the retina does from their physical life-process.[21]

But how can we get to the roots of philosophy without at the same time being philosophical ourselves?

Korsch cites a lengthy extract from the *Communist Manifesto* where Marx and Engels ridicule the pursuit of "eternal truths" as evidence of the fact that they

> were not just combating specific philosophical systems—they wanted eventually to overcome and supersede philosophy altogether, by scientific socialism.[22]

But the discussion in the *Manifesto* on "eternal principles" and exploitation points to a conclusion which is diametrically opposed to the postures of "revolutionary" praxis—the conclusion that these "principles", far from being "superseded" acts of speculation which do not need to be debated, represent, on the contrary, theoretical expressions of private property, a mystification of the truth which needs to be thoroughly understood. Every ruling class has embraced a metaphysical philosophy because all ruling classes have suffered from the misconception that while earlier classes may come and go, they (like Tennyson's brook) "go on for ever". History has ground to a halt, so that current ideas about society must—since fundamental change is inconceivable—be consciously or unconsciously endowed with eternal verity and cast into theological or quasi-theological form:

> the selfish misconception that induces you to transform into eternal laws of nature and of reason the social forms springing from the present mode of production and form of property—historical relations that rise and

---

[21] *The German Ideology*, p. 37.
[22] *Marxism and Philosophy*, pp. 44–45.

disappear in the progress of production—this misconception you share with every ruling class that has preceded you.[23]

It follows then that not only is it quite wrong to speak of theory as having no practical consequences—the real question is whether these consequences are conservative or revolutionary—but similarly it is misleading to speak of Marx and Engels as "superseding" philosophy as though it were possible to supersede one philosophy without putting another in its place. For how can one reject a bourgeois conception of "eternity" without producing a higher and more historically conscious concept of the absolute in its stead? It is no use ridiculing the "timeless" laws of nature about which the earlier bourgeois economists spoke without presenting at the same time a rather more scientific formulation of the same phenomena? In short, an old, discredited philosophy cannot be superseded without a new one, and the *Communist Manifesto* contains a number of brilliant formulations of this new philosophy—historical and dialectical materialism. A new philosophy with universal principles? Yes indeed, a philosophy whose principles are intended to explain what we know so far of the universe. A philosophy which purports to present the absolute truth? Most certainly, as much of the absolute truth as it is possible for us to grasp at this point in time. A philosophy which does not seek to transcend reality, but relies solely upon science and history in its reflections of the real world—a philosophy which expresses

in *general* terms, actual relations springing up from an existing class struggle, from an historical movement going on under our very eyes,[24]

a philosophy which does not reflect these relations unconsciously, but which expresses them in a deliberate and systematic manner. All philosophy, as we have seen, is ultimately practical, but Marxism is the first philosophy to become really aware of this fact. Hence it is a philosophy whose practice is immersed in history, grounded in science, and explicitly directed towards revolutionary ends.

What Korsch, Lefebvre and the other praxis theorists fail to grasp is that Marxism does not diminish the importance of theory (and thus in *this* sense, philosophy), it greatly enhances it, and precisely because Marxism does really understand the actual relation between thought and reality, it demands that *more* rather than less attention be paid to questions which may appear rather abstract. After all, where is the revolutionary who devoted a major slice of his active life to the pursuit

---

[23] *Communist Manifesto*, pp. 67–68.   [24] Ibid, p. 69.

of theory as Marx did? Marx was untroubled by the philistines who carped at his "German philosophy", for he and Engels understood full well that without a *scientific* grasp of capitalism the success of the proletariat could not be assured. The question was not whether one was "active" or "merely theorised": the question was whether one sought to build up a revolutionary movement in a correct and therefore scientific manner. For one thing is certain: if theory "without practice" is no recipe for success, practice without theory, "philosophy-free praxis", is a guaranteed recipe for ignominious failure.

When Engels speaks then of the fact that Marxism is "no longer a philosophy", he makes it perfectly clear what he means. Marxism is not a philosophy in the quite *specific* sense that it does not stand outside of the world of developing science: philosophy has traditionally been idealist, Marxism is materialist—that is the matter in a nutshell:

> it is no longer a philosophy at all, but simply a world outlook which has to establish its validity and be applied not in a science of sciences standing apart, but in the positive sciences. Philosophy is therefore "sublated" here, that is, "both overcome and preserved"; overcome as regards its form, and preserved as regards its content.[25]

Our concern with the question of truth and the correspondence of ideas and reality: all this must *remain*. We can make no progress unless we *build* upon the past: even revolutions require that we develop what has gone before.

> The communist revolution is the most radical rupture with traditional property relations; no wonder that its development involves the most radical rupture with traditional ideas.[26]

But without a continuity with the past, such a radical rupture would not be possible. It is precisely because "the communist revolution" heralds such radical change that, in order to break with exploitation in *all* its forms, we must get to the bottom of philosophy "in the hitherto existing sense of the term". We cannot, as Engels says, overcome the past, unless at the same time we "preserve" it on a higher level. And what does this mean? It means, not rejecting philosophy out of hand in absurd praxical fashion—a childish attempt at the impossible—but overcoming its form, while "preserving its content": retaining our concern with the nature of the universe, in order to bring into being a

[25] *Anti-Dühring* (Foreign Lang. Publ., Moscow), p. 191.
[26] *Communist Manifesto*, p. 74.

new development in its history. Only by *absorbing* the philosophy of the past can we transform it from a dogma into a guide for revolutionary action.

It is not really surprising—to make our last point about Karl Korsch's praxis in this chapter—that by rejecting the criteria of truth and falsehood as superseded philosophical standpoints, Korsch is only able to judge theory according to whether it is "practical" or not, a position incidentally which is no less "philosophical" for the fact that it happens to be hopelessly idealist. But if *this* is our yardstick—whether theory is "praxical" or not—it is not only Lenin who was guilty of spinning "philosophical ideologies", "purely theoretical critiques", it was Marx and Engels. See where Korsch's "defence" of Marx (and in his case, Engels) leads him:

> Marx and Engels had initially conceived their revolutionary theory in direct relation to the practical revolutionary movement, but when this died down, they could only continue their work as theory. It is true that this later development of Marxist theory was never just the production of "purely theoretical study" . . . nevertheless it is clear that the *theory* of Marx and Engels was progressing towards an ever higher level of theoretical perfection although it was no longer directly related to the *practice* of the workers' movement.[27]

Now this can only mean that when Marx and Engels found, following the diminution of militant class struggle in the 1850s (in England where they lived), that they could only "continue their work as theory", then this theory lost "its practical consequences" (i.e. was not immersed in specific political struggles) and ceased to have a revolutionary content. Creating theory "without practice", one is compelled to conclude that in fact Marx and Engels had both become idealists. For nobody can deny that in the period after 1852 both Marx and Engels felt that the most practical thing they could do under the circumstances was to withdraw from ordinary politics and concern themselves predominantly with theoretical matters.[28] This withdrawal was the result not, of course, of idealism, but of science: a correct materialist understanding of the fact that England's industrial

---

[27] *Marxism and Philosophy*, p. 104.

[28] ". . . since 1852 I was no longer connected with *any* association and was firmly convinced that my theoretical works were of greater benefit to the working class than participation in associations whose days on the Continent were over", Marx to F. Freilgrath, 29/12/1860, *Selected Correspondence* (Foreign Lang. Pub. House, 1953), p. 147.

monopoly over the world market and its concomitant advantages for the working class had for the moment punctured class consciousness so that, as Engels could observe as late as 1885, "since the dying out of Owenism, there has been no socialism in England".[29] But if man is the maker of his world, are not revolutions acts of *will*? Was it not a dangerously "idealist" thing to do for Marx and Engels to allow objective circumstances to dictate their actions? As far as Korsch is concerned, this "theory without practice" was the beginning of the end:

> in spite of his famous statement that he was "not a Marxist", Marx himself was not entirely free from this dogmatic and idealistic conception of the relationship of his Marxist theory to later manifestations of the working-class movement.[30]

Korsch had particularly in mind Marx's *Critique of the Gotha Programme*. Not that Korsch is arguing that what Marx actually had to say about the Gotha Programme was wrong or inaccurate: there is not one word about the *content* of Marx's critique—it is simply, says Korsch, that Marx made the mistake of judging the proletariat "theoretically". Perhaps he should rather have encouraged the German workers to continue imbibing the muddle-headed illusions of Lassalle?

The truth is that the praxis conception of theory is inanely nihilist. It is a conception which all the praxis theorists (whether they think of themselves as philosophers or not) share to some degree, and Korsch's version deserves special stress, for Korsch himself shows that if the arguments are taken to their logical conclusion, then it is not only Lenin and the "orthodox Marxists" who embraced "philosophical ideologies" and "pure theories", but Karl Marx himself. Can it not be said, from Korsch's standpoint, that the greatest of Marx's endeavours, the volumes of *Capital*, was nothing more than a "theoretical critique", and that when Marx drove himself to exhaustion and well nigh ruined his health in writing the work, he was simply "philosophising" and thus, his heroic efforts notwithstanding, was guilty of idealism and dogmatism? For if, as Korsch says, the *Critique of the Gotha Programme* is "theory" and not "practice", what are we to say of *Capital* itself? As for the direct political work of Marx and Engels—for example in the First International—even this falls foul of Korsch's pragmatist criteria. These struggles—for Irish and Italian independence, in support of

---

[29] English Preface to *The Condition of the Working Class in England*, in Marx and Engels, *On Britain* (Moscow, 1962), p. 31.

[30] Korsch, op. cit., p. 101.

Lincoln against the slave-owners in the American civil war—were not in many cases immediately concerned with the achievement of socialism, so that their practical significance only makes sense when evaluated in terms of a *theoretical* standpoint which understands the differing stages through which the masses may have to pass on the road to socialism. In other words, their practice can only be understood in the light of a Marxist theory of history, the *philosophy* of historical materialism itself.

Korsch's claim then that Marxism cannot, in any sense of the term, be a philosophy involves a childish misreading of what Marx and Engels actually had to say on the subject: their dicovery that all theory was by its nature tied to practice, no matter how idealist the theory, and however blind and foolish the struggle. *This* was what they meant by the unity of theory and practice, a phrase much beloved by praxis writers, but in reality, how feebly understood! It goes without saying that this discovery itself required, as an essential expression of its "practice", the development of consistent materialist premises which alone can furnish the philosophical foundations of Marxist thought. For philosophy stripped of its traditional mystique is simply the generalised expression of all theoretical statements, from simple everyday words to grand embracing concepts. And although it is typical of the intellectual posturing of praxis writers that they should imagine in some cases that one can actually do away with philosophy by some sort of heroic act of will, the truth is that just as Marxism, theoretically considered, is a philosophy, so too is Praxis. Despite the torrent of angry words and menacing gestures against those who, it is alleged, have converted Marxism into an "ideology", "a theory of the universe", a vulgarised, dogmatic, idealist outlook, praxis theory has, of necessity, its very own philosophical basis, and however little its practitioners are actually *conscious* of the fact, its very own "theory of the universe", upon which its more immediate principles and concrete observations rest.

What is this elusive theory which pretends not to exist? Which mentions the debate between materialism and idealism in order to abstain from the contest? Which chatters incessantly about Man and Nature and the Universe and yet claims only to be concerned with revolutionary praxis?

I shall try to answer these and other questions as I go along: all I have sought to establish in this chapter is two basic points. Firstly that Marxism, despite the praxical sound and fury to the contrary, *is* a philosophy; and that, secondly (whatever their other differences), so is Praxis! With this initial methodological stumbling-block out of the way, the argument can now proceed.

4

IS THERE A DIALECTIC OF NATURE?

Fundamental to the theory of praxis is the view that dialectics can only be a part of *human* activity, the practical dimension of *man*, the creator of a *social* world. The idea that dialectics is more comprehensive in scope, that dialectical theory theoretically expresses *all* movement in the world of material reality is fiercely contested, and the notion of a "dialectic in nature" is considered unanimously by praxis writers to sum up all that is mechanistic, dogmatic and positivistic in "orthodox Marxism".

How, asks Sartre, can men be creative and free unless dialectics are *exclusively* human and social in character? Dialectics "without men" perverts Marxism into a "paranoid dream". The only dialectical materialism which makes sense is historical materialism—the dialectics of human relations.[1] Jeff Coulter agrees. A dialectic outside of human activity rules out the possibility of man becoming "an autonomous subject in a total praxis",[2] and leaves him as the victim of a "non-libertarian society", "permanently incorporated into a determinate ontological system". A most terrifying prospect! People will still have to pay attention to objective laws of nature! The concept, praxis writers insist, is both philosophically absurd and politically reactionary. The dialectic in nature puts, says Gustav Wetter, a curse on the dialectic,[3] and promotes, adds Zivotic, bureaucracy, authoritarianism and alienation.[4] Few concepts of Marxist "orthodoxy" anger the praxis thinkers as much as this one.

And who is actually responsible for putting this curse on to the dialectic? An outraged unanimity prevails: the villain of the piece is Frederick Engels. It is Engels who inflicted upon his comrade's theory the ugly naturalistic stigma that has so confused succeeding generations of Marxists and done so much damage to the movement.

Engels ventured where Marx had feared to tread, and the outcome was

[1] *Search for a Method*, op. cit., p. xiii.
[2] "Marxism and the Engels Paradox", op. cit., p. 137.
[3] Cited by Coulter, op. cit., p. 129.
[4] Miladin Zivotic, "The Dialectics of Nature and the Authenticity of Dialectics", *Praxis*, 1965.

dialectical materialism; an incubus which has not ceased to weigh heavily upon his followers. . . .[5]

These are grave charges, and they are by no means new.

As early as 1907, Victor Chernov, described by Lenin as "a Narodnik and a sworn enemy of Marxism",[6] can be found setting up Marx against Engels, and accusing the latter of "naïve dogmatic materialism" and of "the crudest materialist dogmatism".[7] Twelve years later—despite Lenin's exposition in *Materialism and Empirio-Criticism*—George Lukacs in his *History and Class Consciousness* forcefully advanced substantially the same view, claiming that Engels' philosophical formulations differed radically from those of Marx, and that, in particular, the attempt to apply dialectics to nature was an erroneous venture, foreign to Marx's theory, and solely the responsibility of Engels. It is of the first importance, wrote Lukacs,

> to realise that the method [of dialectics] is limited here to the realms of history and society. The misunderstandings that arise from Engels' account of dialectics can in the main be put down to the fact that Engels—following Hegel's mistaken lead—extended the method to apply also to nature.[8]

And there is no doubt that Lukacs' critique of Engels struck a responsive chord. Lukacs explicitly acknowledged this when he later commented that his book fell in with a basic tendency in the history of Marxism that has taken many forms, all of which

> have one thing in common, whether they like it or not and irrespective of their philosophical origins or political effects: they strike at the very roots of Marxian ontology. I refer to the tendency to view Marxism exclusively as a theory of society, as social philosophy, and hence to ignore or repudiate it as a theory of nature.[9]

Lukacs, one of the founding fathers of "praxis" (though by no means the earliest as we shall see), has been followed with enthusiasm by most other members of the praxis school—Avineri, for example, arguing that Lukacs and his disciples are "perfectly right" in maintaining that the dialectics in nature, in Engels' sense of the term, has very little in common with the way Marx understood materialism.[10]

How true is the alleged division between Marx and Engels? *Prima*

---

[5] George Lichtheim, *Marxism*, op. cit., p. 247.
[6] *Materialism and Empirio-Criticism*, op. cit., p. 85.
[7] Ibid., p. 86.
[8] Lukacs, op. cit., p. 24.
[9] "Preface to the New Edition" (1967), op. cit., p. xvi.
[10] Avineri, op. cit., p. 69.

facie, from what we know of Marx and Engels' intimate political and intellectual co-operation, it seems highly improbable that a rift of this magnitude could have divided the two men, but the charge is made so frequently (and fiercely), and not only by advocates of praxis theory, that it cannot simply be ignored. Nor is the matter merely one of academic interest: if millions of Marx's followers have got his position on this basic philosophical question completely cockeyed, then the quicker we face the fact the better. Of course, if an investigation shows that in fact Marx *himself* suffered from the same "dogmatic" and "positivist" tendencies as Engels (in the dialectics of nature as on other issues), then it is important that the praxis writers should be made aware of this fact, for only a charlatan or an opportunist can wish to continue advocating a theory in the name of a thinker whose *own* position in fact flagrantly contradicts the one ascribed to him.

Before actually considering the charges themselves which have been levelled against the dialectics in nature, it is necessary, first of all, to sort out Marx's own views on the subject.

(i) *Did Marx reject the Dialectic in Nature?*

As far as Lenin was concerned, Engels' comments on nature and the universe in *Anti-Dühring* (one of the works singled out by praxis writers for sharp criticism) were "in full conformity" with the materialist philosophy of Marx.[11] Both in his commentaries on Marx and in his *Materialism and Empirio-Criticism*, Lenin lays great stress on the basic unity which existed between the two founders of Marxism: he comments, for example, that

> Marx frequently called his world outlook dialectical materialism, and Engels' *Anti-Dühring, the whole of which Marx read through in the manuscript*, expounds precisely this world outlook[12] (stress in original).

And if there *was* any sharp divergence between Marx and Engels on these matters, Engels for his part was certainly not aware of it. As he puts it in the 1885 preface to *Anti-Dühring*,

> Marx and I were pretty well the only people to rescue conscious dialectics from German Idealist philosophy and apply it in the materialist conception of nature and history.[13]

---

[11] *Karl Marx*, op. cit., p. 17.
[12] Op. cit., p. 229.
[13] *Anti-Dühring*, op. cit., p. 16.

But is it true that it was really Engels who was interested in the natural sciences and that Marx, with a shrewder sense of what was "authentically dialectical", was only concerned with society and man? Certainly this is what some of the praxis school suggest: Petrovic, for example, asks

> what is Marx's attitude toward the dialectic of nature? Here and there Marx used to remark that dialectical laws hold not only for society but also for nature. But he never became so interested in the dialectics of nature as to try and write more about it.[14]

These remarks "here and there" are, as I shall show in a minute, of the utmost importance: but how true is it that Marx was never really interested in these matters and so, as Lichtheim argues, "wisely left nature (other than human nature) alone"?[15] It is certainly true, as Engels comments, that he and Marx

> could keep up with the natural sciences only piecemeal, intermittently and sporadically,[16]

and we know of course, that it was Engels rather than Marx who was to write at some length on the question of dialectics in nature and of the value of dialectical thinking in the natural sciences.

But why was this? Because Marx lacked a real interest in the natural sciences and was able to somehow sense, anticipating his praxis "champions", that dialectics could only really exist in the social world of man?

There are a number of good reasons for believing that this inference is basically false and that no real or significant difference exists between Marx and Engels on the question which arouses such ire from praxis quarters, the dialectic in nature. Marx's alleged "lack of interest" in the natural sciences can be quite simply explained from the division of work which he and Engels had worked out between them; it is moreover strongly refuted by evidence of Marx's real concern with a science of nature in even his earliest writings, in his joint writings with Engels, in the two men's correspondence, and indeed within *Capital* itself.

I shall say something about each of these points in turn.

Firstly—a simple point which it is vital to bear in mind but which is invariably ignored by praxis critics—is the fact that once it was clear to

---

[14] Petrovic, op. cit., p. 28.
[15] Lichtheim, *Marxism* (London, 1964), p. 247.
[16] *Anti-Dühring*, op. cit., pp. 16–17.

Marx and Engels that they were both moving towards a scientific understanding of capitalism, they decided to divide up the work between them. This fact is important not simply because it explains why Engels was to devote more time than Marx to discussing philosophical questions, but also because it points to a basic unity of outlook which made such an agreement possible. The *German Ideology*, the *Holy Family*, and the *Communist Manifesto*, all joint works, are three outstanding testimonies to the essential unity which existed between Marx and Engels on political and philosophical questions, and it is not surprising that Marx, as he looks back upon his collaboration with Engels, should refer to the fact that Engels in his splendid treatise on political economy in 1844 and his *Condition of the Working Class in England*, completed in the following year, "had arrived by another road . . . at the same result as I",[17] and that when in 1845 Engels came to Brussels

> we decided to set forth together *our* conception as opposed to the ideological one of German philosophy, in fact to settle accounts with *our* former philosophical conscience (stress mine).

Now this would be an astonishing thing to say if in fact Engels' conception of dialectics was "mechanistic" and "vulgar" and radically opposed to the "praxis" theory of Marx. There is not the *slightest hint* of such a disagreement, and although the comment refers to an earlier period, it was in fact written in 1859.

The fact then that Marx and Engels decided upon a division of labour in order to elaborate their new outlook in all its variegated aspects[18] is itself evidence that both felt a basic underlying agreement with the other on all essential issues. Nor is it only Engels who refers to the agreement to divide the work up between them: Marx refers to it explicitly in his work against *Herr Vogt* when he says, alluding of course to Engels, that "both of us work according to a common plan and in accordance with an earlier arrangement".[19]

Why then did the division of labour take the form it did? Engels answers this question in his Preface to the *Housing Question*:

> as a consequence of the division of labour that existed between Marx and myself, it fell to me to present our opinions in the periodical press, and,

---

[17] Preface to the *Critique of Political Economy* (Lawrence and Wishart, 1971), p. 22.

[18] Engels, *History of the Communist League* in Marx-Engels, *Selected Works* (Lawrence and Wishart, 1970), p. 442.

[19] Marx-Engels, *Werke*, Vol. 14, p. 472 (trans. mine).

therefore, particularly in the fight against opposing views, in order that
Marx should have time for the elaboration of his great basic work.[20]

The fact then that Marx himself did not devote much time to discussing
the philosophy of Marxism *as such* (as he would have had to do had *he*
had to "fight against opposing views") and therefore, time to the
dialectics of nature, the question which concerns us here, is no evidence
at all that these matters did not interest him or that his views about
them differed in any real way from the views of Engels. It is rather to
the "common plan" and "earlier arrangement" worked out between
Marx and Engels which we should look, if we want a serious
explanation.

   This then brings me to my second point, for the truth is that even in
Marx's earliest writings, in fact long before Marx worked out a
consistently materialist theory of society, it was clear to him that a dialectical understanding of man and society was impossible without a
dialectical understanding of nature and the universe. Here Marx (like
Engels) followed Hegel, and whatever their differences with the
"mighty thinker" they accepted with Hegel that the truth was "the
whole"; both nature and man had to be considered philosophically, if a
mere relativism and subjectivism were to be avoided. A science of man
was impossible unless it was based upon a science of nature.

   Consider, for example, how in 1842—when Marx's position is
coloured by idealism—he still argues, in the objectivist manner of
Hegel, that social institutions must be based upon the natural laws of
the external world. It is true that Marx's politics are still somewhat
conservative (the argument is directed against laws allowing divorce
on the wishes of either marital party), but that is not the point. The
point is that even here, although still under the influence of idealism,
Marx clearly sees the link between society and nature, and the need to
understand one in terms of the other. The legislator cannot, he insists,
permit his whims "to prevail against the nature of things",[21] for he
does not in fact "make" or "invent" the law

   just as a swimmer does not invent nature and the laws of water and
   gravity.[22]

Human activity, in other words, cannot be understood in abstraction
from the natural world. If this stress on an independently objective

---

[20] *Housing Question* (Progress Publ., 1970), p. 8.
[21] See Marx's article in the *Rheinische Zeitung*, 19.12.1842, trans. in *Writings of the Young Marx on Philosophy and Society*, eds. Easton and Guddat, p. 141.
[22] Ibid., p. 140.

nature is "positivism", then it must be said that such positivism enters into the fibres of Marx's thought long before he ever encounters Frederick Engels.

The truth is that from his earliest days Marx is impressed by the fact that the natural sciences are of crucial importance to the student of society, both because of the disciplined manner in which they investigate reality, and because without understanding nature one cannot really understand man. In the first weeks of 1843, in investigating the economic hardships of the peasants in the Moselle district of the Rhineland, Marx stresses the need to examine relationships objectively, as they really are, and adds

> one can determine this with almost the same certainty as a chemist determines under which *external* circumstances some substances will form a compound.[23]

But it is not simply that Marx believes that one must emulate the nature scientist in the way in which one investigates objective reality. More profoundly there is, in *Paris Manuscripts* of 1844, for example, the clear grasp of the fact that a science of nature is as much a part of the communist outlook (Marx has by now mostly rejected idealism) as a science of man. There can be no question of an interest in one to the exclusion of an interest in the other. On the contrary, Marx argues, it is the great sin of "philosophy" that it has remained "alien" to the "constantly growing mass of material" which the natural sciences have developed[24] and

> even historiography pays regard to natural science only occasionally, as a factor of enlightenment and utility arising from individual great discoveries.

Are communists to ignore the natural sciences because our basic concern is with the freedom of man? This may be the argument of certain praxis theorists but it was never the position of Karl Marx: for natural science, declares Marx, constitutes the practical force which has "invaded and transformed human life" through the development of industry, and thus even though it is still the basis of human life "in an estranged form", it has prepared the conditions for "human emancipation".[25] A concern with the natural sciences is vital. For natural science directed consciously towards human ends can thereby

---

[23] "Defence of the Moselle Correspondent: Economic Distress and Freedom of the Press", *Writings of the Young Marx*, op. cit., p. 145.

[24] *Economic and Philosophical Manuscripts*, op. cit., pp. 102–103.

[25] Ibid., p. 103.

begin to lose its exclusive character, and become the basis of a science for man. Indeed, the very division between natural and human science can then be overcome and the real nature of industry as "the *actual*, historical relation of nature, and therefore of natural science to man", can be properly understood.

> Natural science will in time subsume under itself the science of man, just as the science of man will subsume under itself natural science: there will be one science.

It is of course true (as I shall show in a later chapter) that these youthful exuberant formulations have their weaknesses (which praxis writers ruthlessly exploit), but they make one point absolutely clear. As far as Marx was concerned, the understanding of nature holds the key to an understanding of man: as Marx says elsewhere in the *Manuscripts*, "only when science proceeds from nature—is it *true* science".[26] And yet it is argued in all seriousness by praxis writers that Marx was not really concerned about the natural sciences or dialectics in nature and left that questionable area to the mechanistic formulations of the "positivist" Engels.[27]

This position is reiterated in *The German Ideology* where the two sides of history—the natural and the human—are considered "inseparable",[28] while in *The Holy Family* Marx and Engels ridicule the idea that it is possible to even begin to understand historical reality if one excludes

> *from* the historical movement the theoretical and practical relations of man to nature, natural science and industry.[29]

Now unless the unity of man and nature is simply asserted as a purely abstract (and thus rather pretentious) axiom, it must mean that a study of nature is fundamental to an understanding of man and that an

[26] Ibid.

[27] Valentino Gerratana, in his recently translated essay, "Marx and Darwin", *New Left Review*, No. 82, confirms the importance of these passages in the *Manuscripts* in understanding Marx's attitude towards the natural sciences.

[28] *The German Ideology*, op. cit., p. 28. The passage in which this particular comment is made is in fact crossed out, indicating possibly that Marx and Engels were searching for something more historically precise than the mere assertion that men are united with nature. For the limitations of their earlier formulations, see the discussion in Chapter 8.

[29] *The Holy Family* (Moscow, 1956), p. 201.

understanding of the activity of one rests upon an understanding of the "activity" of the other. Just a cursory glance at Marx's earlier writings reveals what praxis writers try to deny: that a passionate concern with and interest in the natural sciences is as evident in the work of Marx as it is in the writing of Engels.

Consider our third point: the evidence of the Marx-Engels Correspondence and the light which it throws on Marx's attitude towards the natural sciences and Engels' ideas in particular.

It is clear that Marx and Engels frequently discussed questions of natural science. We find Engels in a letter on July 14th, 1858, asking Marx to send on Hegel's *Philosophy of Nature* and entering into a lengthy discussion on the way in which the progress of the natural sciences would have given Hegel "facts . . . from every side" with which to flesh out his dialectical concepts—from the discovery of the cell to the law of the transformation of energy to recent advances in comparative physiology.[30]

In the course of this correspondence, we see not simply that Marx listens to Engels' ideas on the natural sciences, but that the subject is one of great interest to him. On June 27th, 1867, Engels referred in a letter to Marx to the work of Hofmann on chemistry, arguing that it demonstrated, despite the author's mechanistic outlook in general, how the atom, "formerly represented as the limit of divisibility", is in fact nothing more than a relation. Between the divisions of matter there exist quantitative differences which turn into qualitative ones—a fundamental law of dialectical movement. How does Marx respond? In view of the persistent misrepresentations of Marx on the natural sciences it is worth quoting his reply in full:

> You are quite right about Hofmann. You will also see from the conclusion of my Chapter III [of *Capital*], where the transformation of the handicraft master into a capitalist—as a result of merely *quantitative* changes—is touched upon that *in that text* I refer to Hegel's discovery—the *law of quantitative changes turning into qualitative changes*—as holding good alike in history and natural science. In a *note* to the text (at that time I was attending Hofmann's lectures) I mention the *molecular theory*[31] (stress in original).

So much then for Marx's alleged lack of interest in the natural sciences. And so much for his supposed belief that dialectics were purely social in significance and had nothing to do with the natural world. Marx's comments speak for themselves. Not only do they

[30] *Selected Correspondence*, op. cit., p. 131.
[31] Ibid., p. 229.

directly refute the "Engels ventured where Marx had feared to tread" thesis, but they show that Marx considered the *universality* of dialectics to be of sufficient importance to explicitly incorporate it into Volume I of *Capital*.

On May 30th, 1873, Engels wrote an extraordinary letter to Marx outlining some "dialectical ideas on the natural sciences" which had just come into his head that morning—ideas which of course he was to later elaborate at much greater length in *Dialectics of Nature*. Engels consults Marx:

> seated as you are there at the centre of the natural sciences you will be in the best position to judge if there is anything in it.[32]

And what is Marx's response? That these ideas are absurd and untenable—wholly at variance with his own, human-based, dialectical conceptions? That Engels had uncritically taken over from Hegel romantic notions of nature which are mechanical, metaphysical and purely speculative? Alas, Marx had not had the good fortune to encounter the dazzling arguments of praxis theory on the subject! Instead he replies:

> I have just received your letter which has been most edifying for me. However, I don't want to hazard a judgment until I have had time to think the matter over and at the same time consult the "authorities".[33]

His letter then delves into the problems of economic theory which he has on his mind (along with the international situation), but he ends up by saying that one of the "authorities" he has in mind, Carl Schorlemmer,

> after reading through your letter considers himself to be essentially in agreement with you, although he reserves judgment over the details. . . .[34]

It is clear then that Marx takes Engels' ideas on dialectics extremely seriously although it is not clear on this particular occasion how he follows them up, for there follows a break in the correspondence until August 29th when other matters are discussed. But we do know that Marx was not simply *interested* in the line of thought which Engels spent so many years exploring, but was in *basic agreement* with it. Valentino Gerratana draws attention to a letter of Marx to Engels on

[32] Ibid., p. 343.
[33] Marx to Engels, 31.5.1873, *Werke*, 33 (Dietz Verlag, Berlin 1966), p. 82 (trans. mine).
[34] Ibid., p. 84.

July 4th, 1864, in which we find Marx—immersed in works on physiology, histology and the anatomy of the nervous system —commenting

> you know that (1) I get round to everything late; and (2) I always follow in your foot steps. So it is likely that now in my free time I will devote myself a lot to anatomy and physiology, and also that I will attend courses (with demonstrations *ad oculos* and dissections).[35]

As Gerratana adds, the fact that Marx is affectionately joking in these passages should not allow us to conceal the real significance of these expressions.

> From them it is clear that (1) Engels acted as an important intellectual stimulus to Marx and (2) Marx attributed great value to the field which was systematically developed by Engels in *Anti-Dühring* and the *Dialectics of Nature*.[36]

How astonished Marx would have been to hear a confident George Lukacs (and his praxis disciples) assert that the dialectic in nature was a foreign importation into Marxist theory by the "mechanistic" Frederick Engels!

Indeed, nowhere do we see Marx's real concern and interest in the natural sciences more graphically displayed than in the enormous enthusiasm with which he greeted Darwin's *Origin of the Species*. He wrote to Engels on December 19th, 1860, that

> this is the book which contains the natural-historical foundation of our outlook,[37]

and scarcely one month later, he confirmed this judgment, in almost identical terms, in a letter to Lassalle, January 16th, 1861: Darwin's book, he exclaimed,

> is very important and serves me as a natural scientific basis for the class struggle in history.[38]

What precisely Marx meant by "the natural-historical foundation", a "natural scientific basis" for the class struggle will become clearer in a moment: his excitement about Darwin's work (Marx sent Darwin a complimentary copy of Volume I of *Capital* and tried unsuccessfully to

---

[35] *Werke*, 30, p. 418.
[36] "Marx and Darwin", op. cit., p. 77.
[37] *Werke* 30, p. 131. I am indebted to Gerratana's article for this reference.
[38] *Selected Correspondence*, op. cit., p. 151.

dedicate Volume II to him) simply crystallises what emerges irrefutably from the correspondence, namely Marx's deep interest in the natural sciences and his essential agreement with what Engels had to say.[39]

It is not surprising therefore, to take briefly my fourth point in this argument, that Marx should have incorporated some of the ideas he worked out with Engels into his life-work, *Capital*, where, as we shall see in the next section, he defended both Hegel's law of the transformation of quantity into quality *as it applies to nature* and the vital importance to dialectical and historical materialism of Darwin's work.

The dialectic in nature, then, was no invention of Engels: it was worked out in collaboration with Marx and had his full agreement. But what of the concept itself? Because of the immense prestige Marx enjoys as a thinker and revolutionary, praxis theorists, it appears, prefer to manufacture imaginary differences between Marx and Engels, so that they can then carp at Engels rather than forthrightly criticise Marx himself, for it is Marx after all who is the real target of their attacks. But this rather shoddy manœuvre should not side-track us into overlooking the actual criticisms themselves which praxis writers level against the dialectics of nature. True, these are the ideas of Marx as well as Engels: but how valid are they? It is to answer this question that I now turn to consider

(ii) *Nature and Rational Dialectics*

We must begin with Marx's attitude towards the dialectics of Hegel. It is well known that Marx, in a preface to the second German edition of *Capital*, decided in view of prevailing philistinism towards Hegel to openly avow himself "the pupil of that mighty thinker", even here and there "coquetting" in the chapter on value with modes of expression peculiar to him. Marx adds that

> the mystification which the dialectic suffers in Hegel's hands by no means prevents him from being the first to present its general form of working in a comprehensive and conscious manner. With him it is standing on its head. It must be turned right side up again, if you would discover the rational kernel within the mystical shell.[40]

What precisely was involved in this process of demystification? Why indeed did Hegel's version of the dialectic need to be inverted before it

---

[39] Gerratana gives a minor example of where in a matter of detail Marx and Engels differed. See op. cit., p. 77.

[40] *Capital*, I, op. cit., p. 20.

could be said to be wholly rational? Unfortunately the praxis writers are no help here, because not only do they fail to understand the Marxist dialectic (which they ascribe to Engels), but they are also confused about Hegel's own position on the subject.

Let me return for a minute to the criticism of Engels made by Lukacs in a passage in *History and Class Consciousness* which I have earlier referred to. In this passage Lukacs argues that Engels mistakenly followed Hegel's lead in applying dialectics to nature without realising that

> the crucial determinants of dialectics—the interaction of subject with object, the unity of theory and practice, the historical changes in the reality underlying the categories as the root cause of changes in thought, etc., are absent from our knowledge of nature.[41]

But this is irony indeed—for the very conception of dialectics as the unity of subject with object, of theory and practice, is *itself* Hegelian, and all Lukacs has done (while criticising Engels for following Hegel's lead) is to reproduce a somewhat subjectivist rendering of Hegelian idealism and thus adopt a position which leads into the same mystical bog in which Hegel himself becomes ultimately entrapped. It is, in other words, not Engels but Lukacs himself who has "mistakenly followed Hegel's lead". True enough, Hegel has worked out some dialectical theses on nature (which Marx and Engels found enormously valuable), but these theses suffer ultimately from Hegel's idealist belief that if nature is rational then it can only be animated by Universal Reason, the absolute world of Spirit. This means then that reality is ultimately the force of Reason who is sovereign and creator of the universe, while the world of matter is simply a formless, chaotic flux—"prey to boundless and unchecked contingency"[42]—which assumes an ordered substance only as Reason actually creates the universe. In other words, the Spirit is *prior* to the world of nature, for in so far as nature exists *at all*—even as mere "externality"—it exists as "a representation of the Idea".

The notion then, as Lukacs puts it, that the crucial determinants of dialectics are represented by the interaction of subject with object, theory with practice, is ultimately an Hegelian conception; for although Hegel does speak of dialectics in nature, he rejects (like the praxis school) the materialist view that nature is in itself, independently of *all* consciousness (cosmic or individual), dialectical in character. The

41 Op. cit., p. 24, fn. 6.
42 *The Philosophy of Nature* (Oxford, 1970), p. 17.

difference between the Hegelian dialectic and the rather enfeebled praxis version is simply the difference between objective and subjective idealism: the world spirit which, for Hegel, exists independently of particular men—hence Hegel preserves the *objective* idealism of traditional theology—is somewhat diminished in stature by praxis theory, so that it simply becomes the practical energies of men in society. Whereas for Hegel nature exists as a rational system, a spiritually manufactured reality in its own right, for the praxis writers nature only becomes a dialectical reality when, in the words of Alfred Schmidt, it has been drawn into "the web of human and social purposes":[43] it has no objective rationality of its own. The material world *in itself*, considered in abstraction from "the practico-intellectual form of its appropriation",[44] i.e. human activity, can be of no interest to Marxism, for Marxism is about dialectics, and nature only becomes dialectical

> by producing men as transforming, consciously acting subjects confronting nature itself as forces of nature. . . . Nature is the subject-object of labour. It's dialectic consists in this: that men change their own nature as they progressively deprive external nature of its strangeness and externality, as they mediate nature through themselves, and they make nature itself work for their own purposes.[44]

A mouthful indeed, and one which reflects all the weaknesses of Hegelian idealism without any of its strengths! For now dialectics is stripped of all objective reality (albeit of a divinely immanent kind), and simply conceived of as, in the words of one writer, "an affair of the mind". It is only, says Schmidt,

> the process of knowing nature which can be dialectical, not nature itself.[45]

It is no wonder then that this hollowed-out, weak-kneed version of the Hegelian dialectic is subject to the same devastating criticism which Marx levelled against Hegel's *Science of Logic* in one of the fragments of the *Paris Manuscripts*—what the editor calls Marx's "Critique of the Hegelian Dialectic and Philosophy as a Whole".

For what is the gist of Marx's argument? Marx concedes that the notion of the Spirit as historical *activity*, as practice, is an extremely important one, for there is no doubt that Hegel drew this conception from an idealised expression of *human labour* and, in speaking of the

---

[43] *The Concept of Nature in Marx*, op. cit., pp. 58–59.
[44] Ibid., p. 61.
[45] Ibid., p. 195.

spirit as a force which creates itself, points towards an understanding of "the self-genesis of man as a process". But precisely because this creative process is ultimately spiritual, the unfolding of an Idea,

> the only labour which Hegel knows and recognises is *abstractly mental* labour.[46]

The dialectic simply *breaks down*. Why? Because it assumes to start off with "a non-objective spiritual being"—a creator who has yet to create—"a pure restless revolving within itself"—sheer subjectivity, in other words, God himself. Now, says Marx, this initial position is absurd, and it is absurd according to Hegel's *own* conception of the dialectic as the unity of theory and practice, subject and object. For how can a subject exist without an object? It must lack even the *objectivity* of being a subject, and is consequently nothing at all. Hegel must either confess that his abstract reason is so abstract as to be non-existent—in which case it can hardly play its role as world creator—or he must somehow or other persuade this abstract reason to "go forth freely from itself as nature".[47] But how is this possible? The Spirit must, says Hegel, *resolve* to go forth as nature, but an act of resolution is an act of mediation—the mediation of the Spirit with its opposite—and hence in order to "go forth" the Spirit must *already* be in unity with the very material world which it is supposed to create. The conception of dialectics as an *Idea*, as spirit, ultimately dissolves reason into unreason, for it presents us with a creative historical force which is necessarily prevented from answering the supremely creative historical question—"what creates the creator?" Dialectics, which is supposed to be everything in theory, turns out in practice to be nothing at all. The entire *Logic*, declares Marx,

> is the demonstration that abstract thought is nothing in itself; that the Absolute Idea is nothing in itself; that only Nature is something.[48]

That is to say, unless dialectics are themselves ultimately natural, they cannot be anything at all.

Everybody agrees that dialectics have something to do with activity, with practice, with history, but the problem is this. History is only really intelligible as history if it moves consistently and ceaselessly from one stage of development to another, dispensing therefore both with any idea of a First Cause or—at the other end of the line—with any

---

[46] *Economic and Philosophical Manuscripts*, op. cit., p. 141.
[47] The words of Hegel, quoted by Marx, op. cit., p. 154.
[48] Ibid.

ultimate "resting place". This is why, of course, in the last analysis, the dialectics of Hegel's *weltgeist* are not dialectical because they cannot account dialectically for their own origins. Instead Hegel must shore up his spiritual dialectic by granting it a purely miraculous quality of being able to create itself *out of nothing*,[49] and this means therefore denying it the ability, in any meaningful concrete sense, of creating itself at all. In short, unable to explain its own history, the idealist dialectic ceases to be authentically historical and ends up ignominiously, as Marx so eloquently points out, in a slough of mysticism. And if this is the fate of the majestic Hegelian dialectic, what is in store for its watery alter-ego, timidly wallowing in its own subjectivism—the "dialectic" of the praxis school?

According to Schmidt, "nature becomes dialectical by producing men", but how is such an act possible? How can nature produce men, if it is not already a productive force? And how can it be a productive force, endowed with historical creative capacities, if it is not at the same time essentially *dialectical* in character? The problem of course is that the praxis writers vociferously deny the dialectical "nature of nature": Schmidt holds, as we shall see, that nature is mechanical, not dialectical, while Lukacs, following yet again "the mistaken lead of Hegel", accepts an essentially pre-Darwinian view of nature as a chaotic set of forces which go round in a circle "repeating the same thing".[50] But if this is so, "whence cometh man?" To understand human dialectics dialectically, we must understand their *genesis*. And the genesis of man cannot be understood in terms of a nature which is only deemed capable of going round in circles, for surely no one is going to argue in all seriousness that a development as dramatic and far-reaching as the birth of man occurred simply as the miraculous spin-off from a mechanistic merry-go-round dumbly awaiting the human kiss of life before it could "become dialectical".

But praxis persists with its stubborn scepticism. How, asks Merleau Ponty, can matter, if one applies this word strictly, "contain the principle of productivity and novelty which is called a dialectic?"[50] But why, may *we* ask, should matter, if one applies this word strictly, necessarily contain the *principle* of productivity and novelty—i.e. the theoretical reflection of an objective fact—before it can move or create? This is an absurd idea and yet it has always been embraced by

[49] "Spirit may be defined as that which has its centre in itself. It has not a unity outside itself, but has already found it", *The Philosophy of History* (Dover Books, 1956), p. 17.

[50] Cited by Schmidt, op. cit., p. 210 (footnote).

traditional philosophy (whose idealist prejudices praxis theory uncritically accepts), precisely because, as I argued in an earlier chapter, traditional philosophy, soaked in the mentality of the exploiter, has always believed that it is *mind* which moves matter, subject object, the abstract the concrete—the "thinking" master his obedient slave. That creativity—the development of history—comes *from below*, from the bowels of the earth and not from the "aethers of heaven", is an idea which radically subverts the centuries-old arrogance of exploiting classes, and thus at the same time that *idealist* conception of authority and supremacy upon which their entire apparatus of repression ideologically rests. No wonder a scientific understanding of the universe as a world which is real in its own right, independently of mankind and its "divine" consciousness, is an epistemologically repulsive thought! Of course, idealism in our own time increasingly teeters on the brink of outright absurdity, so that rational questions about the nature of the universe and the origins of man are no longer asked. The simple truth is that unless matter *does* contain that "productivity and novelty which is called a dialectic", then its historical development cannot be rationally explained; and if the development of matter is inexplicable, so too is the development of man. The "dialectics" of praxis becomes as theoretically nonsensical as it is practically absurd, for how can we take seriously a concept of practice which is unable to explain its own *concrete* origins? How practical is a "praxis" which must somehow or other "create itself" and, as an impoverished echo of the great Hegelian dialectic, is condemned to take its place with the other innumerable myths in history which have enjoyed "immaculate conception" in the same way? The fact of the matter is that the only way in which dialectics can come about is *dialectically*, and unless reality has *always* been dialectical, it cannot be dialectical at all.

Of course it goes without saying that men through their practice transform nature with the result that nature begins, as it were, to assume an increasingly human appearance. And it is, naturally enough, out of the very human creativity we see all around us, in agriculture and industry, that the understanding emerges that men are not mere passive contemplators of the outside world—they are also its active creators. But the decisive question to answer if dialectics (and thus historical practice) is to be understood, is not whether men and nature interact—it is obvious they do—but rather the thornier chicken-and-egg riddle, *which comes first?* The decisive question, that is to say, is not interaction: it is *priority*, because unless we can answer *this* question, dialectical thought collapses, and in place of the rational, we must rely upon the accidental and the arbitrary for an explanation.

How then is the praxis school to rescue its concept of practice from the paralysing subjectivism which afflicts all who persist in denying an objective, and thus ultimately natural, dialectic? Schmidt, perhaps more than any other praxis writer, is determined to try. Certainly he is aware that "loose" formulations of the praxis concept lead straight to subjective idealism, for if it is argued that dialectical nature is simply a product of human praxis, then can we not say with Lukacs that "nature is a societal category",[51] and that outside of praxis, nothing really meaningful exists at all? Such absurd subjectivism cannot, Schmidt concedes, be squared with Marxism; and indeed he himself cites a good number of Marx's own statements, all of which clearly emphasise the fact that men could in fact produce nothing at all unless an independent material world existed in its own right. In stressing this point, Schmidt of course is quite correct: no meaningful conception of practice is possible unless we accept a materialist theory of the universe. Unfortunately, however, these concessions to materialism simply increase Schmidt's difficulties in trying to reject subjectivism on the one hand, while still defending praxis on the other! For if it is argued that

> all natural being has already been worked on economically and hence *conceived*[52]

what are we to say of that world of nature which natural science insists has in fact existed *long before* the development of human praxis? "This question is particularly annoying for the philosophy of Mach and Avenarius . . ." notes Lenin,[53] and it is a question which is no more palatable to the praxis school. For Schmidt cannot have it both ways: either he must hold that there is no world of nature outside of praxis, in which case the geologist and the zoologist are simply mistaken, or if there is such a nature, then it must—by virtue of the fact that it exists at all—have an historical reality, the capacity to develop, and thus an objectively dialectical character.

How does Schmidt get round this problem? By reviving the agnosticism of Immanuel Kant! He writes:

> like all materialism, dialectical materialism also recognises that the laws and forms of motion of external nature exist independently and outside of any consciousness. This "in-itself" is, however, only relevant in so far as it

[51] Lukacs, op. cit., p. 234.
[52] Schmidt, op. cit., p. 60.
[53] *Materialism and Empirio-Criticism*, op. cit., p. 58.

becomes a "for-us", i.e. in so far as nature is drawn into the web of human and social purposes.[54]

And what does this mean? It means that until we relate ourselves practically to the world of nature, nature has "no relevance", so that as far as *we* are concerned, nature does not in fact exist. It only becomes real (and thus dialectical) when men make use of this nature in organising their lives, in which case it must follow that Schmidt's assertion that nature "exists independently and outside of any consciousness" cannot be proved. To say that nature as a thing-in-itself is "irrelevant" is to argue that objective nature is unknowable, and if *this* is dialectical materialism then it is a "dialectical materialism" which is indistinguishable from old-fashioned solipsism with its childish confession (in the words of Boltzmann, whom Lenin cites) that

to be consistent, one would have to deny not only the existence of other people outside one's self, but also all conceptions we ever had in the past.[55]

The praxical argument that nature only becomes dialectical through social activity suggests to Sartre, that whether we see a dialectic in nature or not is a matter for each individual to decide...

each one is free to *believe* that physico-chemical laws express a dialectical reason *or not to believe it*[56]

but this position does not satisfy Schmidt. As far as Schmidt is concerned, objective nature is not only non-existent, but he can *prove* its *non*-existence by stating with certainty what in fact nature *is*.

Before the existence of human societies, nature could only achieve polarities and oppositions of moments external to each other; at best interactions but not dialectical contradictions.[57]

A most remarkable statement indeed! For nature, despite its objective state of "non-existence", is not simply *not* dialectical, it operates like some static "eighteenth century" *machine*. Of course, how *mechanical* nature produces *dialectical* man is nowhere explained—Schmidt simply assumes that human history is able to leap miraculously out of a void of timelessness! His statement is not only absurd, but it makes a complete

[54] Schmidt, op. cit., p. 58.

[55] Lenin, op. cit., p. 84.

[56] *Critique de la Raison Dialectique*, cited by Coulter, op. cit., p. 143. Of course, this line of argument leads to its own problems, for if each one is free to believe in natural dialectics, so too must each one be free to believe in determinism, reflection theory, etc., the very concepts against which Sartre so passionately argues.

[57] Schmidt, op. cit., p. 60.

nonsense of his *own* praxical theory of knowledge. For it is Schmidt's view, as we have already seen, that

> when understood critically, Marxist materialism does not attempt to assert anything of the material world in abstraction from the practico-intellectual forms of its "appropriation" by a given society,[58]

but what now emerges is that this position is not only not true of "Marxist materialism"—it is also not true of the theory of Alfred Schmidt. For what we are told here is that nature *outside* of society and thus independently of human praxis, can be categorised and has been categorised: it is non-dialectical.

> In its strange alternation between the old mechanics and the strict dialectics of Hegel and Marx, Engels' concept of dialectics corresponded to the pre-dialectical character of nature itself,[59]

and yet these bold assertions as to what nature is or is not *in itself* occur quite independently of those practico-intellectual "appropriations" which are, according to Schmidt, supposed to be the source of all knowable reality.

The attempt to rescue praxical dialectics from an ignominious subjectivism flops wretchedly, and in place of a materialist praxis all we have is a melange of confusion and contradiction. A dismal failure. In the name of materialism, Schmidt argues firstly, that objective nature is unknowable, secondly that it is therefore mechanical so that it only remains to be seen, thirdly, why the dialectics of nature cannot really exist.

The problem, says Schmidt, is that what Engels calls the "dialectics of nature" is simply a series of "abstract metaphysical theses". They are divorced from any concrete historical situation and cast in the form of natural laws—the law of the transformation of quantity into quality, the law of the interpretation of opposites, the law of the negation of the negation—which merely "stand over against reality", "strikingly empty or commonplace", in the words of another praxis writer, "compared with the exact concreteness of the dialectical concepts in the economic or socio-historical writings".[60] Now it is of course true

[58] Ibid., p. 10.
[59] Ibid., p. 60.
[60] Marcuse, *Soviet Marxism* (Pelican, 1971), p. 120. This "comparison" with the economic or socio-historical writings is, as we shall see, a complete red herring. For praxis theory finds the dialectical conceptions as applied to *this* field quite as unacceptable as the dialectical principles of the world of nature.

that Engels formulates his statements about dialectics in nature in general, universal terms; but because these statements are expressed as universal principles, does this mean that they therefore lack "exact concreteness" and "stand over against reality"? The praxis objection is so revolutionary as to be nothing more than a reiteration of that old, tiresome empiricist complaint that there can be no authentic principles of universality in the world, because everything exists as a given *particular*. "Matter only exists in particular forms of being",[61] says Schmidt, and hence nothing universal or general can be said about these "particular forms". Engels' dialectical principles (which apply to *all* forms of matter) must therefore remain "external" to their subject matter and constitute "a dogmatic metaphysic". But how, one may ask, can these principles be "dogmatic" or "metaphysical" if *nature itself* has revealed through the evolution of one form of motion into another, that it "does not move in the eternal oneness of a perpetually recurring circle, but goes through a real historical evolution"?[62] For note that neither Schmidt nor any of his colleagues actually question the *scientific facts* upon which Engels' dialectical principles are based and which point irrefutably to nature as an objective material process in ceaseless historical (and thus dialectical) change. Indeed, Schmidt for all his diatribe against "dogmatic metaphysics" and "speculative principles", has nothing specific to say at all about the *content* of Engels' theory: what he objects to is simply its *form*. One cannot say anything scientific about nature "in the abstract"—as a "supreme principle"—one can only examine it in its particular forms. But this argument is quite as childish and self-defeating as the position we tackled in the last chapter—the argument that it is possible to theorise without philosophy. For now it is being asserted that if something is a particular, it cannot be a universal, and that what is universal cannot at the same time be particular. The truth is, however, that nothing can exist which does not have the dimensions of *both*. All concepts are universal, for they clearly refer to a class or type of things: even everyday words are for this reason universal abstractions.[63] But if all concepts are universal, they are *only* universal because they relate to a given body of *particulars*, and indeed if this were not so, no universal

---

[61] Schmidt, op. cit., p. 57.

[62] *Anti-Dühring*, p. 36.

[63] "By means of his *word* man wrenches [Nature's peculiarities] out of the vortex in which they are swept away and vanish. . . . We are so accustomed to the word that we forget the magnitude of this grandiose act—the ascension of man on the throne of the universe." Herzen, *Selected Philosophical Works*, p. 137.

concept could possibly exist. Even the notion of infinity must refer to something which can be differentiated from its opposite. Hence the mere fact that Engels speaks of matter in *universal* terms—abstracting certain characteristics, motion, mutability, etc., which are to be found in all forms of matter regardless—does not and cannot mean that he is no longer concerned with matter in its *particular* forms; for the only way that one can in fact *identify* these particular forms is by abstracting from them those universal features which they have in common. It is true that when Engels speaks of certain universal laws of motion he is speaking "in the abstract", but it is also true that no thinking *of any kind* is possible unless it is to one degree or another "in the abstract". If Engels is guilty of "metaphysics" because he has something general to say, then so too is each and every one of us, for we necessarily employ a multitude of "metaphysical generalities" every time we speak. If we speak of food when we mean fruit, fruit when we mean cherries, and "cherries" when in fact we mean a given cherry at a given time at a given place, then, according to Schmidt, we must be guilty of "dogmatic metaphysical theses" which stand outside of reality. Of course, as we have seen, all words and thoughts are to some degree or other *abstract*: as Lenin points out, we cannot

> imagine motion, we cannot express it, measure it, without interrupting its continuity, without simplifying, without vulgarising, disintegrating and stifling its dynamism. The intellectual representation of motion is always vulgarised and devitalised and not only through the thoughts but the senses as well.[64]

But if all thought is necessarily abstract, so too is it necessarily concrete, for nobody can abstract from a given set of particulars which are not there. The fact is that *all* knowledge without exception, from the simplest word to the most generalised theory, involves a search for the universal *within* the particular, the eternal *in* the transitory, the absolute *in* the relative, and this "unity of opposites" encompasses both the "particular determinations of matter" and the "supreme principles". Need we add that Schmidt's conception of praxis is no exception?

Schmidt's argument rests, as we have seen, on the view that nature is intrinsically mechanistic and undialectical—able only to achieve "polarities and oppositions of moments external to each other". But is this proposition not as universal and generalised as any which Engels makes? Indeed, whereas Engels' points are properly argued and

[64] Lenin, *Philosophical Notebooks—Collected Works*, vol. 38 (Lawrence and Wishart, 1961), p. 259.

rationally explained, relying not merely upon assertion but on a conscientious examination of natural-scientific discoveries which furnish practical proof for the view that "nature is the test of dialectics", Schmidt's "abstract" and universal theses are simply *assumed* and turn out to be in radical contradiction with everything that has been discovered about nature over the last one hundred and fifty years. The question then is not whether Schmidt and the other praxis theorists have been able to avoid general statements about the natural world (obviously they haven't), the question is why have they been unable to progress beyond the mechanistic notions of the 18th century—both Schmidt and Lukacs embrace these *explicitly*—thus absorbing childish ideas which no thinking scientist could possibly take seriously today in his practical work. As Engels pointed out long ago about the natural scientists, they

> may adopt whatever attitude they please, they are still under the domination of philosophy. It is only a question whether they want to be dominated by a bad, fashionable philosophy or by a form of theoretical thought which rests on acquaintance with the history of thought and its achievements.[65]

There is not much doubt about which form of philosophy dominates the world-outlook of praxis with its arrogant and unthinking rejection of the dialectical character of the natural world. After all, as Engels adds, "those who abuse philosophy most are slaves to precisely the worst vulgarised relics of the worst philosophies"; and after reading about a "pre-dialectical nature" able only to "achieve polarities and oppositions of moments external to each other" in the work of a 20th-century writer, it is surely difficult to disagree.

As for the argument that universal theories must be metaphysical, we concede that when such theories fly in the face of accepted scientific fact, this may be true. But when universal theories are scientifically derived and formulated, precisely the opposite holds. What seems more "abstract" and "metaphysical" is in fact far more *concrete* precisely because, through its very dimension of universality, theory expresses the interconnections of a vast number of particulars: such a theory is not abstract because it is general, on the contrary, it is a thousand times more concrete because it encompasses in its scope a far greater slice of reality than more limiting, particularising concepts. Thus, says Engels,

> the general law of the change of the form of motion is much more concrete than any single "concrete" example of it,[66]

[65] *Dialectics of Nature*, op. cit., p. 213.

[66] Ibid., p. 226.

since, as Lenin has pointed out, it represents a much more profound, complete and faithful reflection of the real world. Hence it is not surprising that although the germs of a dialectic in nature are implicit in the writing of Marx and Engels from their earliest periods, the concept itself only begins to assume a coherent, systematised shape after prolonged investigation into the actual character, the detailed anatomy and physiology, of society and nature—a lengthy encounter with precisely those facts which (as Engels noted in one of his letters) all helped to "flesh out" and at the same time demystify the profound and brilliant analysis of Hegel himself.

It is no wonder that Marx and Engels were highly delighted with a work which despite "its crude English method", magnificently combined universal theory with specific fact: Marx, as we have seen, told Lassalle that Darwin's *Origin of Species* provided him with a natural scientific basis to the class struggle, while Engels, in one of many comments, declared that

> Darwin must be named before all others. He dealt the metaphysical conception of nature the heaviest blow by his proof that all organic beings, plants, animals, and man himself, are the products of a process of evolution going on through millions of years.[67]

Avineri may argue that

> the origins of Engels' views must be sought in a vulgarised version of Darwinism and biology, with the Hegelian terminology serving only as an external and rather shallow veneer,[68]

but this rather ungracious comment does not reflect Marx's view. Marx, as we have seen, had the highest regard both for Engels' scholarship and his ideas, and it was Marx himself who paid specific tribute to the importance of Hegel and Darwin in the development of his own theory. In a well-known passage in *Capital* (which Avineri must have overlooked) Marx made his famous comment on the dialectics of nature (to which he had already referred in a letter to Engels):

> the possessor of money or commodities actually turns into a capitalist in such cases only where the maximum sum advanced for production greatly exceeds the maximum of the middle ages. Here, as in natural science, is shown the correctness of the law discovered by Hegel (in his *Logic*), that

---

[67] *Anti-Dühring*, op. cit., p. 36.
[68] Avineri, op. cit., p. 70.

merely quantitative differences beyond a certain point pass into qualitative changes.[69]

Was it really only Engels who used "Hegelian terminology" in emphasising the dialectical character of the natural world? The praxis writers appear to believe that because human practice is creative, we can simply make up "facts" about the world as it suits us, there being no objective external reality. Before we assert confidently that for Engels,

> the dialectic becomes a *Weltanschauung*, a positive principle for explaining the world, something it most definitely was not for Marx,[70]

should we not perhaps pause to ask what Marx could have possibly meant when he spoke of the correctness of dialectical laws of logic as applied both to society and to the natural sciences? As for the "vulgarised version of Darwinism", as Valentino Gerratana has shown so well, both Marx *and* Engels carefully studied Darwin's work, and Marx in *Capital* pays generous tribute to its "epoch-making" character. What was "vulgarised" about this? On the contrary, it was precisely Marx' and Engels' creative appreciation for the work both of Darwin and Hegel that has enabled Marxism to transform dialectics from a brilliant idea into a materialist science and to develop a conception of practice that is authentically universal and totally free from the pathetic subjectivism and mystifying arbitrariness of the praxis idea. When Marx enthusiastically championed Darwin's *Origin of Species*, he did so because the work drew specific attention to the importance of *pre-human labour*, a dialectical practice *before man*, and referred ingeniously to the natural organs of plants and animals as having "different kinds of work to perform".[71] Praxis theorists may still prefer to believe that nature goes round in circles and that anyone who denies this is being "dogmatic" and "metaphysical"; but as far as Marx and Engels were concerned, the historical character of nature furnished the very lynch-pin of the dialectical universe. Without a natural scientific basis, class struggle could not be properly understood: without its natural-historical foundation, the whole of Marxist theory is built on sand. After all, how can we really explain the production of man and his society through labour, unless we can also explain what produced this production?

[69] *Capital*, I, op. cit., p. 309.
[70] Schmidt, op. cit., p. 57.
[71] *Capital*, I, op. cit., p. 341.

Darwin has interested us in the history of Nature's technology, i.e. in the formation of the organs of plants and animals, which organs serve as instruments of production for sustaining life. Does not the history of the productive organs of man, of organs that are the material basis of all social organisation, deserve equal attention?[72]

The production processes of nature and human technology are intimately linked, not because, as praxis writers imagine, human history is somehow able to endow nature with a dialectical character, but rather because the dialectics of nature are the sole source of the dialectics of man. Dialectics do not require the helping hand of consciousness before they can become a reality: on the contrary, nature is dialectically prior to man as being is to thinking. And in making this assertion, Marxism has broken decisively from the exploitative traditions of thousands of years of abstract philosophical thought. It has not only replaced metaphysics with dialectics, but has freed dialectics from Hegelian mysticism: it has presented for the first time to the world a critical and revolutionary concept which, as Marx puts it, "lets nothing impose upon it"[73]—the dialectic in its consistently rational form. A dialectic which can only exist *in* human society because it existed before it.

But how does the one form of dialectics relate to the other? This will become clearer as we turn to consider what praxis theorists have to say about the theory of reflection—cornerstone of Marxist epistemology—and the role it plays in understanding the real world.

[72] Ibid., p. 342.
[73] Ibid., p. 20.

5

CONSCIOUSNESS AS THE REFLECTION OF REALITY

Lenin's *Materialism and Empirio-Criticism* must be one of the most controversial books ever written in defence of Marxist philosophy, and it has certainly scandalised the praxis school. The work, we are told, is mechanistic and dogmatic, metaphysical and "naïvely realist", deterministic and, it goes without saying (in the words of Petrovic),

> incompatible with Marx's conception of man as a creative being of praxis.[1]

What is it about *Materialism and Empirio-Criticism* which the praxis writers find so unacceptable? It is undoubtedly Lenin's fierce defence of the theory of reflection—his militant and repeated assertions that reflection theory constitutes the philosophical *heart* of Marxist materialism and is crucial to its inner theoretical consistency. For basically Lenin's argument is this: in order to be a materialist one must acknowledge the existence of a material world *beyond* the mind. Being is necessarily prior to consciousness since it is from the world of material being that human consciousness has historically evolved. But how is this provable? How do we in fact *know* that the objective world exists independently of what we think it is, that reality is not itself a mere concocted tissue of our own ideas? Only because we understand the fact that human ideas and sensations are themselves *reflections* of this objective world, a series of "images", pictures or representations which enable us to understand the ultimate primacy of the material world and its historical role as the creator of man.

> To regard our sensations as images of the external world, to recognise objective truth, to hold the materialist theory of knowledge—these are all one and the same thing.[2]

Indeed, says Lenin, the question of whether there is an objective reality which is independent of mankind, and yet which corresponds to the perceptions and conceptions of mankind—this is "the only philosophical question",[3] and it is a question which places the theory of reflection at the centre of the Marxist conception of truth and the universe.

[1] Petrovic, op. cit., p. 63.
[2] Op. cit., p. 116.
[3] Ibid., p. 171.

Interestingly enough, this point is all but conceded by some of the praxis theorists. Petrovic, for example, argues that *if* one holds to the primacy of matter over mind, nature over spirit, then the theory of reflection does indeed seem "to be the most adequate complement to the materialist thesis".[4] Of course, he hastily adds, "creative praxis" wants nothing to do with this kind of "materialist thesis". But whether Marx is considered a materialist or not—and the praxis writers are divided on this point—all agree that the theory of reflection as defended by Lenin in his classic work is crude and indefensible. Alfred Schmidt, for example, who *claims* to endorse a materialist view of the universe, vigorously rejects, nevertheless, any suggestion that human ideas reflect this world of matter, and refers angrily to the dogmatic theory of "image realism" which, he complains, Lenin "codified" in a book more relevant to the history of the party than to philosophy.[5]

The battle-lines are sharply drawn and the polemics are to be conducted in fighting spirit! As far as Lenin is concerned, the professors of philosophy who specialise in trying to refute materialism are nothing more than "learned salesmen of the theologians",[6] and their muddled idealism, though abstract in form, is political *poison*: it must be fought in the most uncompromising manner. Since many of the positions held by the praxis writers are identical to arguments dealt with Lenin "for the thousand and first time", it is hardly surprising that his polemic infuriates them and they are determined to give as good as they get. Sartre in a lengthy footnote all but dismisses Lenin as a philosophical charlatan, arguing that when Lenin speaks of consciousness as the reflection of being he removes, "by a single stroke", "the right to write what he is writing".[7] So unpraxical is Lenin's philosophical demeanour that he is thereby disqualified! For the very idea of reflection in epistemology is thoroughly anti-dialectical: "a useless and misleading intermediary" which could be profitably "suppressed".

How was Lenin led into embracing such a position? The culprit predictably is Engels, for it was Engels after all who pointed to the indissoluble unity that exists between materialism, on the one hand, and reflection theory, on the other. For if it is true, said Engels, that man is ultimately a natural being who has evolved from the animal world, then his brain must be an organ of matter—"matter which

[4] Petrovic, op. cit., p. 62.
[5] *Beiträge zur marxistischen Erkenntnistheorie*, ed. Schmidt (Suhrkampf, 1971), p. 8.
[6] *Materialism and Empirio-Criticism*, op. cit., p. 322.
[7] *Search for a Method*, op. cit., p. 32.

thinks"—and his thoughts part and parcel of the material world. It must, after all, be

> self-evident that the products of the human brain, being in the last analysis also products of nature, do not contradict the rest of nature's interconnections but are in correspondence with them.[8]

But how do we *know* that they are "in correspondence" with the rest of nature? There can only be one answer: there exists a relation of *reflection*. Unless it is understood that consciousness reflects reality, there would be no way of understanding that there is any correspondence between mind and matter: the relation between them would remain simply *unintelligible*, a mere mystery. The theory of reflection, it should be added, does not originate with Engels: it was used by Hegel in an idealist manner to demonstrate that the world of matter was a *reflection* or representation of the Idea; and indeed, without reflection theory, how could Hegel have possibly demonstrated that there is a *knowable* relationship (let alone a creative relationship) between ideas and reality? For if it is asserted that a Divine Spirit creates the material world and yet bears no intelligible resemblance to it (i.e. is not *reflected* by it), then what we argue on the one hand we simply mystify on the other. Of course, in Hegel, the capacity of consciousness to reflect is nowhere historically explained, but this is not the fault of reflection theory: it is the fault of Hegelian idealism. Engels (along with Marx) sought, as we have already seen, to preserve what was genuinely *rational* in the theory of Hegel, and to preserve it in the only way which is possible, by reconstructing it on the premises of materialism. It is not reality which reflects ideas, but ideas which reflect reality. And without this reflection, how could we assert with any confidence that consciousness is intrinsically linked to the real world?

But praxis is convinced, these arguments notwithstanding, that the theory of reflection leads to philosophical positivism, political conservatism and a radical departure from the praxis of the real Marx. Avineri is prepared to refer to Marx's "materialist epistemology",[9] but insists that this has nothing to do with Engels' "mechanistic invention" which simply leads to absurdity:

> if man is a product of material conditions, he can never emancipate himself from their impact. If the world is not of man's own making, how can he change it? That such a reflectionist view of consciousness was adopted by the German SPD under Engels' influence may perhaps explain, on at least

[8] *Anti-Dühring*, op. cit., p. 55.
[9] Avineri, op. cit., p. 39.

one level, the ultimate conservatism and quietism of German social
democracy despite its overt radicalism.[10]

Lukacs, for his part, remains convinced that the normal concomitant of
reflection theory is "mechanistic fatalism"—a "deeply abhorrent"
passivity in the face of external events.

> Against this my messianic utopianism, the predominance of praxis in my
> thought rebelled in passionate protest.[11]

The view that ideas reflect reality must, argued Lukacs in 1919,
undermine the dialectical unity of thought and being upon which
Marxist theory is based; the priority of being to consciousness which
reflection theory presupposes robs man of that creative, activist role
which is surely the essence of Marxism.

But before I answer these criticisms of reflection theory or consider
the now familiar claim that it was invented by Engels, it is necessary to
return to the position of Lenin, for it appears that the praxis theorists
have, in the course of their attacks on the philosophy of Lenin, brought
to light a most extraordinary fact. The fact that Lenin, despite the
stubborn persistence with which he defends the theory of reflection in
his *Materialism and Empirio-Criticism,* came to see, just a few years later,
the error of his ways. In his famous *Philosophical Notebooks*—after a
careful reading of Hegel—he turned his back on "reflectionism" and
threw out the mechanistic and undialectical theory of knowledge
which he had unthinkingly borrowed from Engels. Like Marx before
him, even Lenin, it seems, was unable to resist the charms of praxis
thinking.

This contention is so remarkable, and so utterly uncharacteristic of
what we would expect of Lenin, that it merits at least some
investigation.

(i) *Reflection Theory and Lenin's* Philosophical Notebooks

There can be no doubt that if a thinker of Lenin's stature was indeed
forced after a closer reading of Hegel to drastically reformulate the
entire thesis of *Materialism and Empirio-Criticism*—"the only question in
philosophy"—this would at least add some fuel to the praxis protest
against the mechanistic ways of "orthodox Marxism". What precisely
is the argument? Petrovic asserts that

[10] Ibid., p. 67.
[11] Preface to *History and Class Consciousness,* op. cit., p. xxv.

in the "young" Lenin we ... find a nondialectical theory of reflection according to which our consciousness is only a reflection of the external world, which exists outside and independently of it. The "old" Lenin, in his *Philosophical Notebooks*, also corrected this sin of the "young" one. "Man's consciousness not only reflects the objective world, it also creates it."[12]

The notebook concerned is Lenin's "Conspectus on Hegel's *Science of Logic*", written after Lenin had "discovered" Hegelian philosophy in 1914–15[13] and its contents point to a major intellectual transformation of Lenin's work, and of course his hitherto "mechanistic" theory of knowledge in particular. In Avineri's view,

> Lenin himself ultimately gave up the mechanistic approach initially developed in his *Materialism and Empirio-Criticism*. Lenin's *Philosophical Notebooks* of 1914–16 include extensive excerpts of Hegel's *Logic* and point strongly to the conclusion that under the impact of this confrontation with Hegel, whom he hardly ever studied before, Lenin came to appreciate the non-mechanistic character of Marx's epistemology and its indebtedness to the German idealist tradition.[14]

What is the truth of these arguments? Certainly Lenin intensively studied Hegel's philosophy between 1914–16, but it is quite misleading to suggest that he became aware for the first time of Marxism's "indebtedness to the German idealist tradition". He is perfectly aware of the importance of Hegel's contribution to the development of Marxism in *Materialism and Empirio-Criticism*, and stresses, for example in his section on the philosophical idealists, that the basic truths of the materialist position should not lead to

> forgetfulness of the *valuable* fruit of the idealist systems, Hegelian dialectics—that pearl which those farm-yard cocks, the Buchners, Dührings and Co . . . could not pick out from the dung heap of absolute idealism.[15]

These are hardly the words of one who has yet to appreciate the true importance of Hegel or make his theoretical acquaintance. Of course it is correct to say that in 1914–16 Lenin certainly continued to *deepen* his understanding of Hegel, but can it be said that the *Philosophical Notebooks* "point strongly to the conclusion", as Avineri urges, that Lenin actually abandoned the theory of reflection as a result?

Let me look briefly at Lenin's notes on Hegel in the "Conspectus" and see what in fact Lenin had to say about reflection theory.

[12] Petrovic, op. cit., pp. 28–29.
[13] Lucien Goldmann, "Reflections on history and class consciousness", op. cit., p. 67.
[14] Avineri, op. cit., p. 70.
[15] Op. cit., p. 225.

According to some of the praxis theorists, after closely reading Hegel, Lenin rid himself of this mechanistic invention of Engels. Here is the truth:

on p. 171: *Essentially,* Hegel is completely right as opposed to Kant . . . *all* scientific (correct, serious, not absurd) abstractions REFLECT nature more deeply, truly and completely.

on p. 180: Hegel actually proved that logical forms and laws are not an empty shell, but the REFLECTION of the objective world.

on p. 182: Logic is the science of cognition. It is the theory of knowledge. Knowledge is the REFLECTION of nature by man. . . . [But] man cannot comprehend = reflect = mirror nature as a whole . . . he can only *eternally* come closer to this, creating abstractions, concepts, laws, a scientific PICTURE of the world, etc., etc.

on p. 183: Very profound and clever! The laws of logic are the REFLECTIONS of the objective in the subjective consciousness of man.

on p. 195: Cognition is the eternal, endless approximation of thought to the object. The REFLECTION of nature in man's thought must be understood not "lifelessly", not "abstractly", not devoid of movement. . . .

on p. 201: Life gives rise to the brain. Nature is REFLECTED in the human brain. By checking and applying the correctness of these REFLECTIONS in his practice and technique, man arrives at objective truth.

on p. 202: The idea of including *Life* in logic is comprehensible—and brilliant—from the standpoint of the *process* of the REFLECTION of the objective world in the (at first individual) consciousness of man and of the testing of the consciousness (REFLECTION) through practice.[16]

(Capitals throughout are mine.)

Now the praxis theorists are certainly correct to stress the fact that Lenin is impressed by his close reading of the *Science of Logic*, and finds fresh and deeper insight into the essentially dialectical, militantly "non-mechanistic character of Marx's epistemology". But *how* does Lenin deepen his knowledge of dialectics? By an ever greater understanding than before that at the heart of the dialectical theory of knowledge—a theory pioneered by Hegel—lies . . . the theory of reflection! Now one may wish to argue that in fact the theory of reflection is incorrect or (more problematically) that it was not endorsed by Marx: but to claim that Lenin rejected it after reading Hegel is simply a lie. And the

---

[16] "Conspectus of Hegel's *Science of Logic*", *Collected Works*, vol. 38 (Lawrence and Wishart, 1961).

quotations prove it.[17] Nor is it surprising that a thorough reading of Hegel should in fact have confirmed the correctness of reflection theory: for the theory derives from a "materialist reading" of Hegel himself. The truth is that the praxis theorists, despite the extravagant lip-service they sometimes pay to Hegel, do in fact reject the rational core of the Hegelian dialectic—its objectivity—and the *reflective* relationship which this necessarily presupposes between consciousness and the material world. All that is taken from Hegel are his idealist and subjectivist weaknesses.

And yet, if praxis misrepresentations on the subject of Lenin and reflection theory are basically without foundation, this is not through any lack of trying. Avineri, for example, cites one of Lenin's comments in the *Notebooks* (already quoted above) where Lenin says that

> cognition is the eternal, endless approximation of thought to the object. The *reflection* of nature in man's thoughts must be understood not "lifelessly", not "abstractly", not devoid of movement, *not without contradictions*, but in the eternal *process* of movement, the arising of contradictions and their solution.[18]

And he prefaces this quotation with the comment:

> orthodox Leninism may find it slightly embarrassing to be confronted with the following conclusions. . . .

But with respect, it is not "orthodox Leninists" who need worry here, it is Shlomo Avineri. For it is Avineri who has boldly asserted that the theory of reflection is conservative and mechanistic, and who then proceeds to quote a statement of Lenin's *in explicit defence* of the same theory, declaring that for orthodox Leninists the revelation can only be a fearful embarrassment.[19]

[17] We should also note that in other philosophical writing of the "later" Lenin, e.g. *Karl Marx, The Question of Dialectics*, the theory of reflection is also *explicitly* upheld.

[18] *Notebooks*, p. 195, cited by Avineri, op. cit., p. 70.

[19] Avineri is determined to make the *Notebooks* into some kind of startling find. "These notebooks," he writes, "were virtually unknown under Stalinism where *Materialism and Empirio-Criticism* reigned supreme" (p. 70). Is he wholly unaware of the existence of the famous *Textbook of Marxist Philosophy* (Gollancz, n.d.) prepared by the Leningrad Institute of Philosophy under M. Shirokov for all Soviet institutions of higher education? The book (written some time in the 30's) quotes *extensively* from the "virtually unknown" *Notebooks* including, I might add, the precise quotation which Avineri finds so "embarrassing" (see pp. 148–149). The reader should remember, however, that S. Avineri is a critic who abhors all "partisanship"!

Of course, it is true, as I have already pointed out, that many of Lenin's formulations are sharpened and strengthened by his intensive reading of Hegel, but there is nothing new in the *substance* of what he has to say in the *Notebooks* on the theory of reflection which had not been already stated in *Materialism and Empirio-Criticism*. Indeed, in this earlier work, Lenin quotes the words of Marx which the praxis writers are so fond of misinterpreting, that the dispute over the reality or non-reality of thinking which is isolated from practice is a purely scholastic question, and proceeds to emphasise (in a specific sub-section devoted to the question) that the correspondence between our ideas and the objective nature of things we perceive can only be proven through the "success" of human practice. There is no hint here that cognition can be anything other than a *practical* activity, nor is there any suggestion that reflection is some sort of static reproduction of the universal truth. On the contrary, asks Lenin,

> if the world is eternally moving and developing matter (as the Marxists think), reflected by the developing human consciousness, what is there "static" here?[20] ... the sole conclusion to be drawn from the opinion held by Marxists that Marx's theory is an objective truth is that by following the path of Marxian theory we shall draw closer and closer to objective truth (without ever exhausting it); but by following *any other path* we shall arrive at nothing but confusion and lies.[21]

No one denies the value of the *Notebooks* with their renewed emphasis upon the "activity" of thinking, but it is quite wrong to suppose that "the criterion of practice" had not been stressed before. But what of Lenin's assertion which Petrovic cites as proof that his "non-dialectical theory of reflection" had been superseded? After all, does not Lenin actually say in the *Notebooks* that "man's consciousness not only reflects the objective world but creates it"?[22] Is this not, as Petrovic contends, a significant "correction" to an earlier formulation? Petrovic has managed to overlook all the other comments on the theory of reflection (cited above) which are made by Lenin in the "Conspectus" and has found one which presents a slightly different formulation (so it seems) of the epistemological problem. How significant is the finding? If we look at Lenin's comment on the page in which it was penned, we find next to it, the statement (printed in boldface): "practice in the theory of knowledge", and just above it, the remark that

[20] *Materialism and Empirio-Criticism*, op. cit., p. 123.
[21] Ibid., p. 129.
[22] *Notebooks*, op. cit., p. 212.

Marx . . . clearly sides with Hegel in introducing the criterion of practice into the theory of knowledge: see the Theses on Feuerbach.[23]

Now although this is an important comment, it is a comment which reinforces what Lenin (as we have seen) had already said in *Materialism and Empirio-Criticism*: namely, that it was vital to rescue Hegelian dialectics, crucial to understand the role of *practice* in the process of cognition, and thus important to bear in mind Marx's *Theses on Feuerbach* which establish this point. There is absolutely nothing in *Materialism and Empirio-Criticism* to suggest that reflection is anything other than an *active* process, or that contemplation in a purely passive sense is either desirable or indeed humanly possible.

It is true that some of the formulations of Lenin in *Materialism and Empirio-Criticism* can be misconstrued by those who fail to really understand materialism. Consider, for example, Lenin's statement[24] that

> the objective reality is copied, photographed . . . by our sensations, while existing independently of them.[25]

Does not the imagery of the "photograph" or the "copy" imply a measure of passivity in the process of thought and sensation, so that the later statement in the *Notebooks* plays an important role in *correcting* an earlier contemplative bias? Knowledge not only reflects reality, it creates it. This argument, though plausible, still seems to me to overlook two important points. Firstly, Lenin in *Materialism and Empirio-Criticism* is not *primarily* concerned with distinguishing between mechanical and dialectical materialism: the work is an attack on subjective idealism and thus a defence of materialism in general. Thus while Lenin is aware of the weaknesses and inconsistencies in Feuerbach, he can still make use of a number of Feuerbach's statements because they are of a *broadly* materialist character. They do acknowledge an objective reality beyond the mind. As Lenin makes it clear,

> one can be a materialist and still differ on what constitutes the criterion of the correctness of the images presented by our senses[26]

and there is a section of *Materialism and Empirio-Criticism* which does

[23] Ibid.
[24] "Lenin and Philosophy", *Marxism Today*, June 1970, p. 182.
[25] *Materialism and Empirio-Criticism*, op. cit., p. 116.
[26] Ibid., p. 100.

discuss the role of practice as the *Marxist* criterion "of the correctness of the images presented by our senses", and hence the way that the criterion of practice differentiates dialectical materialism from the less consistent (and thus ultimately metaphysical) materialism of the Enlightenment. But if the role of practice is stressed, the key emphasis of the work is on the fundamental point (which *all* materialists accept), namely that matter exists as an objective reality beyond the mind. If Lenin emphasises the strengths of Feuerbach's materialism (in contrast to the glaring subjective idealism of the Machists), there is nothing to suggest in the work that he endorses his weaknesses: on the contrary, it is explicitly stated that materialism can only be ultimately defended on a dialectical basis, and this means *not* rejecting the notion of reflection, but understanding its *practical* character. Thus when Lenin later says (in the passage Petrovic cites) that we not merely reflect reality (i.e. reflect it in some kind of contemplative, passivist way), we *create* it (i.e. *reflect* it in practical, active fashion), he merely re-emphasises a point already made in *Materialism and Empirio-Criticism* in that section where he *does* discuss the "internal" differences between consistent, dialectical materialism and the inconsistent, metaphysical materialism of the mechanist school. What is at stake therefore is *not* reflection theory as such (as Petrovic contends), but reflection theory construed in a consistent, dialectical (and thus ultimately materialist) manner. For what we have in dialectics, as Lenin puts it elsewhere, is

> an immeasurably rich content as compared with "metaphysical" materialism, the fundamental *misfortune* of which is its inability to apply dialectics to the Bildertheorie [theory of reflection], to the process and development of knowledge.[27]

The "Bildertheorie" remains.

But even if we accept that Lenin does stress the role of practice in cognition in his "earlier" work, is it not true that certain formulations in *Materialism and Empirio-Criticism* are misleading? Is not the imagery of the "photograph" and the "copy" liable to a passivist misconstruction? The problem, however, is this: unless we follow Plekhanov's position[28] and question the very premise that ideas do resemble reality in some intelligible way, how can we possibly *avoid* imagery which is liable to be misconstrued by those who cannot understand the practical nature of the reflection process? After all, even

---

[27] "On the Question of Dialectics", *Philosophical Notebooks*, p. 362.

[28] See Lenin's discussion on Plekhanov's "theory of symbols" in *Materialism and Empirio-Criticism*, op. cit., p. 221.

in the *Notebooks* Lenin refers to ideas as a *picture* of the world[29] and speaks of how we "comprehend=reflect=mirror" nature, and these terms, like of course the very term reflection itself, can be misconstrued by those who reject the basic epistemological point at stake—that ideas are, when all is said and done, *subordinate* to the world of reality. To one who thinks that praxical ideas breathe order into chaos and make life itself, the materialist position sounds very passivist indeed! "Copying", "photographing" and "reflecting" are all practical and creative activities in human cognition, and only by emphasising and re-emphasising this point, can we avoid the misunderstanding which may otherwise arise from individual words.

What the so called discovery of the "two Lenins" clearly indicates is that the praxis theorists are not concerned with producing a serious critique of Lenin's epistemological standpoint, they are simply concerned with seizing any "evidence", however flimsy, which they feel may help to discredit the reflection theory which of course is irreconcilable with all subjectivist notions of "praxis". Because Lenin deepens his knowledge of Hegel between 1914–16 this fact is twisted to mean that he has become a belated convert to the praxis school. And yet, as we have seen, there is no serious evidence at all to support this argument.

Nor, unfortunately, is that the end of the matter. For the praxis writers also claim that, like the dialectic in nature, the theory of reflection is the misleading contribution of Engels and cannot justifiably be ascribed to Marx. Although I shall try to avoid covering the same ground twice, for I have already said a good deal about the agreement between Marx and Engels, it is still necessary to devote at least some attention to

(ii) *The Epistemological Question in Karl Marx*

The issue at stake here is a simple one: what is Marx's standpoint on the relationship of consciousness to being? As everybody knows, Marx's earlier writings were influenced by idealism, so that this question, whether being reflects consciousness or consciousness reflects being, is not, at any rate before 1845, satisfactorily cleared up. For example, in a famous passage in Marx's *Critique of the Hegelian Philosophy of Law*, we read that "philosophy cannot be made a reality without the abolition of the proletariat", but what is yet to be explained is the *source* of this philosophy and how its ideas actually come into people's heads.

[29] *Collected Works*, vol. 38, p. 182.

Likewise in the *Paris Manuscripts* of 1844, although Marx tackles many social problems, the question of the priority of being to consciousness is not consistently stated. Consider, for example, Marx's comment that

> it is just in the working up of the objective world, therefore, that man first really proves himself to be a *species being*. . . . Through and because of this production, nature appears as *his* work and his reality. The object of labour is therefore the *objectification of man's species life*: for he duplicates himself not only, as in consciousness, intellectually, but also actively, in reality, and therefore contemplates himself in a world which he himself has created.[30]

Clearly in this passage the *ultimate* priority of nature over man—of being over consciousness—is not really evident and man the creator still bears traces of the Hegelian *Weltgeist*. And yet what *is* clear about this passage, is that although the priority of being to consciousness has yet to be properly sorted out, the relation between ideas and reality remains a *reflective* one: man's ideas and the external world in which they objectify themselves in fact *mirror* one another, because without this reflective relationship how could Marx possibly say that man "contemplates himself in a world which he himself has created"? Even while traces of idealism remain, Marx still embraces the theory of reflection, and like Hegel (who thus differs in this respect from the praxis theorists), Marx is a rationalist and never held the view—in either his early or his scientific writings—that, as Petrovic contends, a reflective relation between ideas and reality is simply unprovable.[31]

Moreover, if the theory of reflection as expounded in the *Manuscripts* still has an idealist hue, the position is very different in *The Holy Family* where Marx and Engels explicitly defend and develop a materialist stance. It is true that they can still say (1845) that Feuerbach represents their position "theoretically": but in "practical" terms, they are now, they proclaim, for socialism and communism, so that even "theoretically" we find materialism expounded with a dialectical rigour which Feuerbach's position lacks.

The comments by Marx and Engels in *The Holy Family* are worth noting carefully—for there have been Marxists, including for example Antonio Gramsci, who have argued that

> Marx never called his conception "materialist" and when speaking of French materialism, criticised it. . . .[32]

[30] *Economic and Philosophical Manuscripts*, op. cit., p. 72.
[31] Petrovic, op. cit., p. 195.
[32] *The Modern Prince* (International Publishers, New York, 1957), p. 103.

and just a glance at *The Holy Family* shows that assertions like these are simply not true. Marx and Engels never rejected the materialism of the Enlightenment: even when they criticised it, they built nevertheless upon its foundations, and at no time did they ever have occasion to revise the judgment of 1845 that materialism is *necessarily* "connected with socialism and communism": that in fact it provides its *logical* basis.[33] The philosophical viewpoint which Gramsci describes as "reactionary", "common-sensical", and "of religious origin"—the view that "the external world is objectively real"[34]—was for Marx and Engels the cornerstone of real science. It is true (and this is what Gramsci seems to be getting at) that objective idealism, like materialism, also asserts that the world is objectively real; but for Marx, the *difference* between dialectical materialism and objective idealism is far weightier than this (rather trivial) similarity. After all, an objective idealist like Hegel, as Marx and Engels complain, "stands the world *on its head*"[35] and denies what is scientifically irrefutable: the absolute priority of nature to man. The simple truth is that

man has not created matter itself. And he cannot even create any productive capacity if matter does not exist beforehand.[36]

The clear-cut assertion of the materialist standpoint represents an important philosophical break-through, and it is a break-through which has been brought about by a growing concern with not simply the conditions of the working class but the problems of practical politics. For the question of whether being creates consciousness or consciousness being is a question of pressing social and political import and demands a consistent answer to the very question which the praxis theory of Young Hegelians continued to dodge—the question of *priority*. In a number of highly significant passages, Marx and Engels stress the fact that it is crucial to be able to distinguish between the *material reality* of the proletariat and its ideological "appearances". The workers are not gods—abstract "makers of the world" who can be used by philosophers as the practical vehicle of the Hegelian world-spirit—they are active members of society "who suffer, feel, think and act as human beings". And what compels them to act is not philosophical ideas but "practical necessity"—"the stern but steeling

[33] *The Holy Family* (Lawrence and Wishart, 1957), p. 254.
[34] *The Modern Prince*, op. cit., p. 106.
[35] *The Holy Family*, op. cit., p. 254.
[36] Ibid., p. 65.

school of labour".[37] It is this "massy" fact which makes the *distinction* between consciousness and being—a distinction which idealism naturally smothers—so vital if the social and political importance of the proletariat is to be understood. For

> the question is not what this or that proletarian, or even the whole of the proletariat at the moment *considers* as its aim. The question is *what the proletariat is*, and what, consequent on that *being*, it will be compelled to do.[38]

It is crucial, in other words, to make the distinction between what workers may *think* they are, and what in fact they are. But how can this distinction be made if one questions the very existence of a real world which exists in its own right independently of consciousness? Materialism and communism are, as Marx and Engels stress, closely interlinked, and "mere philosophy" which smudges the truth about an objective world thus leads to impotence, to what Marx and Engels aptly describe as a "practice *in abstracto*",[39] a practice dangerously inclined to mistake its own illusions about life for the real world. Subjective idealism, that is to say, and this of course is where the praxis rendering of Hegel leads, is not merely philosophically absurd: it is an intellectual luxury which no practical worker can possibly afford:

> these *massy*, communist workers, employed for instance in the Manchester or Lyons workshops, do not believe that "pure thinking" will be able to argue away their industrial masters and their own practical debasement. They are most painfully aware of the *difference* between *being* and *thinking*, between *consciousness* and *life*. They know that property, capital, money, wage labour and the like are no ideal figments of the brain but very practical, very objective sources of their self-estrangement and that they must be abolished in a practical, objective way for man to become man not only in *thinking*, in *consciousness*, but in massy *being* in life.[40]

Marx was a materialist, and those who assert to the contrary simply have not read (or at least digested) what Marx wrote on the subject. *The Holy Family* (like *The German Ideology* which soon followed it) shows beyond all shadow of a doubt that for Marx as for Engels, "the great basic question of all philosophy" was the relation between thinking and being, and that Marx both posed this question and answered this question in an unequivocally materialist manner. If this means that the question of the *primacy* of matter to mind, of being to consciousness, is only possible, as Petrovic argues, "given certain

---

[37] Ibid., p. 205.   [38] Ibid., p. 53.   [39] Ibid., p. 56.   [40] Ibid., p. 73.

dualistic assumptions which Marx's naturalism-humanism excludes",[41] then this so called "dualism" is as evident in Marx (I shall say something about "naturalism-humanism" later) as it is in Engels and Lenin. *The Holy Family* itself proves it.

Now Alfred Schmidt (as we have already seen in the question on the dialectics of nature) accepts the view that Marx is a materialist. Indeed, he shows how *The Holy Family* alone irrefutably establishes this point. And yet, having made this point, he argues quite as firmly as his other praxis colleagues that Marx rejected the theory of reflection. Although Marx was a materialist,

> we must insist that Marx did not see in concepts naïvely realistic impressions of the objects themselves, but rather reflections of the historically mediated relations of men to these objects.[42]

Ideas, in other words, do not actually reflect the *real world itself.* But what do Marx and Engels say on the subject in the work which Schmidt himself acknowledges clearly establishes their materialism, *The Holy Family?* They make it absolutely clear that it is impossible to be a consistent materialist and yet not embrace the theory of reflection. For consider their scathing criticisms of the speculative method of thought which every idealist employs—the belief that reality takes its substance from the "principles" of the universe. Hegel, for example, in his *Encyclopedia of the Philosophical Sciences* argues that the "idea" of fruit is more basic than the empirical fruits we find in the real world, so that he imagines

> that my abstract idea "Fruit", *derived from real fruit*, is an entity existing outside me (stress mine).

The idea abstracted from the reality comes to imagine that it is the reality which has been abstracted from the idea. As far as the speculative thinker is concerned,

> what is essential to these things is not their real being, perceptible to the senses, but the essence that I have extracted from them and then foisted on them.[43]

Marx then is in no doubt that the idealists have got hold of the opposite of the truth. They forget that their "essential ideas" which supposedly create reality, can only in fact have been drawn from this same reality in the first place. Ideas are abstractions from reality, but

---

[41] Petrovic, op. cit., p. 62.
[42] Schmidt, op. cit., p. 111.
[43] *The Holy Family*, op. cit., p. 78.

this assertion is itself only provable (as we have already seen) if ideas are seen to actually *reflect* the reality from which they have been abstracted. That is to say,

> the apples, pears, almonds and raisins that we get in the speculative world are nothing but *semblances* of apples, *semblances* of pears, *semblances* of almonds, and *semblances* of raisins.[44]

And it goes without saying, of course, that it would be quite impossible for Marx and Engels to say that the ideas were "semblances" of reality unless they actually *reflected* the real world. The one exists independently of the other.

But what of Schmidt's argument that ideas do not in fact reflect objects themselves, but rather the "historically mediated relations of man to those objects"? After all, is it not true that fruit, for example, are not "purely" natural objects themselves, but have in many cases been cultivated by man who has thereby "historically mediated" them? The fact of the matter is that whether objects are "purely natural" or have already been cultivated or created by man, the proposition still stands: the material world exists independently of ideas which reflect it. This material world may be "purely natural", i.e. untouched by human activity or, through agriculture and industry, display the marks of man's expanding productive capacities, but the epistemological point still remains the same: the real world whether natural or social is still a *material* world, and it is *this* which is reflected in the mind. Schmidt's argument is simply a red herring, for the truth is that something does not cease to be an object-in-itself merely because it has human labour mixed in with it: there is all the difference in the world between what a particular economic system in fact is and what people may *think* it is. It does not cease to be an object-in-itself reflected by the mind, simply because human energies have gone into making it. Indeed, even conscious activity itself is objectively material, and we can make no scientific progress in philosophy until we are able to distinguish between what the activity of consciousness *really* is as "matter which thinks", and what idealists may imagine it is. The distinction between appearance and reality—a distinction which cannot be logically sustained *without* a theory of reflection—remains whether the reality is "wholly natural" or partially man-made, and it is no exaggeration to say that this distinction which praxis theory blurs and smudges, forms the philosophical kernel of scientific socialism.

[44] Ibid., p. 80.

No wonder Marx stresses it throughout his work. In *The German Ideology*, we find Marx and Engels arguing that one cannot explain "practice from the idea", one must explain "ideas from material practice". It follows that in any historical epoch

> the ruling ideas are nothing more than *the ideal expression* of the dominant material relationships:[45] (stress mine)

and it can only be said that ideas *express* material relationships because they in fact *reflect* them. Naturally, the fact that ideas reflect reality does not mean that they need reflect reality accurately or objectively: as *The German Ideology* points out (and as we have already noted), because the division of labour in society divides the thinker from the actor, these reflections may well be warped and distorted, presenting an *illusory* picture of the real world. But even illusions are reflections, and indeed, if they were not, how would be able to actually *distinguish* them from truths?

The point then which Marx and Engels have stressed repeatedly in the writings of 1845 that

> there is a world in which *consciousness* and *being* are distinct; a world which continues to exist when I do away with its existence in thought . . .[46]

proves of crucial relevance as Marx begins to extend and develop his critique of bourgeois political economy. If the idealist historians have confused concrete reality with abstract illusion, the economists, acting according to their own analytical "theory of praxis", have blithely imagined that categories and principles rule the world. Denying a materialist theory of reflection, they necessarily turn the world on its head, overlooking the basic fact that

> economic categories are only the theoretical expressions, the abstractions of the social relations of production. . . .[47]

> the same men who establish their social relations in conformity with their material productivity, produce also principles, ideas, and categories, in conformity with their social relations.[48]

And what would our praxis writers say to that? That when Marx speaks of "principles, ideas and categories" *conforming* to social relations, he does not also mean that these categories necessarily *reflect*

---

[45] *The German Ideology*, op. cit., p. 60.
[46] *The Holy Family*, p. 255.
[47] *Poverty of Philosophy*, op. cit., p. 92.
[48] Ibid., p. 93.

them? Over and over again, Marx shows that he takes the reflection theory for granted, and it is not surprising why. As the *Communist Manifesto* stresses,

> the theoretical conclusions of the Communists are in no way based on ideas or principles that have been invented, or discovered by this or that would-be universal reformer. They merely express, in general terms, actual relations springing from an existing class struggle, from a historical movement going on under our very eyes.[49]

Marxism itself, that is to say, stands or falls *as a scientific, truthful reflection of the real world.*

Nor is it accidental that Marx persistently refers to *all* reality whether natural or man-made as *material*, for it is material reality which is *distinct* from consciousness, which determines consciousness, and which is therefore the realm which consciousness reflects. This position receives of course its most celebrated formulation in the Preface to the *Critique of Political Economy* where it is stated that "definite forms of social consciousness" *correspond* to the economic structure of society. This economic structure Marx calls society's *real* foundation, and it is a structure whose transformation we can determine with the precision of a natural science, because we are, after all, talking not about categories and principles, but about material reality. We cannot understand reality from principles, we can only understand principles from reality: "consciousness must be explained from the contradictions of material life", and this is only possible because material contradictions are reflected in the conscious mind.

Reflection theory, that is to say, is an intrinsic part of both historical and dialectical materialism, and hence, not surprisingly, the most compelling evidence of its crucial significance is to be found in the crowning work of Marx's life-long studies, *Capital* itself. At the heart of *Capital* lies the assertion that commodity production (from which capitalism itself emerges) is a deeply deceptive social formation: its appearances belie its reality. To elaborate this point, let me briefly retrace some of the steps which Marx's argument in fact follows.

The commodity, as everybody knows, is a good produced *for exchange*. But in order for goods to exchange, the labour which makes them—concrete, particular labour—has to be stripped of its historical qualities so that it is rendered "abstract", and exhibits a measure of value which enables products as far removed from one another as tins of boot polish and crystal palaces to "change places" in the equalising

[49] *Communist Manifesto*, op. cit., p. 62.

exchange process. Now this process of abstraction, as mysterious as it sounds, is nevertheless perfectly *real*—indeed, as Marx puts it, as real as "the resolution of all organic bodies into air".[50] After all, without the existence of abstract labour, all sorts of different objects simply could not exchange. But here is the rub. Because in the course of the exchange process, concrete labour loses its social and particularistic qualities, it *appears* that when objects exchange they merely exchange as *things* and that social relationships have got nothing to do with it. In other words, as Marx puts it, as the result of commodity production a definite social relationship between men "assumes, in their eyes, the fantastic form of a relation between things".[51] To imagine that "things" can somehow just exchange as disembodied entities is of course absurd, it is an *illusion* but it is at the same time an illusion *created* by the practical character of commodity production which strips human labour of its social character and therefore makes it *appear* as though men were not actually involved. In other words, like the illusion that "ideas create the world", it is an illusion which has been created by the "topsy turvy" character of the real world. The commodity, says Marx, displays a variety of "theological whimsies" and is, of necessity, surrounded by "magic and necromancy", because unless we can scientifically get to its social and concrete roots which the exchange process essentially mystifies, we will imagine that "the fantasic form of a relation between things" is not simply an illusion, but the reality itself.

At first glance, Marx tells us,

a commodity seems a commonplace sort of thing, one easily understood. Analysis shows however that it is a very queer thing indeed, full of metaphysical subtleties and theological whimsies.[52]

Analysis shows us that the commodity of necessity veils itself with what are illusions, but at the same time illusions which have their roots in reality. And how is this remarkable analysis, with its irony and wit, its profundity and penetration, possible? Because Marx proceeds as a materialist scientist who is able the whole time to firmly grasp the essential distinction between appearance and reality: universal labour is an abstraction but it is an abstraction which is at the same time a concrete, social reality. In this way, Marx is able to achieve two things: he is able to show what the commodity *in fact* is and yet at the same

[50] *Critique of Political Economy*, op. cit., p. 30.
[51] *Capital*, I, op. cit., p. 72.
[52] *Capital*, I, p. 71.

time can demonstrate why the commodity has the squid-like capacity to veil in illusion the truth of this reality. But this entire analysis only makes sense because it assumes that our ideas are a *reflection* of reality. Initially these reflections are superficial and misleading:

> man's reflections on the forms of social life, and consequently also his scientific analysis of those forms, take a course directly opposite to their actual historical development,[53]

because, of course, we begin with social life as it *currently* is: we assume, as the bourgeois economists do, that the exchange process is simply something natural, and that commodity relations have always taken the form they display under capitalism. In other words, it is only through protracted *scientific* analysis that we begin to work towards the historical truths which lie beneath contemporary appearances, so that we can explain the illusions in terms of a deeper reality. We can show that in fact, appearances notwithstanding, it is people who are socially involved when objects exchange. But these truths are not obvious, and their discovery is only possible because of a dogged materialist resolve not to accept "metaphysical subleties and theological whimsies" at their face value. For it is no coincidence that Marx, in a celebrated chapter in *Capital*, likens the *fetishism* which surrounds the commodity to the world of religious illusions which is itself "a reflex of the real world". Indeed, he argues that the character of the religious illusion, whether it is tribal or medieval or bourgeois, depends upon how men actually relate to nature in the material world: Christianity, he comments, and especially Protestantism, with its stress upon abstract equality and atomistic individualism, is ideologically appropriate to express the needs of commodity production under capitalism because, as we have seen, it is precisely commodity production which *abstracts* labour into an "individualised" thing. But what of the forms of religion in communities where commodity production (as in medieval societies) exists only on the fringes, so that relations between people are correspondingly narrow? This narrowness, says Marx,

> is *reflected* in the ancient worship of nature, and in the other elements of the popular religions[54] (stress mine).

And as for religious reflections as such? The religious reflex of the real world can only

[53] Ibid., p. 75.
[54] Ibid., p. 79.

finally vanish when the practical relations of everyday life offer to man none but perfectly intelligible and reasonable relations with regard to his fellowmen and to nature.[55]

It is surely plain from what I have said that in order to understand Marx's analysis of the commodity and of commodity fetishism, the theory of reflection is absolutely crucial: for without it, the scientific distinction between appearance and reality smudges and blurs and the *entire* analysis falls to the ground.

Consider for a moment how Marx's analysis of commodity production continues to develop. The creation of money, for example, arises directly out of the need which commodity production has for abstract labour: to facilitate commerce a commodity must be set aside whose *sole* purpose is to act as the medium in terms of which all other commodities can exchange. This means that "metaphysical subleties and theological whimsies" further compound, for now we have a commodity which only exists to express abstract labour in concrete form. Its use-value is to *exchange*; its particularity arises solely from its *universal* function, for money of course, as a "doubly abstract", "universally universal" commodity

> reads all prices backwards, and thus, so to say, depicts itself in the bodies of all other commodities.[56]

It is therefore the *social* role of money to ensure that social relations do in fact assume the fetishistic appearance of *things*: money, more than any other commodity, is dedicated to turning things upside down and confounding illusion with reality. No wonder a materialist science is needed to sort it all out! For now, it can be shown in down-to-earth, matter of fact terms wherein the secret of money lies: a "visible god" that "speak'st with every tongue to every purpose", "that solder'st close impossibilities/and makes them kiss"[57] can be thoroughly demystified once and for all. But not if we reject reflection theory, not if we cannot understand that illusory appearances are simply the *semblances* of a material world.

But having shown that money is in fact simply the "commodity of commodities" and hence "doubly abstract", how is Marx to explain that exploitation itself and production of profit take place? For here

---

[55] Ibid.
[56] Ibid., p. 110.
[57] These words, cited by Marx with some relish, come from Shakespeare's *Timon of Athens* (Act IV, sc. iii).

yet another paradox is involved: having stressed the *equalising* character of commodity production (which makes for abstract labour in the first place), now we have to show that *despite* the fact that commodity exchanges under capitalism are (in theory) equal, exploitation takes place and the capitalist makes a profit. Here Marx extends his analysis of the commodity to embrace not merely money but the worker himself, and explains that the worker's labour power is a commodity in the precise scientific sense (it is worth the value of its production), but a commodity with a difference. Labour power is a special commodity whose value is always less than the value of the commodities which the worker's exertion of labour power is able to produce, and this difference supplies the surplus-value from which capital derives its profit.[58] In the discovery of surplus value we find "the secret of profit making": that secret upon which the entire edifice of capitalist exploitation rests. A discovery, as Engels rightly stressed, to rival Darwin's evolutionary theory, but how was it made? To discover surplus value, Marx tells his reader, we must leave the "noisy sphere"

> where everything takes place on the surface and in the view of men, and follow them both into the hidden abode of production, on whose threshold there stares us in the face "No admittance except on business". Here we shall see not only how capital produces, but how capital is produced.[59]

Instead of the fairy tale appearance of the goose which lays the golden eggs, we find the grim reality: the exploited labourer, the human commodity whose fate it is to produce something "out of nothing". Philosophers who specialise in translating practical misery into transcendental bliss, have spoken lyrically about the universal spirit which creates itself . . .

> the substance of my being, my universal activity, and actuality, my personality, . . .[60]

but here we find what this "self-creativity" actually looks like in material terms.

When Alexander Herzen demanded to know from the idealists why "under this absolute scheme of existence workmen starve in Birmingham and Manchester",[61] he had a real point. Puncture the

---

[58] Technically profit is really a *part* of surplus value, if we separate it from what the capitalist must pay out in rent and interest.

[59] *Capital*, I, p. 176.

[60] Hegel, *The Philosophy of Right* (Oxford, 1967), p. 54: but the quotation of course appears in *Capital* itself, p. 168.

[61] Herzen, *Selected Philosophical Works* (Moscow, 1956), p. 88.

mystery and the bombastic ecstasies which surround the "self-creating spirit" and what do we find? The exploited worker from the sale of whose labour-power values worth two or three times its own value are produced—a miracle indeed! Commodity fetishism assumes even more monstrous disguises when the worker himself is involved.

The philosophical weapon which enables Marx so effectively to combat this dense fog of illusions is, as we have seen, the materialist distinction between reality and appearances, and it is the essence of my argument that this distinction can only be based on the theory of reflection. It is not merely that Marx implies a need to sort out things as they appear from things as they really are: he *explicitly* and repeatedly stresses that without this distinction no science is possible. All science, he says in the third volume of *Capital*,

> would be superfluous if the outward appearance and the essence of things directly coincided,[62]

for the truth is that phenomena like the commodity are deceptively simple "on the surface of things". It is always easier to be "vulgar" (i.e. superficial) than to be scientific and record "the estranged outward appearances of economic relations" while ignoring "the internal relationships" upon which these are based. The truth is often seemingly paradoxical: profit is made under capitalism and yet goods exchange under perfect competition *at their values*. This undeniably happens and yet it is "contrary to everyday observation".

> It is also paradox that the earth moves round the sun, and that water consists of two highly inflammable gases. Scientific truth is always paradox, if judged by everyday experience which catches only the delusive appearance of things.[63]

But how can we distinguish truth from appearances unless we say that one is a misleading *reflection* of the other? And how can we fight for the truth *in place of* appearances (a relative journey towards absolute truth), unless we understand science as a truthful reflection of what is really going on? Marx not only emphasises the need to distinguish reality from appearances,[64] he explicitly links this point with his basic theory of reflection. In a passage dealing with Ricardo's "great

---

[62] *Capital*, III (Lawrence and Wishart, 1966), p. 817.

[63] *Wages, Price and Profit* (Moscow, 1947), pp. 31–32.

[64] There is further discussion on this in N. Geras, "Essence and Appearance: Aspects of Fetishism in Marx's *Capital*", *New Left Review* 65, and David Goldway, "Appearance and Reality in Marx's *Capital*", *Science and Society*, 1967.

historical significance for science", in his *Theories of Surplus Value*, Marx explains how Ricardo's stress on the determination of value by labour time creates the means for understanding the very *basis*, the "internal organic coherence and life process" of the bourgeois system: it enables him

> to elucidate how far a science which in fact only *reflects* and reproduces the manifest forms of the process, and therefore also how far these manifestations themselves, correspond to the basis on which the inner coherence, the actual physiology of bourgeois society rests; and in general, to examine how matters stand with the contradiction between the apparent and actual movement of the system[65] (stress mine).

I shall return again to this extremely significant passage, but for the moment it is stressed in order to emphasise how, for Marx, the distinction between the apparent and the real, the inner and the outer—distinctions crucial to living science—necessarily *presume* the theory of reflection. Unless ideas reflect reality, then talk about reflecting the manifest forms as opposed to reflecting the inner structure would make no sense at all. The Marxian concept of science hinges pivotally on this crucial point.

It is therefore no exaggeration to say that the famous words in Marx's preface to the second (German) edition of *Capital* actually summarise the philosophical importance of the theory of reflection to his *entire* thesis. For Hegel, Marx says, the real world is "only the external, phenomenal form of 'the Idea'", while

> with me, on the contrary, the ideal is nothing else than the material world reflected by the human mind and translated into forms of thought.[66]

We have seen from just a glance at some of the ideas in *Capital* why this remark is profoundly significant: but what is the praxis response to black-and-white testimony to the fact that Marx *himself* endorsed reflection theory? Coulter quotes these words and says bravely: this

> will not suffice, of course, for the imputation to Marx of a mechanistic representationism,[67]

but what evidence do we need? Of course, this comment of Marx's is no isolated, "chance remark" which can be seized upon in abstraction from the rest of his work. On the contrary, it is because Marx's *explicit*

---

[65] *Theories of Surplus Value*, Part II (Lawrence and Wishart, 1969), p. 166.
[66] *Capital* I, op. cit., p. 19.
[67] Coulter, op. cit., p. 131.

endorsement of the theory of reflection in this well-known preface admirably captures the philosophical tone and substance of what is to follow, that the comment stands as irrefutable evidence that praxis inventions about Engels' "deviations" from Marx's "true" theory of knowledge are completely without foundation.

The division between Marx and Engels on the theory of reflection, like the division between Marx and Engels on the dialectics of nature, is simply another praxis fiction. Praxis theory is at loggerheads not simply with Lenin or Engels: it is at loggerheads with Marx himself.

Marx not only expressly embraced the theory of reflection, but he and Engels expressly repudiated the opposing formulations of the praxis theorists of their own day—the Young Hegelians. When Korsch insists that Marx and Engels have been misunderstood because

> the *coincidence of consciousness and reality* characterises every dialectic, including Marx's dialectical materialism,[68]

he produces the precise argument which Marx and Engels had as early as 1845 categorically rejected as sheer mysticism. *The Holy Family* states explicitly that being and consciousness are of necessity *distinct*, and this means of course that theory and practice cannot, philosophically speaking, form a "mystic identity" which expresses unity at the expense of differentiation.

> The speculative *mystic identity* of *being* and *thinking* is repeated in *Criticism* as the equally mystic identity of *practice* and *theory*,[69]

a "practice *in abstracto*". And yet what is modern "praxis" if it is not an updated version of this old "practice *in abstracto*"?

Lukacs, in a work which he later admits was an attempt to out-Hegel Hegel, argues for the same "mystic identity" which the polemic against the Young Hegelians already rejected: no separation of subject and object is theoretically possible, "the Hegelian-dialectical identification of thought and existence . . . is also in essence the philosophy of historical materialism";[70] he does so again in the most notorious formulation of *History and Class Consciousness*—

> the proletariat is at one and the same time the subject and object of its own knowledge . . .[71]

—a sentiment which might have emanated from the very mouths of the "critically critical" Bauer brothers over seventy years before.

[68] Korsch, op. cit., pp. 77–78.   [69] Op. cit., p. 255.   [70] Lukacs, op. cit., p. 34.
[71] Ibid., p. 19.

But if it is now clear that praxis theory prefers to overlook the polemic fate of its (somewhat obscure) predecessors and persists in ascribing its own position to Marx, it does not necessarily follow that, because the target of their attack is Karl Marx, all their criticisms must be wrong. What are we to say, for example, of the argument that the distinction stressed by Marx between consciousness on the one hand, and being on the other, leads to dualism, or that the theory of reflection implies an inherent passivity.

It is essential therefore, before leaving this subject, to say something on

(iii) *Dualism, Passivity and the Theory of Reflection*

According to Korsch, any attempt to distinguish between objective reality and the world of ideas must lead to a metaphysical dualism which can only undermine the dialectical unity which exists between theory and practice, consciousness and being. Lukacs, likewise, was adamant on this point:

> in the theory of "reflection" we find the theoretical embodiment of the duality of thought and existence, consciousness and reality, that is so intractable to the reified consciousness. And from *that point of view* it is immaterial whether things are to be regarded as reflections of concepts or whether concepts are reflections of things. In both cases the duality is firmly established.[72]

And a similar stance is taken by Lefebvre and Petrovic.

What is the validity of the criticism? Is it not unsatisfactory, indeed even positivistic, to imply that consciousness, on the one hand, and objective reality on the other, inhabit separate worlds? Clearly it is if it is not *also* pointed out—as of course every Marxist does—that the *difference* between consciousness and being in no way excludes their ultimate and absolute *unity*. In other words, Marxism is *dialectical* materialism, and emphatically stresses that the same world of matter exists of necessity in an infinity of *qualitatively* different forms.

Marx and Engels, and Lenin after them, explicitly repudiated the view that materialism could make no progress beyond the mechanical conceptions of Holbach or Hobbes: on the contrary, Engels for example, in *Dialectics of Nature*, pointed out that motion, the intrinsic mode of existence of all matter,

---

[72] Ibid., p. 200.

is not merely crude mechanical motion, mere change of place, it is heat and light, electric and magnetic tension, chemical combination and dissociation, life and finally consciousness.[73]

Now each of these forms is related in the sense that they are all ultimately material: but if they are united, they are also *qualitatively* distinct, for each constitutes matter at a different stage in its process of evolution. The activity of consciousness, in other words, is material, but it is "matter which thinks", and hence has quite distinct properties all of its own. There can be no absolute dualism between thought and being because conscious beings are 100 per cent material from top to toe!

We have then something which is linked with the rest of the material world and at the same time, as a *specific* form of matter, has peculiarities of its own. What is the problem? The problem is this: that praxis theory for all its dialectical gestures and Hegelian phraseology has yet to grasp the basic point that nothing in the world is *either* endowed with particular properties *or* simply undifferentiated from everything else, *either* something particular *or* something universal: it is of necessity *both*. Each form of matter is quite specific: but each form of matter is also *related* to every other form, and it is in this relationship that we find its *universal* content. In other words, something which is *purely* unique (is "only" a particular) can no more exist than something which is *purely* universal (i.e. has no specific form). As Lenin puts it,

matter is primary. Sensation, thought, consciousness are the *supreme* product of matter organised in a *particular* way.[74]

The fact that thinking is a specific form of activity does not make it any the less material on that account.

But if we say that consciousness is ultimately part and parcel of the material world as a whole, why do we constantly contrast consciousness and being, mind and matter, as though they were something different? In order to *explain* that consciousness, unlike other forms of matter, has the *specific* capacity to *reflect* the real world. The contrast, in other words, between the two is, as Lenin correctly shows, an epistemological one: it is not intended to suggest that because the mind reflects matter, it cannot at the same time be matter "which reflects". In fact, precisely the opposite is true: it is *because* thinking is a material activity with properties of its own that we are able to explain how it takes place. If consciousness lacked its *distinct* material mode of

[73] *Dialectics of Nature*, op. cit., p. 37.
[74] *Materialism and Empirio-Criticism*, op. cit., p. 44.

existence, then its reflective capacity would be a mystery: and if consciousness had *no* material mode of existence, then its capacity to reflect would be a miracle. Neither the mechanistic position nor the "spiritualist" position makes any sense at all.

To insist then with Karl Korsch that Lenin "goes back to the absolute polarities of 'thought' and 'being', 'spirit' and 'matter'" when these were dualistic polarities which Hegel had "already surpassed",[75] is wrong on both counts. *Firstly* because Lenin explicitly asserts the absolute unity of mind and matter, theory and practice, and *secondly* because Hegel, contrary to Korsch's uncritical comment, *fails* to overcome dualism because in the last analysis (as I have already tried to show) he is unable to explain the origin of consciousness and therefore is obliged to render the contrast between mind and matter not merely epistemologically relative but substantively *absolute*. His dialectic between thought and being dissolves of necessity into mysticism.

The charge then that the theory of reflection is dualistic is both incorrect and ironic. It is incorrect because neither Marx, Engels nor Lenin ever asserted that human consciousness was anything other than a *form* of matter and hence a part of the material world, and ironic because the charge levelled against Marxism can with real justification be put at the door of praxis instead.

Petrovic argues, for example, that it is not possible to establish primacy within Marx's "naturalism-humanism" because thinking is as much a part of activity as all other aspects of a human being whose praxis is indissolubly whole. How "dialectical"! Everything is related to everything else and no element is prior to any other! But merely to *assert* as Lefebvre does that thinking and being are always dialectically related through praxis, does not answer the question, what precisely is this relationship? For here two problems immediately arise. The first is that of the practical impossibility of arguing that it is undialectical to separate (even epistemologically) consciousness and being. If as is alleged, thinking is identical to being in *all* respects, how then can we give it a separate form of its own, for it is not merely "dualistic" Marxists who separate thought from being, it is the theorists of praxis. Petrovic tells us, for instance, that

in his spiritual activity, man is perhaps more creative than anywhere else,[76]

but if it were really true that thinking is even relatively indistinguishable from other forms of being, how could we argue in

[75] *Marxism and Philosophy*, op. cit., p. 116.
[76] Petrovic, op. cit., p. 197.

this way? After all, praxis theorists repeatedly refer to the *unity* of theory and practice, spirit and being, but things which are identical to one another in every particular are not *united* with each other, for they have no *separate* identity to begin with.

One can no more metaphysically separate the universal from the particular than one can tear apart unity and difference. If two things are united together that can only be because they are *also* different. Praxis theory, in arguing that theory and practice, consciousness and being form a unity, thereby acknowledges that "matter" and mind, epistemologically contrasted, are not identical in every respect. Like the "dualistic" Marxists, the theorists of unified praxis are also obliged to "separate" thinking and being.

This is the first problem which their critique on this score runs into. The second problem arises from their argument that because theory and practice form a unity, then no assertion of the primacy of one over the other need follow. As Schmidt puts it, "reality reflects men's practice, as much as their practice reflects reality".[77] No dogmatic "monism" is needed, for what we have is a mechanical see-saw, and all in the name of the Praxical Dialectic. And this means of course that in rejecting the *materialist* distinction between consciousness and being, dualism in its most obvious form emerges; for out of the entanglement of relationships, all we can point to is theory on the one hand, and praxis on the other. Neither is "reducible" to the other: they are united to each other and yet are apart.

In practice, of course, this position is not only superficial: it is quite untenable. For as Lenin rightly observes in *Materialism and Empirio-Criticism*, it is quite impossible to define *two* ultimate concepts of epistemology, both mind and matter, except by means of a definition which brings the one within the more comprehensive scope of the other.[78] And there have been Marxists like Antonio Gramsci who have mistakenly argued that Marxism rejects the materialist outlook because "the nature of man is spirit" . . . as he puts it,

the concept of "objective" in metaphysical materialism appears to mean an objectivity which exists even outside man, but to assert that reality would exist even if man did not exist is either to state a metaphor or to fall into a form of mysticism. We know reality only in its relations with man, and just as man is an historical process of becoming, so also knowledge and reality are a becoming, and objectivity is a becoming etc.[79]

[77] Schmidt, op. cit., p. 224.
[78] *Materialism and Empirio-Criticism*, op. cit., p. 107.
[79] *The Modern Prince*, op. cit., p. 107.

Now this is subjective idealism pure and simple, but it is expressed with a *monistic* consistency—the primacy of thought over reality—which is rarely found in praxis theory where a dualism of "interrelationships" is blandly asserted as the solution to those absolute polarities of thought and being in which Marxism is supposed to indulge.

Of course, even *consistent* idealism lands up in the trough of absurdity—as we have seen with Marx's critique of the Hegelian dialectic, where in order to explain the *origin* of Thought, one encounters the paradox of consciousness really being something without being something real: consciousness has to be given an independent objectivity in order to deny that there is one. In the last analysis, the nonsense of an abstract thought unable to think concretely erodes all idealist epistemology, whatever its consistency: but the shallow dualism in praxis philosophy makes its accusations against Marxism seem especially ironic.

If then the charge that reflection theory leads to dualism backfires, what of the second accusation, that this theory implies a relationship of man to the world around him which is *essentially passive*? By presenting knowledge as a reflection of objective being in subjective consciousness, Lenin and his followers, says Korsch, "present knowledge merely as a passive mirror".[80] This claim is made similarly by Sartre. Coulter refers scathingly to reflection theory as depicting cognition in terms of static isomorphism, a mere photographic image,[81] while Schmidt protests that if all consciousness can do is to mirror the world of facts, how is it possible for men to change it?[82] Lukacs for his part considers the "objectivism" of reflection theory more appropriate to the "reified" thinking which is characteristic of false consciousness under capitalism: it is an attitude which passively accepts the external world as "readymade and unchangeable". Of course we judge thought by reality, but what is reality? It is a process of *becoming*—"and to become, the participation of thought is needed". Once this is realised, "the question of whether thought is a reflection appears quite senseless".[83]

Now clearly if this charge stands—that reflection theory implies passivity—then indeed Marx's theory is in serious trouble, for this would mean that it asserts that men must *change* their world and are themselves productive, creative beings who increasingly mould nature

---

[80] Korsch, op. cit., p. 118.
[81] Coulter, op. cit., p. 131.
[82] Schmidt, op. cit., p. 56.
[83] *History and Class Consciousness*, op. cit., p. 204.

in their own image, and yet would appear to be embracing a theory of
knowledge which condemns them to the role of spectators who look
on helplessly at the world around them. At the heart of Marxism there
would gnaw a dreadful inconsistency, and in fact it is just such an
inconsistency which is alleged by Alfred Sohn-Rethel (a thinker of the
"critical" Frankfurt school), in a reference he makes to

> a certain incompatibility between two materialist ways of thinking, one
> tracing the basic principles of knowledge to a root in "social existence", the
> other deriving them from the "external world" by way of "abstraction"
> and "reflection".[84]

To get to the roots of this problem, the real question to be answered
is this: if Marx, Engels and Lenin consider Marxism to be a reflective
process—a process of abstraction—how do they see this process of
thinking actually taking place? And despite all the sound and fury
about the passivity which reflection theory "of necessity" implies,
nowhere can one find a *single* reference in the classic works of Marxism
to thinking as a *passive* process. On the contrary, in all the texts, the
position is made crystal clear: men are beings who distinguish
themselves from other animals through *producing* their means of
subsistence, but they cannot produce the material means of life without
at the same time producing their conceptions about this life.
Consciousness, that is to say, is an *activity*, a *practical* process, for it is,
when all is said and done, the conscious dimension of the production
process itself. As Marx puts it in the famous passage in *Capital*:

> what distinguishes the worst of architects from the best of bees is this, that
> the architect raises his structure in his imagination before he erects it in
> reality.[85]

It is quite impossible to humanly produce without the aid of human
thinking. No form of human practice is possible without the presence
of theory, so that when Marxism calls for the unity of theory and
practice it is simply demanding the *conscious* recognition of what in
fact has always been the case. The distinction between theory and
being, is a *relative* one: it is not and cannot be absolute, for men cannot
act at all unless they also think.

"Consciousness can never be anything else than conscious
existence": the assertion that consciousness is a practical activity is

---

[84] "Historical materialist theory of knowledge", *Marxism Today* (April 1965), p. 118.
[85] *Capital*, I, op. cit., p. 178.

made throughout Marx and Engels' writing—in the *German Ideology*, the *Theses on Feuerbach*, etc., and of course in the particular works of Engels including *Anti-Dühring* and the *Dialectics of Nature*.[86]

Indeed, not only is there no evidence that Marx and Engels conceived of thinking as a passive process, but it is precisely because they understood consciousness to be a practical activity that they also insisted that it was a process of reflection. Those who reject the theory of reflection have not really understood the production process itself. And why? Because production is only possible because the world has a material reality independent of human production. Unless the subjects of labour—earth, water, timber, mineral ores, etc.—as "spontaneously provided by nature" exist "independently" of man,[87] production cannot take place.

> If we take away the useful labour expended upon . . . [commodities] a material substratum is always left which is furnished by Nature *without the help of man*. The latter can only work as Nature does, that is by changing the form of matter[88] (stress mine).

The objective independence of the external world is an essential *precondition* for all human activity and it is the very production process itself which gives the lie to the praxis view that somehow or other the knowable world is the production of man. Now once we establish the necessity of an objective reality, there is only one way in which man can successfully act upon this objective reality, and that is by reproducing in his head the objects which he needs to transform in the outside world. The earth, the rocks, the fish, the animals, the fruit—man's "original larder" and his tool house—these objects and implements of human production can only be evident to man if, as objective realities, they are reflected in his mind. Otherwise we may well ask: how could he discover them? Human practice would have been stifled at birth if men were unable to reflect with some measure of accuracy the world external to them, for without reflection it is impossible to identify, distinguish, recognise and thus change. When men produce, they do in fact practically *abstract* objects, sticks and stones, plants and animals, from their natural surroundings, and it is only this practical abstraction in material reality which enables theoretical images of the "abstracted objects" to develop in the

---

[86] See for example, Engels' explicit critique of the "empiricism of observation", in *Dialectics of Nature*, p. 233.

[87] *Capital*, I, op. cit., p. 178.

[88] Ibid., p. 43.

mind—ideal abstractions which reflect in one way or another this activity in the real world.

There is nothing passive, in other words, about reflection at all. Were men simply to gaze "contemplatively" at material reality —although to an exploiter this "appearance" seems to fit the facts —they would not only starve their bodies, they would starve their minds, for they would give themselves no reason to think at all. A "contemplative" mind would be universally blank. Anyone who doubts this ought simply to look at the way in which a child learns to speak and think, for there is assuredly nothing passive or static about this process. Reflecting reality is a protracted practical process with even the simplest of abstractions—our everyday words—involving a veritable infinity of practical moments, of active experience. Indeed, it is precisely the failure of mechanical materialism to understand reflection as a practical, creative process that causes it to lurch into subjective idealism, and it is little wonder that Berkeley could turn Lockean empiricism upside down with such brilliant ease. After all, it is only because reflection is in fact an essentially active process, that we can *prove* the existence of that external reality our minds reflect.

And so yet again the tables are turned on the arguments of the praxis school. Not only is the theory of reflection consistent with an understanding of knowledge as conscious *practice*, but it is only because ideas do in fact reflect the real world that human practice is possible. Lukacs himself, despite his fierce attacks on Marxism in *History and Class Consciousness*, was to later realise just how childishly nihilistic the praxis critique of reflection theory in fact is. In view of the persistent obsession with the errors of a Lukacs who is now only of "historical interest", I quote his recent repudiation of earlier praxis follies:

> the most primitive kind of work, such as the quarrying of stones by primeval man, implies a correct reflection of the reality he is concerned with. For no purposive activity can be carried out in the absence of an image, however crude, of the practical reality involved. Practice can only be a fulfilment and a criterion of theory when it is based on what is held to be a correct reflection of reality.[89]

All reflective images are formed through practice, and their truth content can thus only be ascertained in the same way that the images themselves were formed—through practice, for how else can we set about finding out whether the images in people's heads correspond to the reality of the external world?

[89] Lukacs, op. cit., p. xxv.

Of course, this reality comes to be increasingly man-made with the advance of agriculture and industry, but this does not alter the reflection theory one iota, for even reality which is man-made does not automatically correspond accurately to the idea thrown up in people's minds. It still remains a material "thing-in-itself" even though human activity has played a part in its creation: a stratum outside the mind. Men's tools, their social relations, are still *material* realities because, although human consciousness has played a direct part in their formation, what the mind does in practice is a very different kettle of fish from what the mind may actually think it is doing in theory. This is why the fetishism of the commodity itself (as discussed earlier) arises: men by producing in an exploitative and one-sided fashion necessarily mystify themselves in the process. Indeed, it is precisely because theory and practice themselves are objective realities only partially and imperfectly reflected by the mind, that our debate arises in the first place.

It is clear, then, that the praxis critique of the theory of reflection is ironic and mistaken: it is not only that praxis theory is guilty of the charges it levels against Marxism in the matter of dualism, it is not difficult to show that its own rival epistemology (if such it can be called) leads inevitably to the very passivity of which Marxism is accused. One need only look at the theory of Sartre to see the dismal recipe for despair, impotence and confusion which it offers as its "critical critique". Consider, for example, Sartre's argument that the revelation of a situation is effected in and through the praxis which changes it. "The action", Sartre tells us, *"in the course of its accomplishment, provides its own clarification"*,[90] but what does this mean? Supposing we have two contrary courses of action, each providing its own variety of self-clarification in the course of its accomplishment, which would we see as correct? After all, we cannot choose the course which corresponds to the needs of the situation, because then we would be guilty of "mechanistically" viewing active thought as a *reflection* of reality, whereas what we need to do is to find the truth through praxis itself. But how? By some sort of adventurous leap into the dark? It is not too difficult to see that what Sartre's theory boils down to is the belief that there are as many "truths" as there are praxical actors to make them—a paralysing philosophical *relativism* which would make considered and rational action quite impossible. For whenever we acted, we would be trapped in the confines of our own activity, having no external world by which to measure the

[90] *Search for a Method*, op. cit., p. 32.

extent of our failure or success. Slithering towards a suffocating subjectivism, our "praxis", following occasional outbursts of irrational "activism", would simply relapse into that very state of contemplative passivity of which our critics so thoughtlessly accuse Marxism.

Indeed, without the theory of reflection, praxis can only degenerate into some kind of mystical "creativity" (that most beloved of words!) which makes no impact on any world other than that of its own fiery ego. Certainly it seems increasingly far removed from the practice of the every-day world. Engels, for example, is accused of making a "monumental error" when he presumes that by "practice" we mean that human activity which makes things. Not at all, not at all! Praxis is not practice, snaps an outraged Lukacs, fulminating against Engels for asserting in a well-known passage,

> if we are able to prove the correctness of our conception of a natural process by making it ourselves, bringing it into being out of its conditions and making it serve our own purposes, then there is an end to the ungraspable Kantian "thing-in-itself".[91]

Guilty! cries Lukacs of "an almost incomprehensible terminological confusion", for Engels as a materialist seems to think that there is a reality outside of us—"in-itself", which we understand as we transform it, making it into a thing "for-us". Not so! Everything is "for us" since *we* are the creators of the world whether we realise it or not, and since there is no objectivity outside the mind, nothing real "in-itself", there appears to be no need for any practical investigation to find anything out. After all, Engels' "deepest misunderstanding", says Lukacs, consists of his belief that "the behaviour of industry and scientific experiment constitutes praxis in the dialectical, philosophical sense",[92] whereas "in fact scientific experiment is contemplation at its purest". It is not natural science or material production which is "creative": it is only "dialectical praxis" itself. But if praxis is not technology or production, what then is it? Lukacs, an authentic member of that "Holy Family" whom Marx and Engels had ridiculed so many years before, answers: it is that mysterious and purely speculative identity of theory and practice which emerges in our conscious acts of self-creation, for since consciousness is itself "self-consciousness of the object", "*the act of consciousness overthrows the objective form of the object*",[93] and the spirit of "free activity" reigns supreme. For praxis, man is the Secular Creator, and he provides in the

---

[91] *Ludwig Feuerbach*; cited by Lukacs, p. 131.
[92] Ibid., p. 132.   [93] Ibid., p. 178.

course of his creativity all the criteria and the justification his activity needs. Everything is swallowed in the Solipsistic Whole.

The truth is that praxis theory is neither rational, critical nor "activist". By rejecting the existence of an objective world which the mind reflects, it surrenders reason to arbitrariness and subjectivism; by converting human practice into a mystical "divinity", it makes science impossible, and in place of the distinction between appearance and reality (which Marx so frequently stresses) we have only "the illusions of the epoch"—"self-clarifying" and self-vindicating courses of action. Indeed, to search for the truth about praxis behind the mystifying fog of its menacing appearances is to present its theoretical endeavours in a most unflattering practical light. For everything against which the praxis theorists contend turns back against them: the philosophy they deny continues to haunt them, the assumptions about nature they would exclude stubbornly remain, while the theory of reflection which the praxis writers abuse and attack with redoubled fury emerges all the stronger as a result. For what does the praxis theory of knowledge itself prove? It proves beyond doubt that *without* a theory of reflection no theory can extricate itself from mysticism and crippling subjectivity. Even praxis theory, in order to make itself *intelligible*, must employ the weapons of the enemy in its own defence, for it can only make its case on the presumption that its own ideas *reflect* the truth, *correspond* to reality, *copy* things as they actually are, whereas the ideas of "orthodox", "dogmatic" Marxism do not. Without conceding at the start the correctness of the theory of reflection, the theorists of praxis cannot even *begin* to refute it. Indeed, there are times when they acknowledge this unhappy paradox with disarming bluntness.

Karl Korsch, for example, is quite certain: the theory of reflection is not dialectical—it is "naïve realism". But if this is so, how are we to explain the rise of Marxism? There is only one answer: through this self-same "naïve realism"! The development of Marxist theory, writes Korsch,

> was never just the production of "purely theoretical" study; it was always a theoretical *reflection* of the latest practical experiences of the class struggle (stress mine),[94]

and he is of course, his "naïveté" notwithstanding, quite correct, for how else could it be explained? Schmidt who rests his case upon the purely sophistical argument that there is somehow an epistemological distinction to be made between material reality which men have

[94] Korsch, op. cit., p. 104.

helped to mould and material reality which they have not—anything else is "naïve realism"—comments with happy oblivion:

> in modern times extra-human natural existence has been reduced more and more to a function of human social organisation. The philosophical *reflection* of this is that the determinations of objectivity have entered in greater and greater measure into the Subject . . . [95] (stress mine).

And Avineri, who unequivocally condemns the theory of reflection as "conservative" and "quietist", etc., does not hesitate to fall back upon it whenever he finds himself in a tight corner. He tells the reader, for example, that although Marx's categories are the product of a given socio-historical context, this does not mean they have a purely relativist significance, and why?

> Precisely because the categories reflect a historical reality; the more developed and more complex the reflected reality, the more truthful and adequate the categories relating to it.[96]

We can, it seems, all be "naïve" when it suits us. "Naïveté" of course has its strengths as well as weaknesses, and "naïve realism"—it is really *mechanical* materialism to which praxis writers allude—rests upon a dogged conviction born of practice that there is of necessity something "out there". The real problem with "naïve realism" is not that it is materialist, but that it is inadequately or *inconsistently* materialist and, for all its materialist "hunches", it has yet to break free from that exploitative world outlook which poses everything metaphysically, a world where everything is fixed and rigid: the communication is

> "'yea, yea; nay, nay'; for whatsoever is more than these cometh of evil". . . . Positive and negative absolutely exclude one another; cause and effect stand in a rigid antithesis one to the other.[97]

As Engels points out in this memorable passage, the apparently luminous method of so-called sound common sense, happy within his own four walls, is catastrophically unable to cope in the outside world. For how do we prove the reality of the outside world if we are unable to think in opposites? The "naïveté" of mechanistic realism brings it (as I have already argued) to the absurdity of imprisoning the thinker in his own sense-data, precisely because it sees in matter only unity and identity: it fails to see movement and differentiation. If everything is

[95] Schmidt, op. cit., p. 28.
[96] Avineri, op. cit., p. 64.
[97] *Anti-Dühring*, op. cit., pp. 34–35.

matter, then, argues common-sensical realism, it must be all the same: between the musician and nightingale there is only "a difference in organisation". But it is precisely this *difference* in organisation which gives consciousness its own distinct, qualitative identity: which makes consciousness the consciousness of distinctively human practice, endowed with a property which no other mode of existence of matter possesses: the material ability to rationally reflect matter. Common sense thinks mechanically: because the brain is material, it concludes that it responds to its environment as "passively" and purposelessly as appears the case with all other forms. If consciousness is the "same" as matter, how then can it be different?

> It is characteristic of the entire crudeness of "common sense" . . . that where it succeeds in seeing a distinction it fails to see a unity, and where it sees a unity it fails to see a distinction,[98]

and this of course is brilliantly said. *Either* thinking is absolutely identical with all other forms of material activity, *or* it is a self-explaining miracle. Praxis theory naturally enough is too "adventurous" to accept the first: so that in place of the first, it puts the second. Turning common sense inside out, it throws out the realism, but adheres to the naïveté, so that the implicit one-sidedness and subjectivism of mechanical materialism is brought proudly to the fore. It is the theoretical creativity of praxis which rules the world!

"Naïve realism" is not transcended by accepting its assumptions and then standing them on their head. If it is naïve to think that consciousness is "simply" being (without its own properties), so too is it naïve to imagine that being is simply consciousness (i.e. without any material properties at all). Praxis theory, in rejecting the theory of reflection, rejects the strengths of mechanical materialism with its *attempt*, inconsistent as it was, to understand matter, and instead inherits, builds upon and unthinkingly glorifies all its most pivotal weaknesses.

It does not even stand up to the criticisms of common sense.

---

[98] Marx's review, *Die moralisierende Kritik und die kritische Moral*, cited by Schmidt, op. cit., p. 50.

6

BASIS AND SUPERSTRUCTURE

The well-known Marxist analysis of base and superstructure follows on directly from the question discussed in the last chapter, namely the primacy of material being to the human consciousness which reflects it. This link between epistemology and social theory is forged quite explicitly in Marx's famous Preface to his *Contribution to the Critique of Political Economy*, where, elaborating upon a position already expounded in *The German Ideology*, Marx explains how men as social producers enter into productive relations which correspond to a given stage in the development of their productive forces; these relations form a social basis to which correspond legal and political superstructures, and are reflected in definite forms of social consciousness. Being determines consciousness, so that consciousness "must be explained from the contradictions of material life, from the conflict existing between the social forces of production and the relations of production".[1] It is clear then that the Marxist theory of history rests foursquare upon the premises of dialectical materialism, and that unless one accepts the materialist theory of reflection the entire thesis of historical materialism, so admirably expounded in the Preface, simply falls to the ground.

Lenin makes this clear in *Materialism and Empirio-Criticism* when he stresses that reflection theory holds *both* for dialectical materialism and historical materialism, and adds—a famous comment—that

> from this Marxist philosophy, which is cast from a single piece of steel, you cannot eliminate one basic premise, one essential part, without departing from objective truth, without falling prey to bourgeois-reactionary falsehood.[2]

The notion that when we come to explaining social history the materialist theory of reflection no longer holds is self-evidently absurd, because of course it is precisely in the context of society that the dialectical materialist concept of consciousness becomes relevant. The fact that Marx in the Preface above expounds reflection theory in terms of human society does not mean that the primacy of being to

[1] Preface to the *Critique*, op. cit., p. 21.
[2] Lenin, op. cit., p. 306.

consciousness does not hold as a universal philosophical truth: it does, and it holds whether we think of material being as being socially mediated or "purely natural".

This, however, does not go down well with the theorists of praxis. Averneri argues, for example, that

> Marx never said that "being determines consciousness", but that "*social being determines consciousness*"[3]

and to all who can free themselves from non-scholarly "partisanship" it must be obvious that "these are two entirely different statements". Why? Because, says Avineri, according to Marx,

> "productive forces" are not objective facts external to human consciousness. They represent the organisation of human consciousness and human activity. . . . Consequently, the distinction between "material base" and "superstructure" is not a distinction between "matter" and "spirit" (as Engels in his later writings would have it) but between conscious human activity, aimed at the creation and preservation of the conditions of human life, and human consciousness which furnishes reasons, rationalisations . . . for the specific forms that activity takes.[4]

In other words, we can reject dialectical materialism and yet still preserve the distinction between basis and superstructure, but now in an authentically "dialectical" way which accords with the teachings of praxis.

But the argument that "conscious human activity" is involved in productive forces does not in any way undermine the materialist distinction between matter and spirit, for the primacy of being to consciousness has never been taken by Marxism to mean that *human* production can take place independently of human thought. On the contrary, Marx makes it perfectly explicit (in the famous passage about the bee and the architect in *Capital*, for example) that human production is both physical *and* mental, while Engels, in a brilliant but somewhat neglected (in the West) tract on the *Part Played by Labour in the Transition from Ape to Man*, argued that labour could only become human when, as the product of its development, men developed the capacity to speak and to think.

> The reaction of labour and speech of the development of the brain and its attendant senses, of the increasing clarity of consciousness, power of

---

[3] Avineri, op. cit., p. 76.
[4] Ibid.

abstraction and conclusion, gave both labour and speech an ever-renewed impulse to further development.[5]

Once men have become distinct from apes, there can be no doubt that their development of tools requires the complete co-ordination of all mental and manual faculties. So there is no question of arguing that because ideological superstructures reflect a material base, that human production can take place without human thought.

All human activity is conscious activity. It cannot possibly be anything else. When Marx insists that being (whether social or natural) is independent of the consciousness which reflects it, what he is getting at is *not* that human production occurs without thought, but that what happens in the world of production occurs independently of what people may happen to think is happening. In other words, a social base is not external to thought *as such*, it is external to thought *as an interpretation* of what is going on. For this reason, productive forces are indeed objective facts beyond human consciousness, because it is crucial to be able to distinguish between what conscious human activity is *in fact* doing and what conscious human activity (through its ideologists) may imagine is the case. The position is really quite simple.

> Just as one does not judge an individual by what he thinks about himself, so one cannot judge such a period of transformation by its consciousness.[6]

It requires the sophistry of a praxis critic to imply that because we cannot judge a social transformation by its consciousness, that therefore such a transformation is supposed to occur without any human consciousness being involved at all. The distinction between matter and spirit is not (and no serious Marxist has ever argued that it was) an *absolute* one. It is intended only as a *relative* distinction, so that reference to a social basis as material emphasises that it is independent not from consciousness as such (in any absolute sense), but from the particular way in which people imagine it, consciousness in the relative sense, i.e. as it relates to people's subjective beliefs, visions, ideals, fancies, conceptions, etc.

Avineri's praxis version of the base/superstructure analysis which merely distinguishes between "conscious human activity, aimed at the creation and preservation of the conditions of human life" and "human consciousness which furnishes reasons", smudges therefore the crucial distinction which Marx makes between society as it *really* is and society

---

[5] *Dialectics of Nature*, op. cit., p. 176.
[6] Marx's Preface to the *Critique*, op. cit., p. 21.

as it may *appear* to people at any given time. As it stands it is powerless to free the scientist from "the illusion of the epoch", and the latent idealism of Avineri's ambiguous formulation is made perfectly explicit in the work of a praxis writer who followed Weber rather than Marx, and argued that historical materialism was materialist only in name because

> the economic sphere was, in the last analysis, in spite of occasional denials of this fact, a structural interrelationship of mental attitudes. The existent economic system was precisely a "system", i.e. something which arises in the sphere of the mind (the objective mind as Hegel understood it).[7]

Because human production is *conscious* production, therefore, says Mannheim, it only occurs in the mind. Certainly this argument is absurd, but it confirms the point which Lenin makes in *Materialism and Empirio-Criticism*, that it is impossible to think about philosophy consistently unless one ascribes historical priority to the world of matter or to the world of mind. To try to defend a distinction between basis and superstructure, as Avineri does, *without* embracing either a materialist or an idealist theory of reflection simply cannot be done, for all it leaves us with is an idealist muddle.

The inability to grasp the relationship between dialectical and historical materialism, to understand the way in which reflection theory expresses itself in social terms, has created great confusion over the question of basis and superstructure, and nowhere is this confusion more clearly seen than over those celebrated letters which Engels wrote towards the end of his life in which he sought to clarify the materialist conception of history.

Just as the adversaries of Marxism have construed Marxism as mechanical rather than dialectical, so too, unfortunately, have some of its "friends", and in a letter to Schmidt (5/8/1890) Engels warned against those for whom historical materialism serves "as an excuse for not studying history",[8] the arid, one-sided belief that because the economy is ultimately decisive in determining the course of history, that the superstructure can have no causal role to play. The "fatuous notion", as Engels describes it, that "because we deny an independent historical development to the various ideological spheres which play a part in history we also deny them *any effect upon history*".[9] Among the more recent proponents of this "fatuous notion" have been Frankfurt

[7] Karl Mannheim, *Ideology and Utopia* (Routledge, 1960), p. 229.
[8] Marx and Engels, *Selected Correspondence*, op. cit., p. 496.
[9] Ibid., p. 542.

theorists like Erich Fromm who see in Engels' comments a recognition on his part of

> the failure to pay enough attention to the power of ideas in their theory of historical materialism. But it was not given to Marx or to Engels to make the necessary drastic revisions.[10]

But this is a most garbled version of what in fact Engels said. Engels conceded both in his letter to Schmidt (27/10/1890) and in his letter to Mehring (14/7/1893) that he and Marx, in their *general* expositions of historical materialism, had been chiefly concerned in stressing against those who denied it, the overriding importance of economic forces. This emphasis had resulted in a certain neglect of form for content: in other words, the *principle* had been stressed rather than the difficulties and complexities which are inevitably involved in the "concrete analysis of concrete conditions". But this imbalance was in no way the fault of the theory itself, which had never suggested or implied that "only economics matter", and the misunderstanding had arisen only in the minds of those who had simplistically misread the theory in its most general formulation.

Theory can only really be grasped when it is practically applied, and, as Engels adds emphatically,

> when it came to presenting a section of history, that is, to making a practical application, it was a different matter, and there no error was permissible.[11]

In other words, to really understand historical materialism we must look not merely to the general theory, but to how it works out in practice; and it soon becomes clear to anyone who reads Marx's *Eighteenth Brumaire of Louis Bonaparte*, for example, or Engels' *Peasant War in Germany* that the economic basis cannot for a minute exist "on its own", but is itself moulded and shaped by the politics and ideas of the period. Indeed, the absurd and senseless notion that only the base matters can only arise because commentators persist in trying to abstract historical materialism from the living process of history. Put into a concrete context and applied, it soon becomes obvious that the economic basis only exists *at all* because it is related to the superstructure above it. Base and superstructure form an inextricable *unity*, and the difficulty in understanding this arises from the same mechanistic thinking which we encountered before. If something is

---

[10] *The Sane Society*, p. 266.
[11] *Selected Correspondence*, p. 500.

different, then it cannot be the same, and if it is the same, then it cannot be different. The fact that we can differentiate basis from superstructure, the fact that we point to the ultimate primacy of one over the other, does *not* mean that the two are not, at the same time, part and parcel of the same social totality—that "whole vast process" which, as Engels put it, "goes on in the form of interaction". The separation, in other words, between basis and superstructure (like the distinction between being and consciousness) is an *analytical* or epistemological one, intended to *explain* the component parts of a social reality which can only exist *as a whole*. In the real world of course no separation of this kind can be made at all, as would be immediately obvious to anyone who actually tried to abstract the forces of production from the framework of property relations, or to abstract the relations of production from the legal system, State apparatus and world of culture which these relations necessarily presuppose. We can only understand through abstraction—an abstraction which reveals that between the basis and superstructure there is both unity *and* differentiation. There is *interaction* between the component elements, but within this causal cut and thrust there is the ultimate *primacy* of one over the other.

Yet even some of the more diligent commentators on Marxism find this point difficult to grasp. Bottomore and Rubel, commenting on Marx's increasingly well-known *Grundrisse*, argue that

> at no point in his discussion of material production does Marx use such expressions as "in the last analysis" or "ultimate factor". In these manuscripts he is far from expounding the kind of monist determinism from which Engels found it difficult to extricate himself when, after Marx's death, he was obliged to concede the deficiencies of the materialist conception of history as (in his account) he and Marx had formulated it in their various writings.[12]

Now it is true that Marx writes in the *Grundrisse* that "production, distribution, exchange and consumption are not identical, but that they all form the members of a totality, distinctions within a unity".[13] Are we, however, to conclude from this sentence that Marx, unlike Engels, did not regard material production as the factor ultimately decisive in the understanding of history? We must read on ...

> production predominates not only over itself, in the antithetical definition of production, but over the other moments as well. The process always

[12] Introd. to *Karl Marx, Selected Writings*, eds. Bottomore and Rubel (Pelican 1963), p. 34.
[13] *Grundrisse*, trans. Nicolaus (Pelican, 1973), p. 99.

returns to production to begin anew. That exchange and consumption cannot be predominant is self-evident. Likewise distribution as distribution of products; while distribution of the agents of production is itself a moment of production. A definite production thus determines a definite consumption, distribution and exchange as well as *definite relations between these different moments.*[14]

In other words, while *"in its one-sided form*, production is itself determined by the other moments", when looked at as a whole "production predominates". It serves as that self-same "ultimate factor" which Bottomore and Rubel ascribe to a struggling Engels, and confirms the simple point which Engels was making in his letters, that within the interacting organic whole there must of necessity be *priority*. If this is "monistic determinism", it is monistic determinism not because production is not itself "in its one-sided form" determined by the other moments, but because, when all is said and done, "production predominates"—the ultimate but certainly not the only determining factor.

"What these gentlemen all lack," writes Engels in exasperation, "is dialectics. They always see only here cause, there effect. . . . As far as they are concerned, Hegel never existed."[15] How apposite is the comment in describing the critics and commentators of historical materialism today! What they lack is a dialectical understanding of the unity of opposites: an analytical distinction between basis and superstructure is taken to mean the rejection of society *as a whole*; a determinism of superstructure by base is assumed to imply the absence of any interaction between them. The insistence on differentiation *within* unity can only be "mechanistic" and "positivist", for after all it is concerned with explaining reality as it really is. Nothing very much remains of praxical man and his abstract creativity. . . .

The rejection, then, by praxis writers and their ideological allies of dialectical materialism, with its crucial distinction between the dialectics of thought and being, extends itself to the rejection of historical materialism with its distinction between base and superstructure. But it is not simply that the theorists of praxis deem historical materialism "mechanical", thus demoting the "creativity" of ideas in importance, it is held that the distinction between base and superstructure does serious violence to reality. Instead of reflecting life as it develops, historical materialism, it is alleged, suffocates it beneath its alienated abstractions and results in precisely the dogmatism it purports to avoid.

[14] Ibid.   [15] *Selected Correspondence*, op. cit., p. 507.

Arch-critic in this regard is Jean-Paul Sartre who devotes a good deal of his Introduction to the *Critique de la Raison Dialectique* (translated as *Search for a Method*) to attacking this "dogmatism" of the contemporary and classical Marxists. I turn to consider his arguments in a little more detail.

(i) *Sartre's Critique of "Idealist Marxism"*

As far as Sartre is concerned, "idealist Marxism" has the incorrigible habit of conceptualising events *a priori*. Concrete events and real historical people are forced "terroristically" into prefabricated moulds, so that the "particularities" of history are liquidated in the process. "The lazy Marxist puts everything into everything", complains Sartre—real men become mere symbols of the Marxist's myths and analysis boils down to "the bureaucrat's practice of unifying everything". But who are the lazy Marxists whom Sartre has in mind?

One of them certainly seems to be Engels, for Sartre draws his reader's attention to Engels' letter to Starkenburg (25/1/1894), where Engels elaborates his view that all societies are governed by necessity, "the complement and form of appearance of which is *accident*".[16] Take the case, Engels says, of the great man in history—that such and such a man is found at a particular time is pure chance. Cut him out and a substitute will be found, at least in the long run. "If a Napoleon had been lacking, another would have filled his place." Accidents, in other words, play their role in history, but only as the particularised configurations of necessity. The further away a particular sphere is from necessity—i.e. economic necessity—and the closer it approaches the realm of ideology and personality—i.e. "accident"—the more zig-zag will be the curve which links the two spheres.

> But if you plot the average axis of the curve, you will find that this axis will run more and more nearly parallel to the axis of economic development the longer the period considered and the wider the field dealt with.[17]

In other words, no matter how remote the world of "genius" and ideology appears from the world of necessity, its independence is ultimately illusory, and despite the complex and accidental configurations of its forms it follows in the long run the path of economic progress.

Now this argument greatly incenses Sartre: it involves, he protests, a liquidation of particularity, "an arbitrary limitation of the dialectical

---

[16] Ibid., p. 549.   [17] Ibid., p. 550.

movement, an arresting of thought, a refusal to understand".[18] It points to Engels' inability to accept or to understand the existence of the unforeseeable—"the unthinkable changes of birth"—and his insistence on contemplating "a universality limited to indefinitely reflecting upon itself".[19] Marxism, that is to say, is afraid of *life*—a life which can only be understood without *a prioristic* abstract schemas which arbitrarily subordinate some elements to others—a life which men themselves constitute in the course of their praxis—a life which will restore into "the universality of concepts", "the unsurpassed singularity of the human adventure".[20] Marxism, in short, can only become humanly relevant if we "reconquer men within Marxism".

What is the validity of such a criticism? In what sense can it be said that Marxism is *a prioristic*? It is certainly not true that Marxism seeks to impose prefabricated moulds upon reality in the manner Sartre contends. Marx and Engels in *The German Ideology* place especial emphasis upon the fact that the premises from which historical materialism begins are "the real premises"—that is to say, "men, not in any fantasic isolation or rigidity, but in their actual, empirically perceptible process of development under definite conditions".[21] And there are a good many passage elsewhere in their writings which establish the same point. Not least in this regard are the above-mentioned letters of Engels themselves, in which Engels warns (in the letter to Ernst, for example, 5/6/1890), that

> the materialist method turns into its opposite if it is taken not, as one's guiding principle in historical investigation, but as a ready pattern according to which one shapes the facts of history to suit oneself.[22]

A real understanding of history can only spring from the concrete investigation of its realities: how then can it be said by Sartre that Marxism is "limited to indefinitely reflecting" upon its own universals?

What Sartre is getting at, it appears, is this: historical materialism is a *universal* theory which asserts a set of relationships between basis and superstructure which apply *regardless* of given circumstances. In other words, the contradiction between the forces of production and the relations of production exists, of necessity, in *all* societies, and forms, again *without* exception, the material basis upon which the various

[18] *Search for a Method*, op. cit., p. 57.
[19] Ibid.
[20] Ibid., p. 176.
[21] *German Ideology*, op. cit., p. 38.
[22] *Selected Correspondence*, op. cit., p. 493.

superstructures arise. Marxism, in other words, as a science "liquidates" the possibility that things might be otherwise, and thus to a praxical Sartre, for whom mankind makes the world what it is as it goes along, this *universal* theory necessarily jumps the gun. How do we *know*, he protests, that the economic basis of a society always determines its superstructure? We should rather examine each particular situation itself in order to determine

> in each case whether the action or the work reflects the superstructural motives of groups or of individuals formed by certain basic conditionings, or whether one can explain them only by referring immediately to economic contradictions and to conflicts of material interests.[23]

In other words, what Sartre seems to be saying is that at times historical materialism is relevant and at other times it is not. The base *may* determine the superstructure, but then again, it may not. Indeed, it may even happen that neither factor is the crucial one, and instead psycho-analysis with its concern with the conditioning of individuals as a series of unique events will reveal the key to the situation. What is required, says Sartre, is "a supple, patient dialectic" to meet every contingency: whether such a "dialectic" is materialist, idealist or psycho-analytical will all depend.

    Now it is true that every theory, including Marxism, can degenerate into dogma; but what Sartre is in effect arguing is that Marxism, because it is a *universal* theory of history, is for this reason alone, dogmatic. And this is absurd. Marx states quite explicitly in his Preface to the *Critique* that "the general conclusion" at which he arrived and which became "the guiding principle of my studies" was the "outcome of conscientious research carried on over many years". It was not the product of some kind of arid metaphysical introspection, worked out in abstraction from those "particulars" of living history which Sartre claims to prize so highly. The fact that Marxism has been derived from a "concrete analysis of concrete conditions" does not make it any the less universal for that reason: in fact quite the contrary is true. Marx's *certainty* as to the universality of certain contradictions is the product of a truly encyclopaedic grasp of historical fact, and the *a prioristic* manner in which Marx presents his theory, does not mean that it is abstract or dogmatic, but rather that it has been thoroughly and systematically worked out. Indeed, since Sartre is clearly unable to differentiate scientific theory from the mere momentary impressions

[23] Sartre, op. cit., p. 42.

which the observer has of the outside world, it is worth-while elaborating this last point a little further.

In the famous Preface to the *Critique*, for example, Marx is able to set out the theory of historical materialism in an *a prioristic* manner because he has worked out the theory as a whole. Thus he can pin-point the crucial importance of the relations of production into which men enter, explain how in conjunction with the forces of production these form the economic basis of society, and why the real source of all social revolution is to be found in the antagonism between relations and forces of production. In other words, each theoretical conclusion stems from the one *prior* to it, so that the theory is presented logically and in a manner which shows how the process develops. The ease with which the theory can now be assimilated should not mislead the reader into believing (as Sartre appears to do) that a theory can be actually *worked out* in the same *a prioristic* way in which it is finally presented. That each premise logically reveals itself to the investigator one by one! In fact, of course, exactly the opposite is likely to be true. The *basis* from which the theory starts will only be discovered where the investigation begins to end, so that as Marx points out in his valuable discussion on method, "the real point of origin" appears

in reasoning as a summing up, a result. . . .[24]

The explanation for the paradox is this: the practice of acquiring knowledge follows a path diametrically opposite to its subsequent theoretical presentation. In practical investigation one begins by probing the chaos of apparently unrelated facts all around, having to start off with only "a very vague notion of a complex whole". Gradually historical depth and an inner, apparently hidden causality is brought into the open, so that the "complex whole" can be increasingly *explained*. Simple basic definitions become possible (the product of much preliminary empirical work), and from these initial concepts other aspects of the system can be worked out so as to approximate more and more to that social whole which, in practice, is where the investigation began. Thus although, as Marx comments, "it would seem to be the proper thing to start with the real and concrete elements, with the actual pre-conditions",[25] in fact *science* cannot begin with the concrete world in its totality, for that is the object which, in its diversity and complexity, it needs to explain. Science must move

---

[24] *Critique of Political Economy*, Appendix I, p. 206. This is also reproduced as the introduction to the *Grundrisse*.
[25] Ibid., p. 205.

from the abstract to the concrete, it must begin with the simple and move to the complex, so as to actually reveal to the reader *how* stage by stage, "premise" by "premise", the historical development of the social formation took place.

> In this respect it can be said therefore that the simpler category expresses relations predominating in an immature entity or subordinate relations in a more advanced entity; relations which had already existed historically before the entity had developed the aspects expressed in a more concrete category. The procedure of abstract reasoning which advances from the simplest to more complex concepts to that extent conforms to actual historical development.[26]

Capital is itself of course a superb example of this rational and historical *a priorism* at work, for we see how Marx begins with the value form of the commodity—the economic cell of bourgeois society—and proceeds to explain that while the commodity is simple in reality, it is extremely difficult to properly explain, and indeed, as the "first premise" to the understanding of capitalism, has evaded the human mind for over two thousand years. Yet once the commodity as the cell form has been abstracted from its ramifications and interconnections and thoroughly explained then the other aspects of capitalism to which it relates, historically and logically—exploitation, the division of labour, economic crisis, international trade, etc.—fall into place and can be rendered intelligible. The theory, in other words, moves from the abstract to the concrete, thus inverting in its scientific presentation the natural sequence of discovery which *appears* to move from the concrete to the abstract. In this way it is able to explain that concrete world from whose initially mystifying impressions the investigator necessarily begins.

The fact then that Marxist theory expresses itself universally and in an *a prioristic* manner does not and cannot mean that it has not been derived from a most thorough-going investigation of the real world. Indeed, the contrary is true: the universality and *a priorism* of Marxism points not to its abstraction from reality, but to its *concreteness*. Here Lenin is correct when he asserts in the *Philosophical Notebooks* that genuine laws of science, while abstract *in form*, are in substance necessarily more concrete than any of the particular aspects they contain. Historical materialism as a theory of science is abstract in form only because it is concrete in essence, and it is essentially *concrete* because, as Marx puts it in the *Critique*, "it is the synthesis of many definitions, thus representing the unity of diverse aspects".[27]

[26] Ibid., p. 208.   [27] Ibid., p. 206.

Sartre's attack then on the universality of Marxist theory is basically misconceived. It is true that Marxism may be (and not infrequently has been) *misapplied* in a dogmatist manner so that real men dissolve "in a bath of sulphuric acid"; but to argue that Marxism is dogmatic solely because it *is* a universal theory which can be expounded in an *a prioristic* manner is quite wrong. It is wrong because, as we know, the founders of Marxism meticulously derived the general from the particular. But the Sartrian critique is also wrong because it fails to grasp the really rather simple point that *every* theory rests upon its universals, and without premises which hold universally no rational judgment is possible. If Marxism is dogmatic simply because it is (or can be) formulated systematically, then so too is every other theory, and we are back where we started.

It is of course true that Sartrian existentialism as expounded in *Search for a Method* does indeed *appear* to be shorn of system and universality, and is as a result astonishingly eclectic and incoherent. The world it presents is a world in which it seems that ideas may be of primary importance on some occasions, material forces predominant on others, while the individual's environment may be all-significant on yet other occasions still. A world governed by mutually obstructing causal forces is simply a chaos which defies rational understanding, for if Sartre means what he says, then for every idealist explanation of an event there is an antithetical materialist and psycho-analytical counterpart. The evolution of man, the transformation of society, the origin and role of classes, the impact of personality . . . each is to be explained by that "supple and patient dialectic" which, when it comes down to it, also embraces its opposite! Instead of moving closer to reality, we would simply see the world dissolve into a kaleidoscopic chaos where "nothing is but what is not", a world without any *real* meaning at all. In place of practice in any meaningful sense of the term, all we would have is subjectivist impotence; and if in the Sartrian world nothing is prior or subordinate to anything else—"the levels of an act do not represent a dull hierarchy"[28]—then there are no *real* causes and not surprisingly,

> the consequences of our acts always end up escaping us, since every concerted enterprise, as soon as it realised, enters into relation with the entire universe. . . .[29]

How then can we possibly know what lies beyond the subjectivist world of intention and will, i.e. the truth? And the answer is of course

---

[28] Sartre, op. cit., p. 98.   [29] Sartre, op. cit., p. 46.

that *we can't*. As far as Sartre is concerned, we are condemned to remain the prisoners of our own relativism, able only (like poor King Lear) to "take upon the mystery of things"—the mere victims of chance. The *praxis* which preens itself in theory as a revolutionary concept grappling with reality, proves in practice to be no more than an obscurantist veil which prevents us from knowing anything outside of our own helplessness. In fact praxis appears to have nothing to do with reality at all: stripped of its ideological grandeur, it turns out to be sheerest mystification.

> Thus knowing is a moment of *praxis*, even its most fundamental one; but this knowing does not partake of an absolute Knowledge . . . it remains the captive of the action it clarifies, and disappears along with it . . . man is the product of his product.[30]

I have argued throughout that all science rests upon the distinction between appearances and reality—upon this, the whole of dialectical and historical materialism depends. And yet of course it is precisely this distinction which is smothered ˙y Sartre's contention that knowing remains "the captive of the action it clarifies and disappears along with it": indeed, Sartre himself dismisses the materialist distinction between intention and event as "petit-bourgeois", arguing that the "general import" of an action and its individual signification "are equally objective characteristics".[31] But how can this be? How can there be no difference between what different people imagine is the truth and what in fact *is* the truth, particularly as *opinions* about the truth will inevitably differ?

The truth is that even Sartre's stubborn relativism breaks down in practice when he offers (as soon or later every writer must) a *judgment* of events. Do we condemn—an example he gives—the insurgents at Kronstadt who rose in rebellion against the Bolsheviks or do we support them? Sartre's answer is all revealing: while we may admit that the condemnation of the insurgents at Kronstadt was *perhaps* inevitable,

> . . . at the same time this practical judgment (the only real one) will remain that of enslaved history so long as it does not include the free interpretation of the revolt in terms of the insurgents themselves. . . .[32]

Now this answer borders on absurdity, but not quite. Merely to say that one practical judgment (the condemnation) must include its direct opposite (the support) can only lead to outright mystification and

[30] Ibid., p. 92.   [31] Ibid., p. 29.   [32] Ibid., p. 99.

intellectual paralysis. Sartre pulls back from the brink of total nihilism, and smuggles in, in order to salvage a modicum of meaning from amidst a chaos of probabilities and mutually embracing antitheses, the concept of a *practical* judgment which is "the only real one". But what, may we ask, is the source of this practical judgment which is the only real one? It can only derive from an absolute reality beyond the mind: and yet Sartre insists that knowing praxis "does not partake of an absolute Knowledge"; if the judgment of the revolt by the insurgents themselves is a partial or incorrect one, then this means that there is a distinction between appearance and reality, the very distinction which is supposedly "petit-bourgeois". The simple truth is that Sartre, in order to make himself intelligible, must substantially modify in practice the very notion of relativist praxis which he espouses in theory, accepting the same "dogmatic" yardstick of reality for which he reproaches the Marxists. And further. What is true in this particular instance of the Kronstadt rebels, is also evident in his theory as a whole: it contains, amidst a welter of eclecticism, ambiguity and "qualifications", its *own* set of universal principles, its own "abstract schema", indeed its own "a priorism" even though this is nowhere set out in a systematic and readily intelligible manner. It is true, that unlike historical materialism, Sartre's universal theory bears only the most haphazard and accidental correspondence to the facts of reality, but it exists nevertheless.

Although Sartre claims that, unlike Marxism, he has "an open mind" and switches from materialism to idealism and idealism to psychoanalysis as the occasion suits him, the fact is that beneath this eclectic appearance there is a hidden set of priorities, schemas, determinisms and principles which emerge with little probing. What are those "shame-faced" first principles upon which Sartre's version of Marxism rests? Central is the *universality* of the individual—the real *absolute* of Sartre's relativistic universe. Though Sartre claims that, like Marxism, he believes only in men and the real relations between men, he argues that in fact the *relations* between men are mere "collectives" which are only superficially real. They are simply abstractions "parasitically" dependent upon the real actions of men. Now this argument certainly resembles Marxism in so far as it postulates a basis and a superstructure, and a sense of priority between them which is universally true. The only problem is that the content of the two theories is a trifle different. Whereas for Marx, the individual acquires his social reality from the relationships into which he enters (independently of his will), for Sartre it is not the individual who is a secondary appearance, it is his social relationships. As far as Marx is concerned,

> individuals are dealt with only in so far as they are the personifications of economic categories, embodiments of particular class-relations and class interests.[33]

But for Sartre, it is class which is abstract—a mere "reified" construct which shackles that deeper human reality which is of course the praxical individual, an individual who is, whether Sartre likes it or not, the core of a theory which is quite as "universal" as Marxism is (in its *form*), but whose "schemas, priorities, a priorisms" defy rational understanding, obstruct historical prediction and make an objective evaluation of reality well nigh impossible. We object to this theory not because it is "schematic" or "prefabricated": our objection is that it simply reflects uncritically the illusions of a social strata within bourgeois society well known for its ideological frenzies and atomistic acts of faith. It can scarcely rival historical materialism in its ability to explain the real world.

I come back, therefore, to a point which has already been made in the discussion on philosophy and the dialectics of nature, the point of *substance* in every theory. For the real question is not whether a theory "explains everything", has "schemas", is "metaphysical" (i.e. universal), for as we have already seen, all theories are by their nature abstract *and* concrete, particularistic *and* universal. The real question is: do these theories correspond to the real world? Whether historical materialism is true or not does not depend upon whether it is "open-minded" or "supple" and "patient" in its dialectical formulations: it depends upon whether it reflects reality more correctly than its rivals; and irrationalist or anarchist attacks on theory as such cannot serve as a substitute for the answer to *this* question. Indeed, these attacks do not even *begin* to make an impact on the truth of Marxism, for they simply contradict their very substance by virtue of the fact that they can be made at all. It takes a universal theory to disprove one.

But this simple point will not satisfy our praxis critics of historical materialism: as far as they are concerned, it is not merely the "priorities" of basis and superstructure which make the theory dogmatic, it is also its claim to relate to the *whole* of human society as far as we have been able to understand it.

I turn, therefore, to consider the question:

---

[33] Preface to *Capital*, I, op. cit., p. 10.

(ii) How "Historical" is Historical Materialism?

As far as Schmidt, Petrovic and Lukacs are concerned, Marx's theory of history is vulgarised if it is considered to apply universally to all human society. Schmidt, for example, argues that, despite its suggestive hints to the contrary, the famous analysis as presented in the Preface to the *Critique* should not be construed as expounding a *universal* law of social motion, but should rather be understood as sketching a dialectic which relates to a fully developed *bourgeois* society, and extends to pre-bourgeois society only in so far as exchange relations are anticipated in it.[34] Lukacs agrees. Because pre-capitalist societies do not possess the "independence", "cohesion" and "immanence" in their economic life which we associate with capitalism, the categories of historical materialism cannot really apply. They are relevant only under capitalism, and only the "vulgar Marxist" considers them "eternally valid".[35] And Petrovic poses the question to his reader: did Marx imagine that the formula of the Preface extended to "all so-far-known and all now-predictable history", or was he of the view that his analysis was transient and "restricted in time"?

> At first glance, the question may seem improper. There is no apparent temporal restriction in any of the above-quoted texts of Marx and his adherents, and in his famous text Marx says quite plainly: "The *general* conclusion at which I arrived . . ."[36]

But like his colleagues, Petrovic is certain that there is "more" to Marx's position than meets the eye. For now it would seem that just as the dialectic must be ousted from the world of nature where it was illicitly inserted by Engels and Lenin, so too must its role in society be carefully circumscribed. Praxis theory talks a good deal about the Dialectic, but when it boils down to its operation in practice, the enthusiasm of the praxis theorists wanes, and they demand that this unruly ferment must be kept within the confines of bourgeois society and only extended into the past in the most cautious and guarded manner.

Indeed, Lukacs' aversion to historical materialism's "vulgar Marxism" is even more restrictive than that of Schmidt or Petrovic, for he insists that pre-capitalist society has no social dialectics. For what are dialectics? They are, Lukacs tells us, the unity of theory and practice, of

[34] Schmidt, op. cit., p. 181.
[35] Lukacs, op. cit., p. 238.
[36] *Marx in the Mid-Twentieth Century*, op. cit., p. 94.

subject and object, and this means that not only can they not arise in nature, but dialectics have no place in societies which have not developed an abstract concept of subjectivity, and whose members therefore do not see themselves as *subjects* in the abstract individualistic sense. As long as commodity production exists only at the fringes of society, people do not see themselves as producing, distributing and exchanging *as individuals*, and hence the conception of subjectivity which comes to prevail in bourgeois society has yet to arise. "The particular aspects of the economic process," writes Lukacs, "remain separate in a completely abstract way,"[37] and only under capitalism, when the economic elements "interact dialectically", is there real evidence of a separation between basis and superstructure, and that contradiction between the forces and relations of production upon which this analytical separation rests.

In Lukacs' view, then, historical materialism not only arises out of capitalism: it only *relates* to capitalism, so that its *theoretical* genesis coincides with the practical creation of those social facts which give it validity. The dialectic, says Schmidt, "must become absorbed in the actual writing of history if it is not to decay into an empty schema",[38] and this presumably means that it can only create its own theoretical categories as it develops the concrete historical conditions to which these categories apply.

To anyone familiar with Hegel's *Philosophy of History*, this position will be readily seen to reflect the weaknesses of the "old master" without his strengths. For Hegel's philosophy, unlike the dialectics of praxis, is about history *as a whole*, in its objective entirety. It does not confine itself to any one of the stages. On the other hand, Hegel's philosophy of history is also a history of philosophy, and hence Hegel argues that until settled economic conditions and developing agriculture give a people the opportunity to reflect upon life, they lack a *philosophical* consciousness and therefore have no history.[39] Philosophy, therefore, must have an "immaculate conception", for until there is *conscious* historical creativity there is no historical creativity at all. And not for the first time, praxis theory seizes upon the subjectivist

---

[37] Lukacs. op. cit., p. 230.

[38] Schmidt. op. cit., p. 171.

[39] "The periods—whether we suppose them to be centuries or millennia—that were passed by nations before history was written among them—and which may have been filled with revolutions, nomadic wanderings and the strangest mutations—are on that account destitute of *objective* history, because they present no *subjective* history, no annals." *The Philosophy of History*, p. 61.

weaknesses of Hegel and brushes aside his objectivist strengths. The *theory* of historical materialism is somehow deemed to create the concrete historical conditions to which, therefore, it must exclusively apply.

Lukacs quotes Marx:

> in all forms of society where landed property predominates, the natural relation is paramount. In those where capital is predominant, the social, historically created element prevails,[40]

and concludes from this that, because "the natural relation is paramount", historical materialism, which after all relates to society, cannot therefore apply. Pre-bourgeois society is "nature-like and unhistorical", as Schmidt puts it, and therefore lacks the dialectical "self-creativity" which only comes to light under capitalism where relations are no longer "determined by nature, but *set up* by society".[41] It is indeed difficult to imagine a more childish misreading of the words of Marx. Marx after all begins the above-quoted sentence by saying that "in all forms of *society* where landed property predominates, the natural relation is paramount" . . . (stress mine), so that when he goes on to contrast the "natural relation" with "the social, historically created element", it is surely obvious that he is contrasting *appearances* and not reality. The "natural relation" of men under feudalism and slave society is an *illusion*, but it is an illusion based upon the historically undeveloped social facts which therefore conceal from man that *he* is the creator of these social facts. It requires a sophisticated praxis theorist to believe that because these relations appear natural rather than specifically social, that in fact they *really* are. Lukacs and Schmidt, like their Young Hegelian predecessors, are well and truly entrenched in the "illusion of the epoch", and it is therefore quite appropriate that Schmidt should take exception to what he sees as the erroneously "universalist" formulation of historical materialism in *The German Ideology*, for it is precisely against these praxis absurdities that Marx and Engels' polemic is directed. It is after all in *The German Ideology* that Marx and Engels make their famous comment that

> men can be distinguished from animals by consciousness, by religion or anything else you like. They themselves begin to distinguish themselves from animals as soon as they begin to *produce* their means of subsistence . . . ,

---

[40] Lukacs, op. cit., p. 233.
[41] Op. cit., p. 178.

so that as they proceed to elaborate the implications of the point,

> the social structure and the State are continually evolving out of the life-process of definite individuals, but of individuals, not as they appear in their own and other people's imagination, but as they *really* are; i.e. as they operate, produce materially, and hence as they work under definite material limits, presuppositions and conditions independent of their will.[42]

We are, in other words, only interested in what people *think* they are in so far as it helps us get at *the truth*.

Now it is true, as I shall argue in greater detail in the next chapter, that the pivotal insights of historical materialism could only have arisen initially under capitalism where the system's dramatic transformation of nature through technology—its "continual revolutionising of the means of production"—daily impresses upon us the creativity and ingenuity of mankind and their ability to increasingly remould nature in their own image. But it is a ludicrous *non-sequitur* to argue that because scientific insights arise as the result of capitalism, that *therefore* they can apply only to capitalism; for indeed, if this were so, historical materialism would be unable to explain the nature of capitalism at all. Capitalism is *only* intelligible to us because we are able to relate it historically to the societies which preceded it, and to the society which will develop on its ruins. It is moreover no answer to this objection simply to extend Lukacs' thesis, as Schmidt does, to embrace pre-bourgeois society in so far as exchange relations are anticipated in it, for then the question arises: how do these exchange relations themselves arise? How can we explain the development of civilisation (i.e. private property, commodity production and the State) unless primitive communism is itself *dialectically* intelligible? Indeed, will we not *uncritically* embrace as the truth the illusions which these earlier societies had about themselves unless we are able to examine them in the light of a *universal* theory of social progress?

This problem emerges clearly in Petrovic's critique of historical materialism where he argues—somewhat more broadly than Schmidt or Lukacs—that man's essence as tool-maker relates only to the period of civilisation. After all, he says, Marx in his exposition of historical materialism, in the *Preface*, refers to *legal* and *political* superstructures in his analysis and he obviously cannot mean that *these*, for example, existed in primitive communism or will continue to exist in the classless society of the future. The State and its laws are limited to those historical epochs in which private property, the division of labour and

<hr>

[42] *The German Ideology*, p. 37.

the production of commodities predominate, and if the phenomenal forms of the superstructure which Marx mentions are transient, why shouldn't the *entire* analysis on basis and superstructure be similarly transient, and exclude from its point of reference man's earliest societies along with those which are to come? In fact, claims Petrovic, these limitations on the scope of historical materialism were accepted not merely by Marx, but even, on occasions, by Engels himself; and he proceeds to argue that in *The Origin of the Family, Private Property and the State* Engels actually endorses the view that under primitive communism biological factors predominated over material ones, so that it is only with the transition to class society that historical materialism, with its stress on economics as the basis of society, comes into its own. Even Engels, it seems, harboured a certain yearning for that "supple dialectic" of the praxis school.

What is the passage which Petrovic has in mind? In his Preface to the first edition of the *Origin* this is what Engels says:

> according to the materialist conception, the determining factor in history is, in the last resort, the production and reproduction of immediate life. But this itself is of a twofold character. On the one hand, the production of the means of subsistence, of food, clothing and shelter and the tools requisite therefore; on the other, the production of human beings themselves, the propagation of the species. The social institutions under which men of a definite historical epoch and of a definite country live are conditioned by both kinds of production. . . .[43]

Now this comment is not entirely satisfactory and according to an unnamed Soviet commentator whom Petrovic cites, Engels' words are a trifle inexact because they *could* be taken to imply (by someone anxious to distort historical materialism) that there is a dualism of the social and the sexual, and that sexual relations have a social significance independent of the mode of production; and indeed this is precisely what Petrovic contends. He argues that Engels allows for a biological determinism in primitive communism, so that only under civilisation does historical materialism proper fully apply. (It is perhaps worth noting that Engels' "inexactitude" is not specifically delimited to primitive society and it is itself intended universally, but that is by the way . . .)

How shallow and misleading Petrovic's interpretation of Engels' words really is becomes clear from the sentence which follows shortly after the passage cited above where Engels remarks (the words are also quoted by Petrovic):

[45] *Origin of the Family, Private Property and the State* (Moscow, n.d.), p. 6.

the less the development of labour, and the more limited the volume of production and, therefore, the wealth of society, the more preponderatingly does the social order *appear* to be dominated by ties of sex[44] (stress mine).

In other words, the importance of sex ties in primitive society is the product *not* of biology, but of material production, and the domination of sexual considerations is an *appearance* occasioned by the limited volume of production and the low development of human labour. Of course primitive peoples *imagine* that it is the sacred ties of the gens—the ties of blood—which ultimately matter; but there is no reason why (like Petrovic) we should accept these historically inevitable but necessarily naïve *illusions* as the truth of the matter. Certainly Engels didn't: the content of his classic work is profoundly materialist and, outside of the passage which Petrovic managed to "find", there is no ambiguity in his analysis at all. When he describes, for example, the transition from mother right to father right which occurred in the early period of barbarism, he makes it perfectly clear that this dramatic transformation in family structure was brought about by an accumulation of property which gave men a more important status in the family than women. It had nothing to do with sexual reproduction *as such*, but only with woman's role as child-bearer as it was affected by the changing relations of material production. As long as the extremely primitive economy of hunting and food-gathering continued, the household production of women remained crucial and enabled women to enjoy a dignity and respect that disappeared as agriculture and the domestication of animals became the order of the day. Wealthy men accumulating property outside the household were no longer prepared to tolerate a system of inheritance which prevented them from leaving property to their own children. The development of productive forces had rendered the matrilineal relations cumbersome and outmoded—a fetter on further development. The old system had "to be overthrown and it was overthrown",[45] and in a way which admirably confirms, in historically specific terms, Marx's *general* theory of historical materialism as outlined in the famous *Preface*. How in fact could we even begin to understand this process if the materialist analysis of basis and superstructure did not apply to primitive society? The fact that there were not as yet (although the germs of this development can be clearly seen) specifically legal or political superstructures does not alter the key importance of that basic and

[44] Ibid., p. 7.
[45] Ibid., p. 90.

universal contradiction between the forces and relations of material production, in terms of which the emergence of laws and the State can alone be explained.

Just as we can only explain the past scientifically if we understand that historical materialism applies universally, so too, as we move to the other end of the development of human history as we have so far known it, are we only able to have some idea of that future society already nurtured within the womb of capitalism if here, too, historical materialism has something to say. And yet, just as praxis theorists reject the relevance of historical materialism to the past, so too do they dismiss its validity for the future. Petrovic argues, for example, that with the transformation of men into "lords of nature", the ultimate importance of material production will no longer hold. In "the humanistic vision of the non-alienated free being of praxis"[46] men will at last be truly free! Of course, it is true that as socialism develops and begins to transform itself into classless communism, important changes will occur (as of course they are *already* occurring in those countries which are taking the socialist road). The division of labour begins to disappear and with its disappearance go our exploitative illusions about the divine autonomy of the world of ideas. And here the much maligned theory of reflection has a vital role to play in freeing man from idealist illusions which developed with the birth of civilisation itself. But does the fact that the blindfold will be removed from our eyes mean that the basis and superstructure *itself* will disappear and that the forces of production will cease to come into contradiction with production relations? This may of course happen in that ecstatic "vision of the non-alienated free being of praxis" where presumably anything is possible, but as far as Marxists and the real world are concerned, the development of classless society is merely the *beginning* of a real human history. The contradiction between productive forces and production relations must of necessity remain, but now in non-antagonistic form so that, as Marx puts it, social evolutions will cease to be political revolutions, and the immutable force of change, the *mors immortalis*, can take place in a rational, peaceful and controlled manner.

Indeed, the utopianism of the praxis position becomes quite explicit in Alfred Schmidt's comments on this subject. Under class society, notes Schmidt, the distinction remains between economic basis and ideological superstructure: "the classless organisation of society will also have material production at its base. Marx expressly retained this concept."[47] But what will happen to the superstructure? That, says

[46] Petrovic, op. cit., p. 114.　　　　[47] Schmidt, op. cit., p. 141.

Schmidt, will simply disappear. In a footnote he angrily declaims that nothing indicates better the "complete failure of the so-called Marxists in the communist countries" to understand Marx's theory than naïve talk of "socialist ideology" or socialist superstructure.[48] Unfortunately, these "so-called Marxists" are actually concerned with what Marx himself has to say (and not with what some fictional "praxis Marx" has to offer), and they are aware not merely of the elementary distinction between socialism and communism (which Schmidt appears to have missed), but of the fundamentally and militantly anti-utopian character of Marxism itself. It is almost beyond belief that someone who poses as a Marxist scholar (a praxical Marxist of course) can actually refer, as Schmidt does, to socialism as "the realised utopia" which must decide, in its own practice, whether ideology will disappear or religion will be reborn. If Schmidt seriously believes that communism is intended to be a utopia, a world of timeless perfection, then he has not even *begun* to understand what Marxism as scientific socialism is all about. And yet, of course, as Gloucester says of Lear, there is even reason in madness, logic in confusion, and sense in the absurdities of Alfred Schmidt. For his utopianism follows quite logically from the praxis position. If man, through his abstract and idealist praxis, is the creator of the universe, then he can do as he likes. Why not? Up until now, his activity has been fashioned by material forces, but in the "realised utopia" who can be sure? Fourier believed that when communism was "realised" the lions would lie down with the lambs and the sea would be turned into lemonade so as not to taste unpleasant to man. Once praxical man ascends the throne of the universe, the laws of nature can be turned on their head: now the superstructure will mould the base in its own image and at last ideas will rule the roost. Since all reality emerges from the fiery aethers of creative praxis, who can possibly say? It is perfectly logical for praxis theory, in rejecting "dogmatic" historical materialism with its "vulgar" base and superstructure, to substitute an exciting utopia all of its own: but why on earth should this misty idealism and these school-boy dreams be ascribed to the science of Karl Marx?

It is true that in their discussions on historical materialism both Schmidt and Petrovic do concede that Marx does *appear* to be saying in the celebrated *Preface* that the analysis of base and superstructure applies universally. And for once we have encountered an appearance which is a correct reflection of reality. Marx meant precisely what he said: "in the social production of their existence, men inevitably enter

[48] Ibid., p. 230 (footnote).

into definite relations" . . . not solely in bourgeois society, or in commodity producing society, but in *every* society in so far as we have been able to understand it. He makes this point perfectly clear in *Capital* I, where he takes the opportunity of answering one of his critics who takes particular exception to the theses of the *Preface*. His critic protests that while the theory of historical materialism may hold for our own time where in a capitalist society material interests appear to predominate, it cannot be true for the middle ages where Catholicism ruled or in classical Athens and Rome where politics reigned supreme. These objections have a familiar ring. What is Marx's reply? That these criticisms are a timely reminder that what is historically specific to capitalism should not be "dogmatically" universalised? That the dialectics of historical development only take place when commodity production presents subject and object as readily identifiable antinomies? Marx considers the criticisms and noting, by the way, that neither Catholicism nor politics are unknown outside the periods in which they allegedly "reigned supreme", adds drily:

> This much, however, is clear, that the middle ages could not live on Catholicism nor the ancient world on politics. On the contrary, it is the mode in which they gained a livelihood that explains that here politics and there Catholicism played the chief part. For the rest, it requires but a slight acquaintance with the history of the Roman republic, for example, to be aware that its secret history is the history of its landed property.[49]

We come back once again to our old friend, the unity of opposites. The fact that capitalism is a quite *specific* social system and has many features which are peculiar to it, does not mean that there are not *also* basic laws of development which it shares with all other social formations. Unity and difference presupposes one another. There is no contradiction between the fact that in *all* societies there is tension between the forces and forms of production, which in turn creates the division between basis and superstructure, and the fact that in each social formation this *universal* law of motion must work itself out in a highly specific, concrete, particularistic manner. Indeed, to deny this "unity of opposites" neither rescues a theory from "universality" (as we saw in the case of Sartre) nor does it somehow guarantee a theory's "concreteness". In fact, as far as praxis theory is concerned, the opposite is true: in the place of an explicit and systematically worked out unity of the general with the particular, all we find is an abstract "creativity" which is so unpredictable in its varying relationships to

[49] *Capital*, I, op. cit., p. 82.

the external world—it may be religiously conceived, biologically governed, psycho-analytically manipulated, etc.—that all we can say about its mystifying relativism is that it never changes. The world of the relative is only intelligible if it has an *absolute* basis to its own relativity; but whereas praxis theory ends up as the mystified victim of this dialectical law of opposites, Marxism is able to *consciously* explain it. Historical materialism, as the systematic application of materialist dialectics to society, harmoniously unites universality with concreteness. Precisely because it is a universal theory of society, it enables us to concretely evaluate each social formation in the light of its own specific reality: it is "dogmatic" and "mechanistic" to the praxical sceptic only because, as the most advanced social theory of our time, it passionately seeks to approximate to the objective truth.

7

IS MARXISM DETERMINISTIC?

As far as the praxis theorists are concerned, "determinism" is a word of abuse: it represents the very antithesis of that freedom and creativity for which, they believe, the "authentic Marx" really stands. Determinism summarily expresses all that is stifling and "bureaucratic" in the Marxist "orthodoxy"—all that is inimical to the "humanist vision".

The objections to the determinist view seem quite straightforward: determinism insists that the universe, including of course man, is subject to laws of motion which operate with the force of necessity and independently of the human will. How then, asks an angry Coulter, can human freedom be possibly realised if a "mechanistic-materialist" analysis reduces man to the "mere predicate of the movement in external events"—events which trigger "pre-determined responses" thereby denying man his role as *creator*?[1] Freedom and creativity can have no place in the deterministic universe. Petrovic put the praxis case thus:

> no matter how exactly we may formulate and systematise these laws, it seems legitimate to pose the question to what extent the idea of the inevitable, exceptionless general laws of every being can be reconciled with Marx's idea of man as a free creative being of praxis. If all that exists is subjected to dialectical "laws", how can man be exempted? And if man is not exempted, how can we speak of his freedom and creativity?[2]

If the activity of men is governed by laws which operate independently of their intended will, then, argues Sartre, such men are "entirely determined by prior circumstances", the mere "sum of conditioned reflexes" and the passive product of external forces.[3] If we are to "reconquer men within Marxism", it is not only the dialectic in nature, the theory of reflection and the basis/superstructure analysis which must go: Marxism must be freed from these inexorable laws of motion —for it goes without saying, that the "dialect is not a determinism".[4]

On the surface of things, the matter seems cut and dried: one cannot be a revolutionary and an activist if at the same time one is chained to determinism. There is, however, only one problem. The comments and

---

[1] Coulter, op. cit., p. 131.   [2] Petrovic, op. cit., p. 64.
[3] Sartre, op. cit., p. 86.   [4] Ibid., p. 73.

formulations of Karl Marx himself! For as Sartre gloomily observes, there are occasions where Marx himself appears to be one of determinism's most enthusiastic champions. He draws his reader's attention to Marx's response to the formulation of his theory by a critic in the *European Messenger* of St. Petersburg, May, 1872, where Marx is clearly impressed by the defence of his work expressed in the critic's article. This defence is unambiguously determinist in its formulation. The Russian writer quotes from the Preface to the *Critique* and proceeds to emphasise the fact that at the heart of Marx's theory is the discovery of those laws of motion which govern the formation of social orders and the transition of one to the other. Marx, says the writer,

> treats the social movement as a process of natural history, governed by laws not only independent of human will, consciousness and intelligence, but rather on the contrary, determining that will, consciousness and intelligence.[5]

The deterministic essence of Marx's theory is reiterated in almost every sentence of the extract of the critic which Marx himself cites in his afterword to the second German edition of *Capital*. Marx is unequivocally described as a determinist: how does he react?

> Whilst the writer pictures what he takes to be actually my method, in this striking and [as far as concerns my own application of it] generous way, what else is he picturing but the dialectic method?[6]

A "dialectic method" which can only be determinist to the core!

Sartre of course is appalled. Can Marx not see the fiercely anti-praxical implications of the statement which he has just quoted with such glowing approval? Is he not aware that this deterministic manifesto flagrantly contradicts his own demand for the workers' "conscious participation in the historical process which is overturning society" and indeed the theoretical position which he sketches out in the famous *Theses on Feuerbach*, and in particular, Thesis no. 3?

The third of Marx's theses on Feuerbach has, it should be noted, a rather special role to play in the praxis mythology about Marx. It is, as they see it, their ideological trump-card which shatters all "mechanistic misconceptions" and proves conclusively that it was Marx himself who gave the praxis concept its most authoritative imprimatur. "If you still think Marx is a determinist," chorus the praxis school, "then for heaven's sake, read the thesis on Feuerbach, no. 3!" Avineri, for example, believes that it is simply enough to quote the thesis in order to

---

[5] Cited in *Capital*, I, op. cit., p. 17.   [6] Ibid.

dispense with, once and for all, that "conservatism and quietism" inherent in Engels' "distortions" and in the 18th-century materialist view that man is determined by objective conditions.[7]

What exactly does the third thesis say? I quote it in full:

The materialist doctrine that men are products of circumstances and upbringing, and that, therefore, changed men are products of other circumstances and changed upbringing, forgets that it is men who change circumstances and that it is essential to educate the educator himself. Hence, this doctrine necessarily arrives at dividing society into two parts, one of which is superior to society (in Robert Owen, for example).

The coincidence of the changing of circumstances and of human activity can be conceived and rationally understood only as revolutionising practice.[8]

Now what does this thesis mean? Looked at superficially, it appears to suggest that Marx is opposed to the "materialist doctrine that men are products of circumstances" because it forgets that it is men who change circumstances. It is not, Marx seems to be saying, circumstances which make men, but rather men who make circumstances. Naturally, this is how Sartre reads the passage:

. . . to act upon the educator, it is necessary to act upon the factors which condition him. Thus the qualities of external determination and those of that synthetic, progressive unity which is human *praxis* are found inseparably connected in Marxist thought.[9]

But is Marx really saying here that because men change circumstances they are not therefore the product of the world around them and are hence determined by nothing but themselves? The truth of a statement, like the truth of a phenomenon, does not always coincide with its appearances, and the real meaning of the third thesis is a good illustration of this axiom of science. It *appears* to be rejecting materialism and determinism: in fact, it is doing nothing of the kind. Those who see in the thesis an attack on materialism are arbitrarily foisting on Marx an issue which did not concern him. Marx at no time after 1844 *disputes* materialism: he takes it for granted that men indeed *are* the product of their circumstances. Otherwise the repeated affirmations of materialism in The Holy Family and The German Ideology

[7] Avineri, op. cit., p. 67.

[8] *Theses on Feuerbach*, addenda to *The German Ideology*, pp. 651–652. (This is the version as edited by Engels in 1888; it is more or less identical to the original which is also reproduced here.)

[9] Sartre, op. cit., p. 87 (footnote).

which were written at the same time as the *Theses* would make no sense at all. But why then does Marx say that the materialist doctrine "forgets that it is men who change circumstances"? He says this, *not* because he is critical of materialism *as such*, but because he has become critical of a particular *version* of materialism, namely "all hitherto existing materialism"—"that of Feuerbach included" (Thesis 1), "old materialism" (Thesis 10), or what he elsewhere calls "contemplative materialism" (Thesis 9). It is therefore not unreasonable for Marx in the third thesis to refer to this "contemplative materialism" as "the materialist doctrine", for although this is now no longer the case, contemplative or mechanical materialism *was* in 1845 the *only* materialism which has "hitherto existed". What Marx is concerned with is not doing away with materialism (as the praxis commentators sometimes assert), but with *improving it*. A materialist doctrine which forgets that it is men who change circumstances must be replaced by a materialist doctrine which will be capable of explaining human activity as "revolutionising practice". Thesis 10 makes this point crystal clear:

> the standpoint of the old materialism is "civil" society; the standpoint of the new is *human* society, or socialised humanity.[10]

It is only the *old* materialism which is passivist and uncritical: the *new* materialism represents the standpoint of human society because it points to action. Man is the product of his circumstances—Marx does not deny this. All he says is that it is not *enough*: men can, by understanding the circumstances which govern their lives, actually change these circumstances, so that passive contemplation can give way to conscious action. It is this which is the *new* materialism—an activist, dialectical materialism which is clearly delineated in *The Holy Family* where Marx and Engels comment, in *defence* of materialism, that "if man is shaped by his surroundings, his surroundings must be made human".[11] Indeed, the third thesis continues to refer to life, i.e. circumstances, as the *educator* of man, the force which determines his fate: this is not contested. What is contested is the fact which the old materialism omits or "forgets" to add, that this educator is by no means outside of the control of man and can therefore be increasingly "educated" in turn. The new materialism does not *exclude* the old materialism—it builds upon it.

The third thesis therefore in no way rejects *determinism*: what it does

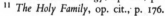

[10] *The German Ideology*, op. cit., p. 652.
[11] *The Holy Family*, op. cit., p. 176.

is to reject a *one-sided* determinism which leads merely to passivity and impotent "contemplation". Indeed, Marx even goes further. For the thesis states that the doctrine of old materialism

> necessarily arrives at dividing society into two parts, one of which is superior to society (in Robert Owen, for example).[12]

Now the implications of this statement are most interesting. If the old materialism produces a dualism between the individual and society, his ideas and the outside world, then in fact the old materialism undermines itself and collapses into idealism: since men are "entirely governed" by circumstances, when they *do* act, they must seek out a Rational Truth from some sort of trans-circumstantial world, for as passive beings who merely contemplate their experience they can derive their motivating principles in no other way. "Contemplative materialism", in other words, is not *consistent* materialism at all, because when it "necessarily arrives at dividing society into two parts", it has to abandon its materialist explanation of the universe. Robert Owen, as Marx points out, is indeed a case in point.

According to Owen, "the character of man is, without a single exception, always formed for him".[13] A position which *appears* to be militantly deterministic:

> Man, therefore, never did, nor is it possible that he ever can, form his own character.

But is it in fact consistently deterministic? It is of course not: firstly, because this determinism cannot explain the origin of those views which oppose it; and secondly, because this determinism cannot account for the forces which are to bring its own perspective to realisation. In the first place, it is not *circumstances* which have shielded people from the truth—it is merely "erroneous maxims"—nor, in the second place, is it the changing of circumstances which will improve society: it is simply "the adoption of principles of truth".[14]

> From this day a change must take place; a new era must commence; the human intellect, through the whole extent of the earth, hitherto enveloped by the grossest ignorance and superstition, must begin to be released from its state of darkness. . . .[15]

[12] Op. cit., p. 652.
[13] *The Life and Ideas of Robert Owen*, ed. A. L. Morton (Lawrence and Wishart, 1962), p. 74.
[14] Ibid., p. 76.
[15] Ibid., p. 167.

In other words, men will only be truly governed by circumstances beyond their control when "enlightened ideas" rule the world. Only outright idealism can rescue mechanical materialism from the impasse in which it finds itself when it sets about (as it necessarily must do) trying to explain activity in the world.

Plekhanov in his brief analysis of French materialism in *The Development of the Monist View of History* confirms this point when he shows how the assertion that the environment is everything easily slides into its one-sided opposite, namely the view that "the world is governed by opinions", i.e. the environment is nothing at all. The stubbornly mechanistic character of the "old materialism" divides society into "two parts", so that determinism is disrupted by dualism, and the materialist standpoint withers at its roots.

The third thesis on Feuerbach does not then, as Sartre contends, reject a materialist determinism: it defends it in the only way in which materialism can be defended, namely as a materialism which is conceived in an activist manner. Materialism which is not activist will cease to be materialism, and its deterministic core will dissolve into the dualism of the "two parts".

Here of course, there is a further irony. Not only is Sartre's anti-deterministic reading of the third thesis unfounded, but it is subject to precisely the same criticism—that it leads ultimately to the dualism of man *and* nature, the individual *and* society, environment *and* opinions—which Marx levels against the *mechanical* materialism of Feuerbach and Owen. When Sartre states that "the qualities of external determination and those of that synthetic, progressive unity which is human *praxis* are found inseparably connected in Marxist thought", he presents a mere *dualism* between the environment and human practice and not an authentically historical *unity* which is only possible when the mechanistic interaction between the "two parts" gives way to that consistently determined whole which Sartre of course rejects.

The third thesis is of profound importance: it is of profound importance because, despite an apparent ambiguity in its formulation which praxis writers try to exploit, it defends materialism, supports determinism, and rejects the very dualistic modes of thought which praxis thinking is forced to endorse.

There is no doubt, then, that Marx is a determinist, although as I have argued, a consistent, practical determinist and not a determinist of the "contemplative", dualist variety. He refers repeatedly to the fact that human life and human history cannot be scientifically understood unless we grasp the fact that men enter into productive relations "independently of their will" in social formations shaped by natural laws of motion. But how are we to understand this position of Marx's? Surely, says the praxis school, Marx is only a determinist when he is referring to the fact that under an alienating and fetishistic system like capitalism men lose control of their circumstances and thus appear to be governed by laws which operate independently of their will. Can Marx really mean that this will also be the situation in a *rational* society, where people will be masters of their lives and be able to consciously control the world of things?

Let me investigate this matter a little further.

(i) *Determinism and Laws: an Illusion of Capitalism?*

Lukacs in his lengthy essay on "Reification and the Consciousness of the Proletariat" in *History and Class Consciousness* paints a graphic picture of how helpless men become under capitalism. It is a point nobody can deny. The *Communist Manifesto* brilliantly describes modern bourgeois society as a society which "has conjured up such gigantic means of production and of exchange" and yet finds itself overpowered by the instruments of its own creation. It resembles "the sorcerer who is no longer able to control the nether world whom he has called up by his spells".[16] Nowhere does this catastrophic helplessness become more evident than when bourgeois society is plunged into economic crisis and is tragically paralysed by its own abundance.

But what does Lukacs deduce theoretically from these economic facts? Man in capitalist society, writes Lukacs,

> confronts a reality "made" by himself (as a class) which appears to him to be a natural phenomenon alien to himself; he is wholly at the mercy of its "laws" . . .[17]

and from this remark, two points emerge. Firstly, that these laws do not really exist, they are merely an *illusion* born of the fetishism of commodities and the reification which results in the minds of men. And secondly, that the existence of these laws or "laws" confirms man's helplessness under capitalism and the depth of his alienation.

To throw some light on this question, let me begin with a few words about the historical significance of the "laws of nature". While it is perfectly true that the concept of "nature" played an important role in medieval and ancient philosophy, before the development of

---

[16] *Communist Manifesto*, op. cit., p. 49.
[17] *History and Class Consciousness*, op. cit., p. 135.

capitalism, no one yet spoke of the "laws of nature". It was the emergence of the market and the massive political upheavals which attended it that cast doubt on the ability of Kings or Princes (or God himself, for that matter) to control social events according to the *Will*: newly discovered laws at work in nature appeared to operate in the social realm as well. Now it is extremely important to note that this conception of natural laws constituted a powerful blow against arbitrary monarchs and despotic priests, for it pointed to the existence of a social and natural order outside the will of "authority" which *all* had to respect. The emerging science of political economy had the most radical implications, as can be seen from the 18th-century Frenchman, Du Pont, who bluntly told the authorities that

> in this science you will discover the indissoluble chain with which He has bound your power and your wealth to the *observance* of the laws of the social order . . .[18]

a Deist God expressing his will through a law-governed universe allows *no one*, not even the Sovereign himself, to do as he likes.

Historically, then, the conviction that society was governed by natural laws—natural in the sense that these laws, whether social or not, operated independently of the wills of men—was not the product of *helplessness* but, on the contrary, of growing strength. The affirmation of natural laws played an important role in the ideological armoury of the rising bourgeoisie against their feudal and absolutist adversaries, as anyone who reads the work of Rousseau or even Tom Paine will readily see. The belief in *necessity*, the understanding that reaction was impotent in the face of those objective social laws which expressed themselves in the bourgeois epoch as the *inalienable* rights of man, strengthened the rising tide of revolution; it did not, as one might suppose from reading Lukacs, weaken it. Indeed, long before the 18th century, titanic thinkers like Hobbes and Bacon saw man's growing mastery over nature in terms of his understanding of its necessary laws. Freedom and necessity were indissolubly linked. Hobbes, who declared that liberty proceeds from necessity—"every act of man's will, and every desire and inclination proceedeth from some cause"[19]—argued in his *Leviathan* that, because man's activity was governed by laws of nature, the State was an *artifact* and therefore could be radically reconstructed in the light of the laws upon which it rested.

[18] Cited by Norbert Elias, *The Break with Functionalism and the Origins of Sociology* (Photo-stat paper, Univ. of Leicester Libr.).

[19] *Leviathan* (Pelican, 1968), p. 263.

This is not to say, as we shall see in a moment, that these earlier conceptions of natural law were not without their limitations; but it is important to remember how and why the ascending bourgeoisie, whom no one can accuse of passivity or helplessness, invoked the laws of reason and nature in their struggle with the old order. The understanding of natural laws was an integral part of revolutionary change. This point is crucial not merely because it throws into serious doubt Lukacs' argument that the existence of natural laws demonstrates man's impotence, but also because it is upon these very conceptions themselves which Marxism has built.

Marx was the first to acknowledge his indebtedness to the scientific political economy of the bourgeoisie and the natural laws of society it revealed.[20] What was erroneous, he argued, about these conceptions of natural law was not that they implied man's inability to control his own existence or that they were, as laws, merely alienated illusions: what was wrong with the laws of nature which the bourgeois economists claimed to discover, was that they were formulated in a way which metaphysically juxtaposed nature to history. They understood capitalism not as an historically determined mode of production, but rather as a timeless system which reflects a purely static human nature and whose laws of motion are therefore incapable of change. It was not the concept of law itself which was at fault, but rather an *ahistorical* interpretation of these laws which made it impossible to understand their genesis and development. In a letter critical of Proudhon, written to his friend Annenkov (28/12/1846), Marx makes this point clear. Proudhon, he says,

> falls into the error of the bourgeois economists, who regard these economic categories as eternal and not as historical laws which are only laws for a particular historical development, for a definite development of the productive forces.[21]

And in a letter to Kugelmann (11/7/1868), he stresses that he is critical of Ricardo, not because Ricardo has discovered a law of value, but because he has inadequately demonstrated it. Noting also that the necessity of distributing social labour in definite proportions cannot be done away with by a particular form of social production, Marx adds:

> no natural laws can be done away with. What can change in historically different circumstances is only the *form* in which these laws assert themselves.[22]

[20] See e.g. his tribute to Ricardo in *Theories of Surplus Value*, II, p. 166.
[21] *Selected Correspondence*, op. cit., p. 45.   [22] Ibid., p. 251.

This conception of a natural law—natural precisely because it is *historical*—lies at the heart of Marx's investigations in *Capital*, which is after all, as he himself said, his search to lay bare the basic economic law of motion in modern society. It is scarcely surprising that Marx should have referred his reader with some enthusiasm to his Russian critic in his second preface to the German edition of *Capital*, because the writer was only rephrasing what Marx himself had already said in the first. Marx could hardly be less ambiguous. Warning the Germans that because England had been used as the exemplar of his teachings they should not imagine themselves exempt from the same historical process, he declared in the first preface that

> intrinsically it is not a question of the higher or lower degree of development of the social antagonisms that result from the natural laws of capitalist production. It is a question of these laws themselves, of these tendencies working with iron necessity towards inevitable results.[23]

There is nothing illusory about these laws at all: these are as real and as concrete as the force of gravity itself.

The scientific discoveries of the bourgeois economists were not, then, rejected out of hand: they were deepened and developed in an historical and materialist manner, for the very conception of a natural law had after all been a revolutionary product of the progressive bourgeoisie.

Not surprisingly, then, as the bourgeoisie ceases to be progressive and its thinkers became cynical, pessimistic and irrationalist, so this conception of natural law was dissolved into subjectivist scepticism. This becomes evident in the "trashy positivism" of Auguste Comte (as Marx called it)[24] where, quite contrary to what some of the praxis theorists seem to imagine, laws of development were seen, not as laws of objective reality, but as simply the constructs of thought, the product of some kind of intellectual "genius" which put the social scientist in the position of a demi-god who breathed order into the chaos of the universe through the "laws" of his system.[25] The sceptical fixation with "appearances" which these so-called positive laws expressed corresponded precisely to what Marx correctly called *vulgar* theory, a theory which mindlessly worships only the *surface* of things; and writers like John Stuart Mill who continued the reactionary work of *dismantling* the rational heritage of the Enlightenment (rather than

[23] *Capital*, I, p. 8.
[24] *Selected Correspondence*, op. cit., p. 218.
[25] For the praxis version of positivism, see Goldmann, op. cit., p. 167.

developing it) always earned Marx's unqualified contempt. For it is precisely as capitalism moves into its moribund monopolistic and imperialistic phase that the helplessness and alienation about which Lukacs writes become so pervasive, and it is precisely in *this* period that the concept of law in bourgeois thinking—of causality, objective reason and scientific determinism—retreats before a rising tide of agnostic despair and irrationalist bewilderment. Once the passivity of "contemplation" with its mystifying absurdities comes to the fore in bourgeois thinking, one of the first concepts to go is the notion of a law of nature operating independently of the human will. For, as I shall show later, there is absolutely nothing passivist about the conception of law and determinism at all.

When it is suggested, therefore, that Marx and Engels regarded the natural laws of capitalism as an "illusion", the truth is turned precisely on its own head. What praxis thinkers like Lukacs think is the "appearance" of capitalism is, indeed, the reality; for the laws of nature under capitalism are perfectly real, and the anarchy and lawlessness of capitalism, which they take at its face value, is the "real illusion". Capitalism *appears* to be governed by nothing but its own chaos, but from amidst all the anarchy the voice of nature still speaks. The fact is, as Engels points out,

> the production of commodities, like every other form of production, has its peculiar, inherent laws inseparable from it; and these laws work, despite anarchy, in and through anarchy.[26]

This is why the society *appears* helpless: not because the laws which govern it are an illusion, but because they are so complex and contradictory that for those who have foresworn science for "hired prize-fighting", these laws are no longer intelligible. Scepticism, empiricism, phenomenalism, positivism, pragmatism—in a word, the infinite varieties of subjective idealism—come to the fore, each asserting in its own specifically obscurantist manner that reality no longer exists and that the only laws we can discover are merely the constructs of our own mind.

But if, as I have argued, the history of capitalism points to the concept of an objective law of nature as a major intellectual breakthrough, cutting deeply into the theological prejudices of the past, a paradox still remains to be resolved: why should a scientific conception of *necessity* have created the intellectual preconditions for

[26] Engels, *Socialism, Utopian and Scientific* (Progress Publ., 1970), p. 63.

the conscious activism of the rising bourgeoisie? Why should the determinist standpoint *facilitate* freedom when it would, on the appearance of things, in fact seem to stifle it?

To tackle this question, I may say a few words about

(ii) *The Dialectical Relationship between Freedom and Necessity*

Quoting one of the well-known passages in the *Communist Manifesto* dealing with the astonishing activism of the bourgeoisie, Avineri comments:

> within the capitalist world two ideas dwell side by side: that man's world is nothing but his *praxis* and that man is impotent to act according to his knowledge.[27]

This is a comment which is more illuminating than Avineri probably realises, for it suggests that the "revolutionary" concept of praxis—an activity in the abstract, a practice in and for itself—is dialectically linked to its opposite: man's tragic impotence to act according to his knowledge. Praxis and helplessness are two sides of the same coin, for each, in its own particular one-sided way, is catastrophically unable to make meaningful contact with the concrete world of reality. *Both* are products of a capitalist system which has nothing positive left to offer an exploited mankind.

The paradoxical unity of the praxical and the passive arises from the contradictory nature of capitalism itself, for it is capitalism's growing *mastery* over nature which increases its impotence. It is a system which chokes on its own creativity, producing that impossible situation in which, as the *Manifesto* says, "there is too much civilisation, too much means of subsistence, too much industry, too much commerce". Capitalist man, like Midas of old, brings poverty through riches and scarcity through abundance. Small wonder that his understanding of practice should become hazy and remote as the consequences of this practice show themselves to be increasingly absurd. The idea of praxis seems to promise him the earth—a majestic if somewhat mystical potential for freedom which must tragically co-exist with the dismal reality of enslavement and helplessness.

The earlier conceptions of practice and freedom which thinkers like Hobbes and Bacon related to *necessity*, now appear to have been betrayed by this objective world. Even Ricardo and Adam Smith had

---

[27] Avineri, op. cit., p. 163.

noted rather pessimistically that advancing mechanisation crippled the human personality while the division of labour increased productivity rather than happiness. Taken as a whole, the ability of man to control society for his own benefit seemed to be slipping from his grasp. To the German Romantics at the end of the 18th century and early 19th, confined by their own circumstances to the role of speculating about the problems of other people's progress, a radical schizophrenia was setting in. Freedom and necessity tragically inhabited antithetical worlds. According to Kant, the world of experience remains governed by natural laws which operate independently of the human will, while the world of thought continues to embody all the potential freedom and self-creativity which capitalism can offer, but now in a self-encapsulated world of its own. A most remarkable combination of reason and metaphysics, of the mystical with the sane. . . .

> whatever conception of the freedom of the will one may form in terms of metaphysics, the will's manifestations in the world of phenomena, i.e. human actions, are determined in accordance with natural laws, as in every other natural event.[28]

Of course, the combination of this antithesis was not to last, for how do we *know* that the world is real and law-governed when our ideas themselves are manufactured in a metaphysical world all of their own? From the 1820s onwards—and it is no coincidence that this is the decade in which economic crisis begins to rock the system—the rationalism of the Enlightenment (with its central concept of the natural law) is pulverised into mysticism and despair—attitudes which *uncritically* reflect the fact that capitalism comes to increasingly deny in practice what it claims to offer in theory. Kantian agnosticism degenerates into a rampant subjectivism so that the principle of *activity* (once founded on a respect for natural laws) becomes, for Schopenhauer, the blind force of Will or, in the case of Carlyle, that wrathful God whose *abstract* labour is the creative force of the Conqueror and Hero. The *energy* of capitalism remains, but now it is the energy of despair, of nihilism, of sheer aggression—in short, the energy of a system whose practice has manifestly ceased to serve the cause of progress and has become openly destructive, divisive and militaristic in character.

It was Hegel, says Engels, who was one of the first to correctly state the true relationship between freedom and necessity, who described freedom as the *appreciation* of necessity. For

[28] *Kant's Political Writings*, ed. H. Reiss, p. 41.

freedom does not consist in the dream of independence from natural laws, but in the knowledge of these laws, and in the possibility this gives of systematically making them work towards definite ends.[29]

But this insight, which of course Hegel developed from the startling evidence presented under capitalism of man's technical mastery over nature, can only be preserved and extended if it is based firmly and squarely on a materialist footing. For Hegel's belief that civil society, with its division of labour and commodity production, could throw up a propertied democracy of "self-willed" individuals was to be shattered by subsequent events, thus feeding the growing pessimism about the "realisability" of freedom. To preserve the rationalism of the Enlightenment (which reached its high-point with Hegel), this rationalism has to be extended; and just as the concept of a natural law is to be reconstructed in an historically conscious way, so too must the concept of freedom under Marxism be shorn of all its abstract metaphysics. Hegel had already noted that freedom was itself the product of historical necessity, of a transformation in material production which, by abolishing chattel slavery, creates the practical possibility of thinking about freedom *for all*. But if Hegel was able to plausibly explain some of the "moments" of his philosophical system, he was hopelessly unable to account for its genesis *as a whole*, and hence his own notion of freedom (tied as it is to private property and exploitation) remains, in the last analysis, ahistorical and abstract. It comes into collision with that very historical necessity which it is supposed to "appreciate", so that even in Hegel there is *implicit* a dualistic despair. The fetishism of the commodity corrupts the work of even the greatest of the bourgeois philosophers, and the spiritual labours of the *Weltgeist* are simply the reflection of that human "abstract labour" which, as a commodity, offers man the form of freedom without its content: the abstract freedom of having nothing. The atomised worker of bourgeois society enjoys only the appearance of freedom and none of the reality. The two ideas dwell side by side: theoretical freedom and practical slavery, abstract *praxis* and a very real passivity.

How uncritical the praxis school really is of this mystified appearance of bourgeois freedom is evidenced both in the work of Sartre and Lukacs.

Sartre of course is convinced that freedom is the opposite of necessity and the deadly enemy of all determinism. He proceeds to tell an

[29] *Anti-Dühring*, op. cit., p. 157.

astonishing story in order to illustrate his point. A coloured member of an airport ground crew is prevented from becoming a pilot because he is black. As a protest against this humiliating discrimination he steals a plane and tries to fly it across the Channel. Of course, lacking any flight experience, he crashes the plane and dies. How should we philosophically evaluate his action?

According to Sartre, this act of tragic and desperate futility is "an emancipating act", and his death, says Sartre,

> expresses at the same time the impossible revolt of his people, hence his actual relation with the colonizers, the radical totality of his fate and refusal, and finally, the inward project of this man—his choice of a brief, dazzling freedom, of a freedom to die.[30]

A freedom to die! Life through death, salvation through suicide! The ghost of the despairing Kierkegaard walks again! For all this merely underlies the precise point which Sartre rejects: the simple truth that an abstract freedom which flies in the face of concrete reality is no freedom at all. *Real* freedom, as Engels stresses, must mean "the capacity to make decisions with knowledge of the subject", and of course it is precisely this "knowledge of the subject"—an understanding of history, of classes, of revolutionary politics—which the coloured pilot in Sartre's story so manifestly lacks. His hatred remains purely *subjective* and hence results in a failure born of despair, "the *impossible* revolt of his people". His abstract freedom turns into concrete slavery, chaining him to that world of necessity which, as Hegel puts it, "is blind only in so far as it is not understood". By trying to ignore these objective laws of motion, the tragic pilot simply ends up as their sacrificial victim. As Carlyle says of Nature:

> answer her riddle, it is well with thee. Answer it not, pass on regarding it not, it will answer itself; the solution for thee is a thing of teeth and claws; Nature is a dumb lioness, deaf to thy pleadings, fiercely devouring. Thou are not now her victorious bridegroom; thou art her mangled victim, scattered on the precipices, as a slave found treacherous, recreant, ought to be and must.[31]

Determinism then is not, as the praxis writers think, the negation of freedom: it is freedom's basic precondition. Without an understanding of necessity, of what is *needed*, activity is impossible, and without purposive activity, how can we be free? The charge that determinism

[30] *Search for a Method*, op. cit., p. 109.
[31] *Past and Present* (Everyman, 1960), p. 7.

leads to fatalism is precisely false, for determinism *alone* makes a meaningful commitment to change possible.

It is not surprising, then, if I may turn from Sartre briefly to Lukacs, that Lukacs himself was to stress the "overriding subjectivism" and "messianic utopianism" of *History and Class Consciousness* (a work usually praised for its mistakes), for the leftism of this work arises out of its inability to resolve dialectically the opposition between freedom and necessity. Though Lukacs concedes in the book that necessity must play a role in the proletarian struggle, thus presenting the workers with the opportunity to change society,

> any transformation can only come about as the product of the— free—action of the proletariat itself.[32]

A "freedom" which can only lead in practice to adventurism, despair and defeat! It was the quality of abstractness which Lenin singled out for criticism in his comment on Lukacs' article "On the Question of Parliamentarianism" published about the same time as *History and Class Consciousness*. G.L.'s article, writes Lenin,

> is very Left-wing, and very poor. Its Marxism is purely verbal; its distinction between "defensive" and "offensive" tactics is artificial; it gives no concrete analysis of precise and definite historical situations; it takes no account of what is most essential (the need to take over and to learn to take over, all fields of work and all institutions in which the bourgeoisie exerts its influence over the masses, etc.).[33]

It suffers, in short, from the same abstract distaste for the world of necessity which empties *History and Class Consciousness* of any real Marxist content: visions, "unities", "resolutions"—all these remain purely messianic yearnings which fail to translate themselves into anything concrete or programmatically specific. Hence the end-product of all praxical fervour is the very "fatalism" of which Marxist determinism stands accused. The vision of "unalienated Man" crumbles inexorably into "the God that failed".

In one of his early polemics against the Narodniks, Lenin pauses to "dwell a little on the attitude of Marxism to ethics", and refers to Engels' words on freedom and necessity. The subjectivist confusion between determinism and fatalism, with its concomitant belief that "freedom of will is a fact of our consciousness", can only end up in

---

[32] Lukacs, op. cit., p. 208. His later reference to the "overriding subjectivism" occurs in the 1967 Preface, op. cit., p. xiv.

[33] Lukacs' article appeared in the Communist International's *Kommunismus* and Lenin's comment appears in *Collected Works*, 31, p. 165.

a utopia or a vapid morality which ignores the class struggle going on in society.[34]

Lenin adds somewhat mischievously:

> one cannot therefore deny the justice of Sombart's remark that "in Marxism itself there is not a grain of ethics from beginning to end"; theoretically, it subordinates the "ethical standpoint" to the "principle of causality"; in practice, it reduces it to the class struggle.[35]

Communism cannot be conceived of as an ideal to which reality must adjust:

> we call communism the *real* movement which abolishes the present state of things.[36]

In other words, the only real standpoint of freedom is that of *necessity*, the real movement which abolishes the present state of things. Free will outside of necessity is simply "an absurd tale",[37] for it is only in terms of necessity that movement can take place. As Lenin expresses it pithily:

> far from assuming fatalism, determinism in fact provides a basis for rational action.[38]

Without determinism, such action would not be possible.

But is it really true that *even under communism* men will still be governed by necessity? This may have been Engels' idea, says Schmidt, but it was not Marx's. The dialectic of freedom and determinism held only for the past: as far as the future was concerned, the laws of nature would "*vanish* through being dissolved by the rational actions of liberated individuals";[39] and yet, of course, Marx actually said nothing of the kind. What he *did* say in a famous passage in *Capital III* is that the realm of freedom in which the human potentiality could be developed "for its own sake" "can only flourish upon that realm of necessity as its basis".[40] It is true that Marx does differentiate freedom from necessity just as he differentiates consciousness from being: but just as not *all* being is consciousness, so not all necessity is *freedom*. *Relatively* speaking,

[34] "The economic content of Narodism", *Collected Works*, I, op. cit., p. 420.

[35] Ibid., pp. 420–421.

[36] Marx and Engels, *The German Ideology*, op. cit., p. 47.

[37] Lenin, "What the 'Friends of the People' are", *Collected Works*, I, p. 159.

[38] Ibid., p. 420.

[39] Schmidt, op. cit., p. 208.

[40] *Capital*, III, op. cit., p. 820.

there is an acute difference between conscious freedom and blind necessity; but in *absolute* terms, freedom and necessity are identical, for freedom can never be anything more a humanly conscious, self-determinism: a creative respect for the laws of reality. A freedom which transcends necessity is simply metaphysical, i.e. it does not exist.

The impossibility of communism as a set of ideals to which reality must adjust becomes starkly obvious if we return to the basis of Marx's theory of society, human labour, itself the outcome of "nature's technology". Once it is understood that all things human must be *produced* (and not by God either!), whether it is human ideas, culture, the family, private property, the State, etc., then it must surely be clear that everything must develop from its own inner necessity, with historically higher forms of this necessity resting upon lower forms. The basis of the spiritual lies in the material world, in that realm of necessity where, in one form or another, men must continue producing in order to satisfy their needs—an historical act which is

> a fundamental condition of all history, which today, as thousands of years ago, must daily and hourly be fulfilled merely in order to sustain human life.[41]

It is not surprising that Schmidt's utopia of "vanishing" laws of nature "dissolved by the rational actions of liberated individuals" comes into collision with this "fundamental condition of all history", the basic premise of Marx's social theory. Schmidt quotes Marx's reference to useful labour as

> a necessary condition, independent of all forms of society, for the existence of the human race; it is an eternal nature-imposed necessity, without which there can be no material exchanges between man and Nature, and therefore no life,[42]

and asks anxiously, does not this sort of thinking lend a somewhat "'ontological' dignity"[43] to the metabolic relations between man and nature? If by "ontological" is simply meant *universal*, then, indeed, Schmidt's concern is well founded. For Marx never made the empiricist's mistake of trying to metaphysically separate the general from the particular, or the universal from the specific. Every society is different and yet it is linked: beneath its own quite specific natural laws there exists that "eternal nature-imposed necessity" which governs *all*

---

[41] *German Ideology*, op. cit., p. 39.
[42] *Capital*, I, op. cit., pp. 42–43.
[43] Schmidt, op. cit., p. 88.

societies without exception. The mistake of the bourgeois economists was not that they believed in an "eternal nature-imposed necessity", it was that they identified this necessity solely with capitalism. They confused, as Marx points out in the *Grundrisse*, the "necessity of the *objectification* of the powers of social labour", an *absolute* necessity, with the "necessity of their *alienation vis à vis* living labour "—a *conditional* necessity springing from "a specific historic point of departure".

Of course this does not mean that because we speak of material production as "an eternal nature-imposed necessity" of human society, this state of affairs can never change. It is absolute only in *relation* to the needs of society and only makes sense in this context. It is not therefore "metaphysical" or "ontological" to speak of metabolic relations between man and nature as an *eternal* nature-imposed necessity because this absolute, like all absolutes, is only meaningful in a specific historical context, in this case the society of mankind. The absolute and the relative, the unconditional and the conditional, "interpenetrate" as opposites, each only being intelligible in relation to the other. Hegel expressed the matter brilliantly when he wrote that "in essence, all things are relative", for that indeed is their *absolute* character. All things relate to the necessity which produces them, and the "eternal nature-imposed necessity" to which Marx refers, is itself, it goes without saying, the necessary product of a prior material evolution.

To assert then, as Shlomo Avineri does, that in "the new society"

> man's relation to nature ceases to be determined by objective necessity: man, now conscious of his mastery over his own nature, creates it,[44]

reduces creativity to some kind of mystical absurdity which immaculately derives from nothing. Alas, the Fool tells a rash King Lear who has just given away his kingdom, "nothing can come out of nothing" and that is not very much! Many centuries before Lucretius made the same point: if, as he put it, *things* were made out of nothing,

> any species could spring from any source and nothing would require seed. Men could arise from the sea and scaly fish from the earth and birds could be hatched out of the sky.[45]

What stands in the path of this crazy utopia, this empiricist nightmare? Necessity. The world is governed by real causes, by natural laws, and human creativity is only possible if it acknowledges the independent

---

[44] Avineri, op. cit., p. 227.
[45] *On the Nature of the Universe* (Penguin Classics, 1951), pp. 31–32.

existence of this universal necessity. It is true that men can transform necessity, but *only on its own terms*. One necessity can only be replaced by another, for creativity itself is only necessity at its most self-conscious. Avineri is right when he says that men create themselves and, indeed, they always have done. But they create themselves only as beings of *nature*, and their "praxis" only materialises when they create themselves in accordance with the laws of this wider being. Creation is only possible as a necessary process. Hence it is no paradox to observe that as men have become historically *more* creative, so they have come better to understand their dependence upon the laws of necessity. In the place of first a magical and then a religious version of necessity—an inverted, but by no means arbitrary necessity—they have gradually developed a clearer picture of necessity as it really is. The more we *appear* to make nature dependent upon man, the more in fact we become aware of our dependence on nature. The more we change nature, the more we become aware of its inner necessity. As Engels points out in the *Dialectics of Nature*, it is man's "victory" over nature which *compels* him to come to terms with the unforeseen results of his own productivity—a fact which the current environmental crisis has made increasingly acute—so that, at every step, writes Engels,

> we are reminded that we by no means rule over nature like a conqueror over a foreign people, like someone standing outside nature, but that we, with flesh, blood and brain, belong to nature, and exist in its midst, and that all our mastery of its consists in the fact that we have the advantage over all other creatures of being able to learn its laws and apply them correctly.[46]

The "new society" does not, as Avineri rather mystically supposes, transcend necessity: it makes man aware of it as never before. Capitalism, it is true, has already revealed to man the existence of natural laws—but it prevents him from understanding these laws *historically* and, like all its exploitative predecessors, the capitalist system must invert human creativity so that it cannot understand its own origins. In its moribund phase, all that remains of capitalist creativity is a subjectivist monster which insanely imagines that it can do "as it likes".

I conclude by returning once again to Avineri's ironic profundity. Under capitalism, *praxis* coexists with the impotence it necessarily implies: it can only be a matter of time before the praxical sorcerer is overpowered by his own spells, and that passivity, which is momentarily veiled by a feverish activism, becomes real. Praxis and

---

[46] *Dialectics of Nature*, op. cit., p. 183.

passivity are merely two sides of the same coin and both are the product of an anarchic, decadent society steadily choking itself to death.

It is ironic that praxis theory in explicitly embracing the one, must implicitly embrace the other: but it is tragic that, in doing so, it should present its "pauper's broth" as Marxism.

8

THE CONCEPT OF PRAXIS AND THE "YOUNG MARX"

Thus far I have sought to tackle the various objections which particular praxis theorists have levelled against "orthodox Marxism", charges that Marxism has been treated as a "philosophy of the universe", that a mechanistic version illicitly extends dialectics to nature, produces a theory of reflection to explain the origin and truth of ideas, interprets historical materialism in a "vulgar" and "dogmatic" way, and finally of course, robs Marxism of its revolutionary activist character by presenting it as scientific determinism. Not all the theorists I have cited from time to time—and this is a point which is worth emphasising—would necessarily subscribe to *all* these criticisms as I have phrased them, but all the theorists would, I think, embrace that basic praxis critique of Marxism with which this work is concerned. A critique which is, I have argued, subjectivist and idealist, and which, contrary to its claims (or even its intentions), represents a fundamental attack on the scientific content of Marx's writing.

No attack on Marxist theory can be expected to make an impact unless it appears plausible, particularly an attack which claims to represent the position of the "authentic Marx" himself. But where is the evidence for this "authentic Marx" to be found? The praxis school rely, for the substance of their critique, upon Marx's own early writings before 1845 where, it must be conceded, not without some reservations, that a measure of support can be found, from within the corpus of Marx's *own* writings, to substantiate the praxis case.

It is essential then to set aside space for some investigation into the problem of the praxis concept and the "Marx before Marxism".

Avineri, for example, lays pivotal stress on the importance of Marx's youthful writings, suggesting that

> the recent discovery of Marx's earlier writings shifted much of the emphasis in the discussions of Marx's theories. . . .[1]

Interest has shifted from economics and materialism to philosophy and praxis, for it has become clear, says Avineri, that it was really Engels who was "interested in economic issues" (a truly remarkable assertion this!) while Marx's "main interest" was philosophical. The early work

[1] Avineri, op. cit., p. 1.

has brought renewed concern with "the richness of Marx's philosophical speculation", involving in the debate groups hitherto unconcerned with Marx and Marxism, so that the study of Marx, says Avineri with a touch of innocent irony, "has even become academically respectable".[2] We wonder why!

As far as Petrovic is concerned, Marx's youth was

a period in which Marx developed the basic philosophical conceptions to which he remained faithful in his later works,[3]

and it is from this period that Petrovic draws the bulk of his quotations which he claims prove Marx's own antipathy to dialectical and historical materialism. Similarly, Lefebvre's "new reading" of Marx relies heavily upon the writings of the pre-1845 period.

Now it is of course possible to present a praxis critique of Marxism without relying upon the early writings. The *Paris Manuscripts* of 1844 were available neither to Lukacs in 1919 nor to Korsch in 1923. The point is, however, that the praxis case appears far stronger if support *can* be found from within Marx's own writings, and this makes it crucial to examine the role of the praxis concept in the intellectual development of Marx himself. To what extent did he *really* embrace praxis theory at all? And how did he come to shed this legacy of idealism as his work developed into that scientific materialism which constitutes its real basis?

I begin with

(i) *Marx and the Concept of Praxis: 1837–1843*

The theory of praxis in a form not basically dissimilar to its modern counterpart came to be widely held among that school of theorists who, developing their position in the Germany of the 1830s and 1840s, called themselves the Young Hegelians: they were the *young* Hegelians because they considered themselves as the *radical* inheritors of Hegel's outlook working to free their master of the apparent inconsistencies in his work, the "gratuitous conservatism" which they believed had been unjustly read into it, and to apply Hegel's teachings to specifically social and political questions. Strauss' famous work, *The Life of Jesus* (1835), produced a secular and highly controversial interpretation of the Gospels which moved beyond even Hegel's by no means uncritical attitude towards the "received truth". August Cieszkowski, a young

---

[2] Ibid.   [3] Petrovic, op. cit., p. 13.

Polish aristocrat, sought in his *Prolegomena zur Historiosophie*, written three years later, to use Hegel's philosophy as an instrument for reconciling ideals and reality in the critical world of the future, and not, as Hegel had done, in the somewhat complacent world of the present. This meant, declared Cieszkowski, that if philosophy wishes to "reconcile", it must also be prepared to change. It must

> descend from the heights of theory into *praxis*. Practical philosophy, or, more correctly, the philosophy of *praxis* (whose concrete impact on life and social conditions amounts to the employment of both within concrete activity)—this is the future fate of philosophy in general.[4]

Hegel had presented critical, rational ideals about human freedom: but they needed to be *realised*, and this meant, said Cieszkowski, consummating philosophy in the social *act*. These arguments were received with much enthusiasm by the Young Hegelian intellectuals in their review journals, for the liberal conservatism of Hegel's politics appeared to his left successors to belie the radical promise of his dialectical theory. And *radicals* the Young Hegelians were. Bruno Bauer was dismissed from his lecturing post in 1842, and it is not difficult, in view of the growing illiberalism among the authorities, to see why. Mankind, proclaimed Bauer, can only be free when it obtains true "self-consciousness", and this can only be done by transforming theoretical principles into practical acts and overthrowing, in order to realise the authentic *essence*, everything that merely *exists*. This, he confided to his friend, Karl Marx, was the "terrorism of pure theory", whose job it was to "clear the ground".[5]

It is not surprising that the young Marx was initially impressed, for Marx's whole background made him sympathetic to radical ideas. In the Rhineland, where Marx grew up, the ideals of the French revolution and the Enlightenment were sympathetically received: at an early age, his father-in-law-to-be had introduced him to the teachings of Fourier and Saint-Simon. In that remarkable essay which he writes on leaving his school in Trier, he declares that it is not enough to be a great scholar, poet or wise man. To be authentically human, one must work for the "perfection and welfare of society itself". It is understandable then that after two further years of study at Berlin and Bonn, Marx was drawn towards the praxical vision of "realising the Absolute". Bruno Bauer at Bonn was one of his instructors, and Marx, always dissatisfied with the idea of study for its own sake, is impressed

---

[4] Cited by Avineri, op. cit., p. 129.
[5] Cited by D. McLellan, *The Young Hegelians and Karl Marx* (Macmillan, 1969), p. 8.

by the Young Hegelian cries for a theory which is practice. In 1837, Marx tells his father that setting out from idealism. he has "hit upon seeking the Idea in the real itself. If formerly gods had dwelt above the world, they have now become its centre".[6] By 1841, when Marx completes his doctoral thesis, he is clearly under the spell of Bauer's "praxis". "It is a psychological law," he writes, "that the theoretical mind having become free in itself, turns into practical energy." The problem with philosophy as such, complains Marx, is that its practice is purely theoretical. This burdens its "innermost essence" with contradictions, for theory has to become practice if philosophical ideals are to become realities. In other words, the world has to become philosophical (i.e. transformed by ideals), and philosophy worldly, (i.e. embodied in practice). Both are transformed in the process, with philosophy losing its idealistic character as "a definite system".[7]

These arguments powerfully display the hold which the apocalyptic vision of praxis—the realisation, once and for all, of the Absolute Ideal—had on the Marx of the early 1840s. Although he tells a sponsor of the *Rheinische Zeitung*—the radical paper he is soon to edit—that "true theory must be developed and clarified in concrete circumstances"[8]—theory is still idealistically conceived as that theoretical heaven which must be brought down to earth so that the real and the ideal are at last One. Hence in his polemic with the conservative *Kolnische Zeitung* over the relations of Church and State, we find Marx following Bauer and the other Young Hegelians in defending what is simply a *radicalised* version (but no more) of Hegel's conception of the State, that "great organism in which legal, ethical and political freedom has to be actualised".[9]

That Marx was influenced by the Young Hegelians and their notion of praxis is scarcely subject to doubt. But the *extent* of this influence was always tempered by the fact that, even during his praxis period, Marx stresses the *concrete* and *objective* in society, and his outlook, in contrast to that of many of the Young Hegelians, remains therefore authentically critical and rational. Like Hegel himself, Marx rejects the idea that principles are somehow above the world and are subjective truths outside objective reality. Marx is always determined to *explain*, to dig out the causes and roots of phenomena, and hence, even during his idealist period, his admiration for the rigour and thoroughness of the natural sciences is evident.

[6] *Writings of the Young Marx*, eds. Easton and Guddat, op. cit., p. 41.
[7] Ibid., pp. 62–63.   [8] Ibid., p. 106.   [9] Ibid., p. 130.

Thus although Marx flirts with praxis ideas, he never accepts the praxis critique of objective reason. He tells his father in 1837 that on reading Hegel

> I wished to dive into the ocean once again but with the definite intention of discovering our mental nature to be just as determined, concrete and firmly established as our physical,[10]

and this is a far cry indeed from the subjectivist fervour of some of the Young Hegelians. Idealism, as far as Marx is concerned, *is* the most concrete way of getting to grips with the material world, so that although he speaks of "philosophy" transforming the world, this "philosophy" is portrayed in a startlingly concrete manner. In a well-known passage he writes:

> the same spirit that builds philosophical systems in the brain of the philosophers, builds railroads by the hands of the workers. Philosophy does not stand outside the world any more than a man's brain is outside him because it is not in his stomach.[11]

Although this position is still idealist, for the *origin* of philosophy is not explained, it is idealism of an extremely concrete and "materialist" kind. It is not surprising that Marx soon becomes increasingly critical of the nihilistic and subjectivist version of Hegel presented by Bauer and the Young Hegelians in Berlin, and he refers contemptuously to the heap of "scribblings" sent by "Meyen and Co." which he dismisses as scribblings written "any old how, pregnant with world revolution, empty of ideas and salted up with atheism and communism".[12] In short, an ultra-leftism of praxical "visions" that has not entirely disappeared today! What irritates Marx about the Berlin *Freien* is not so much their radicalism as their superficiality and dogmatic abstractions that substitute subjectivism for the truth. After all, Marx reiterates the importance of making our judgment reflect the real world when, in a piece at the end of 1842, he stresses that the laws of the legislator can only be respected when they are based on natural necessity—the nature of things;[13] if he defends the *Rheinische Zeitung* at one point against the charge of communism, he does so not because he rejects communism but because he feels strongly that until the theories

[10] Ibid., p. 46.
[11] Ibid., p. 122.
[12] Cited by McLellan, op. cit., pp. 30–31.
[13] *Writings of the Young Marx*, op. cit., p. 140.

have been thoroughly and conscientiously investigated his newspaper cannot decide whether it follows them or not. In his detailed investigation into the conditions of the wine growers in the Moselle area, his dislike of subjectivism and a subjectivist reading of Hegel becomes even more explicit. In studying political conditions, he writes, it is far too easy to "overlook the *objective nature of the relationships*" and to explain everything from the *will* of the people acting. On its own, the will does not exist, for it is precisely these

> *relationships* which determine the actions of private persons as well as those of individual authorities, and which are as independent as are the movements in breathing.[14]

By assuming the *objective* standpoint, one is obliged, says Marx, to look to the *external* circumstances which bring a given phenomenon into being, and this can be determined with almost the same certainty as the determination by a chemist of the particular circumstances under which some substances will form a compound.[15]

This passage in particular seems to me to be of the utmost importance because it shows that, while in these early years praxis ideas influence Marx's thinking, at no time does Marx's position manifest that self-defeating subjectivism, at times bordering on solipsism, which characterises the writing of some of the Young Hegelians and those present-day praxis theorists who follow in their footsteps. It is true that Marx is still impressed by the praxical call to "identify" ideas and reality, so that he remains unclear as to how ideas themselves arise. But despite these weaknesses and ambiguities, nowhere does he repudiate an understanding of objective reality and its law-governed character. As idealist as his early work might be, it is always rational.

By 1843, Marx comes under the sway of a philosopher who is to decisively break the grip of Hegel on the young radicals—Ludwig Feuerbach. Feuerbach's *Essence of Christianity* had been published in 1841, to be followed in 1842 by an even more explicitly anti-Hegelian tract, *Preliminary Theses towards the Reform of Philosophy*, and a few months later his *Principles of the Philosophy of the Future*. These last two works were particularly important for Marx, for they furnished him with a powerful materialist critique of Hegel's philosophy. If Feuerbach was, as Marx later acknowledged, a thinker much inferior to Hegel, the impact of these criticisms was profound and liberating. Although Feuerbach also embraced the praxis idiom, praxis, for Feuerbach, was based on *materialism*, and it is Feuerbach's materialism which appealed

[14] Ibid., p. 144.   [15] Ibid., p. 145.

to Marx's respect for the scientific and the objective. "Thought," wrote Feuerbach, "arises from being, being does not arise from thought,"[16] and it was this *concrete* critique of Hegel which presented Marx with the challenge of going *beyond* the old master: of inverting the causality and determinism of Hegel's system, thus preserving its strengths rather than perpetuating its weaknesses through dogmatic scribblings, "empty of ideas".

The extended critique of Hegel's *Philosophy of Law* begins this work. For materialism does not merely criticise, it seeks to rationally explain, and when applied to Hegel's idea that the family and civil society are no more than "moments" of the State, is a powerful weapon in exposing causal absurdities. For how can the State be said to be responsible for the creation of those institutions upon which it in fact *rests*? Reality is turned on its head when

> the conditioning factor is presented as the conditioned, the determining is presented as the determined, and the producing is presented as the product.[17]

The truth is, says Marx, that it is the people who create the constitution, it is not the constitution which creates the people. This position is clearly an advance; but we should not exaggerate it, as Avineri does when he claims that in this critique Marx has arrived at his "ultimate conclusion regarding the *Aufhebung des Staats*" [abolishing the State].[18] For Marx is still thinking abstractly, and echoes of the praxis position remain. We see this particularly clearly in Marx's reference to democracy as the *true* State, for why is it the true State? Because it represents the perfect embodiment of the ideal—the true unity of the general with the particular. It is true that Marx does comment that for some of the French radicals democracy even appears to go beyond the State, but he still continues to see in democracy that praxis-type unity of theoretical opposites which, when realised, is to bring the whole course of history to a mystifying and messianic Full Stop. The unity of the general and the particular is a purely *ideal* construct which resolves an antagonism which has never in fact existed except as a muddled and distorted reflection of that real struggle which has always existed since civilisation began—the war between the classes. Marx still speaks as a petty bourgeois radical when he refers to the fact that

[16] Cited by McLellan, op. cit., p. 99.
[17] *Writings of the Young Marx*, op. cit., p. 157.
[18] Avineri, op. cit., p. 38.

in democracy the constitution, the law, the State itself insofar as it is politically constituted, is only a self-determination of the people and a particular content of the people.[19]

Scarcely a year later, however, Marx has been disabused of the illusion that the democratic State, indeed any State, expresses the "people's will", for this entire notion of the general will ignores the "natural and spiritual restrictions" which necessarily mould its character.[20] By now Marx's growing interest in political economy is bringing him closer and closer to an understanding of the real factors which only *appear* to separate the general from the particular, ideas from reality.

Feuerbach, for his part, never actually moved beyond the ideal of abstract democracy—"the Head of State", he wrote, "is the representative of Universal Man"—and Marx becomes increasingly impatient with Feuerbach's romanticism and indifference to politics. Marx's essentially practical cast of mind rebels against the continued and futile preoccupation with abstracted unities and perfected wholes, so that in September, 1843, we find him protesting that the communism of the utopians, Cabet, Weitling, etc., is a "dogmatic abstraction" devoid of any real concern for the concrete. We do not, he says, face the world in a doctrinaire fashion with some new principle, proclaiming "Here is truth, kneel here!" . . .

we develop new principles for the world out of the principles of the world . . . one explains to the world its own acts.[21]

But to explain the world, "its own acts", one must take part in the world's struggles, so that our principles can be drawn from reality and not imposed as ideals "from beyond" in a utopian manner.

It is important to remember that throughout the period 1837–43 there is in Marx's intellectual development a combination of a quite *unique* critical depth and incisiveness—which far outshines that of his contemporaries—with ideas which he has taken over from theorists around him like Bauer and later Feuerbach and from socialists like Hess. The form is still borrowed, and at times eclectic; but the critical content is Marx's own. This means that two errors must be avoided when we are discussing the work of the early Marx. One is to insist that by 1843–44 Marx's position had developed to maturity and shed its idealist heritage, for that is clearly not so; but the other—"identically opposite" mistake—is to argue that because Marx was still influenced by the Young Hegelians his work does not still stand *in its own right*,

[19] *Young Marx*, op. cit., p. 175.   [20] Ibid., p. 350.   [21] Ibid., p. 214.

displaying a concreteness and rationality which goes well beyond the limitations of the writers who influenced him. By 1843, Marx does still subscribe to concepts of radical democracy and praxical "unities of opposites", but he does so in a way unique to himself. Ever scathing about subjectivism and philistinism, Marx's theory is at all times astonishingly concrete, and like that world of the 1840s which it reflects, is continually struggling to "go beyond itself".

The Jewish Question is a case in point. We see Marx here still under the influence of Feuerbach but at the same time moving beyond him. Marx is forever dissatisfied with that "truth beneath appearances" for which all the Young Hegelians were searching: he demands to go still further. Just as Feuerbach replaces Bauer's "self-conscious" man with his own rather more earthy anthropological being, so Marx has already become critical of this "universal individual" and wants a deeper reality still. The search for the reality behind alienated appearances must enter the world of civil society itself—the world of commerce and private property—for Marx can no longer accept an uncritical support for "justified egoism" or bourgeois society's much prized "rights of man". "*Political emancipation* by itself", he tells Bauer, "is not *human* emancipation",[22] for as long as civil society remains man is reduced to a mere "isolated monad". And yet, if a "purely political" (i.e. radical democratic) emancipation will not suffice, how is human emancipation to be achieved?

Marx's famous *Introduction to the Critique of Hegel's Philosophy of Law* (written, it should be noted, at the end of 1843, after the *Critique* itself) moves still further along the road towards answering this question. While the *Introduction* embraces a good deal of the phraseology and imagery current among the Young Hegelians, the piece is sharply critical of both the "practical party" led by Feuerbach and the "theoretical party" headed by Bauer. The first attacks philosophy without realising its ideals and hence veers towards positivism; the second makes the same error "but with the factors reversed" and hence *substitutes* philosophy for the concrete world, thus tending towards nihilism. Marx believes that in the *proletariat* he has found a particular class which can emancipate society as a whole, and this is the novel and exciting point which he makes in the *Introduction*. But if Marx is now challenging more pivotally than before the foundations of bourgeois society, his understanding of the proletariat is still abstract and idealist. If "theory" now "finds its material weapons in the proletariat",[23] it is

---

[22] Ibid., p. 232.   [23] Ibid., p. 263.

still "theory" which remains the active revolutionising agency. The proletariat is simply a convenient practical vehicle for the realisation of its aims. It does not exist as a concrete reality in its own right. Even Feuerbach had said that the proletariat provided the *heart* of society, its feeling and passivity, but added that it was philosophy, the *source* of activity and idealism, which provided the head.[24] The influence of Young Hegelianism is still strong, and it is absurd for Avineri to cite passages about philosophy and the proletariat from this work and then claim that they represent Marx's scientific position. It is thoroughly "unMarxist" to picture theory as a flash of lightning which, as an independent force, provides the "will to act"—for where does this theory come from? Avineri himself concedes that even the famous (and quite splendid) passage about theory as a material force which seizes the masses echoes Feuerbach's comment to Ruge, that praxis is the theory which "unites many heads, creates a mass, extends itself and thus finds its place in the world".[25] For how precisely does theory become a "material force"? The problem still remains to be answered, and it is surely impossible not to see in the celebrated passages of the *Introduction* the shadow of the Hegelian *Weltgeist* now seizing upon the proletariat (a truly concrete "universal"!) as the material instrument through which to execute its spiritual will.

It is important to bear in mind that it is not only the proletariat in the *Introduction* which is depicted abstractly: the ideals of philosophy still retain a similarly mystical hue. Because the proletariat has only a human title, we are told, its emancipation will be the emancipation of mankind—a "redemption" of humanity—salvation at last. It is no wonder that an admiring George Lukacs should preface one of his chapters with a motto drawn from the *Introduction*, for he then proceeds to declaim messianically about man as "the perfected whole who has overcome . . . the dichotomies of theory and practice".[26] This of course then appears Marxist provided we forget that the Marx whose words straddle the chapter is the Marx of 1843! "To be radical", runs the motto,

> is to go to the root of the matter. For man, however, the root is man himself.[27]

A sentiment which is still obviously trapped in the *abstract* humanism of

[24] Cited by McLellan, op. cit., p. 105.
[25] Avineri, op. cit., p. 138.
[26] Lukacs, op. cit., p. 136.
[27] Ibid., p. 83.

the Young Hegelians. For if *man* is the root of man, then man has no origins outside of himself, and, immaculately conceived, is simply the secularised version of the Absolute Spirit whose "realisation" redeems humanity and brings history to an end. The millennium at last! What is astonishing is not that Marx is still a Young Hegelian who embraces apocalyptic and abstract ideas about revolution, but that praxis theorists like Avineri should seize upon passages like these to suggest that this was Marx's *real* position.[28] There are still vital developments to come before Marx's theory is transformed into a materialist science. After all, in the *Introduction*, although Marx now refers to the proletariat, he has by no means established the *universal* need for proletarian revolution. It is required in Germany with its philistinism and narrowness but not, apparently, in France where *every* class is politically idealistic and experiences its particular grievances as the grievances of society as a whole. Of course, in the *German Ideology*, two years later, Marx and Engels are to ridicule this political "idealism" as merely an ideological illusion; but in the *Introduction*, Marx still takes it seriously. The German liberals need the proletariat only because they lack "the breadth of soul" to realise philosophy's ideals. Marx's position is extremely radical, but it is *only* radical and hence still abstract and idealist.

This abstractness is, however, steadily dissolving. In the *Introduction* Marx has already acknowledged that "the relation of industry and the world of wealth in general to the political world is a major problem of modern times".[29] In the justly famous *Paris Manuscripts*, written towards the end of 1844, this becomes a problem of *central* importance, and attention is specifically focused on the world of political economy. The *whole* of human servitude, declares Marx, is rooted in the relation of the worker to production, for every relation of servitude is but a modification and consequence of this basic fact.[30] Political economy is the discipline closest to the material basis of society itself and Marx assures his reader that his results have been derived "by means of a wholly empirical analysis". By looking directly at life itself.

Because the *Economic and Philosophical Manuscripts of 1844* are unquestionably the most important of all Marx's early writings, and because they are probably the most frequently quoted source of praxis ideas in recent times, they deserve somewhat closer attention.

[28] Avineri, op. cit., p. 60.
[29] *Young Marx*, op. cit., p. 254.
[30] *Manuscripts*, op. cit., p. 77.

(ii) *Praxis Theory and the* Paris Manuscripts *of 1844*

Martin Jay in his recent but somewhat "praxical" interpretation of the Frankfurt school, refers to Lukacs' *History and Class Consciousness* and Korsch's *Marxism and Philosophy* as the works which stimulated in the 1920s a so-called "recovery of the philosophical dimensions in Marxism".[31] Much of what they argued, he adds,

> was confirmed a decade later with the revelations produced by the circulation of Marx's long neglected Paris manuscripts.[32]

And this is to some extent true: the *Manuscripts* certainly offered support for the praxis view, and although Lukacs has argued that the *Manuscripts* shattered the theoretical foundations of his *History and Class Consciousness* when he read them in the 1930s,[33] this puts the matter far too strongly. Certainly Marx's chapters on alienated labour in the *Manuscripts* provided a much more concrete basis for the concept of praxis than Lukacs in 1919 had been able to offer, but, as we shall see in a minute, these comments on labour by no means transcended the abstract limitations of praxis thought. Not surprisingly, they were seized upon by praxis theorists at the time as a form of ideological manna from heaven—Herbert Marcuse, for example, enthusing in 1932 that the *Manuscripts* would place the whole of historical materialism and scientific socialism on quite new foundations. The *Manuscripts* would confirm the correctness of his own "anthropological" (i.e. subjectivist) views, and present a perspective on Marx which would furnish the key to Marx's work as a whole.[34]

Now it is true that Marcuse's position, though in essence praxical, was not shared by all the members of the Frankfurt school; and, indeed, those who came to lead it, most notably Horkheimer and Adorno, explicitly rejected as naïve and romantic the *Manuscripts'* abstract identities of man and nature. This criticism is also upheld by Alfred Schmidt, the member of the Frankfurt school who has been of chief interest in my work. Schmidt in fact refers scathingly to "the abstract and romanticising anthropology of the *Paris Manuscripts*" and adds caustically that it is not by chance that they remained fragments and

[31] Jay, *The Dialectical Imagination* (Heinemann, 1973), p. 42.
[32] Ibid.
[33] Lukacs, op. cit., p. xxxvi.
[34] "Neue Quellen zur Grundlegung des historischen Materialismus", *Die Gesellschaft*, 1932, cited (unsympathetically!) by Kosing and Richter in *Frederick Engels, 1820–1970* (Dietz Verlag, 1971), p. 12.

were not published in Marx's lifetime.[35] Yet despite these brave words which apparently set him aside from his praxis colleagues, Schmidt in fact finds this "abstract and romanticising anthropology" extremely useful in substantiating some of his own praxis ideas, and like the other praxis theorists, Schmidt is by no means averse to capitalising on the weaknesses and ambiguities of the *Manuscripts* in order to furnish "Marxist" support for the praxis case.

As for the *Manuscripts*, we should remember that they are a highly complex set of documents covering a wide range of issues. My concern here is specifically with their treatment of epistemology, the basic questions of thought and being, theory and practice, ideals and reality, and it is on Marx's comments about these that I shall concentrate.

Marx in a Preface which acknowledges the direct influence of the French, English and German socialists, pays a special tribute to Feuerbach. It is to Feuerbach, he says, that the method adopted in his work, the method of "positive criticism", owes its "true foundation";[36] and although Marx is moving well to the left of Feuerbach, the deficiencies of the latter's views are strongly manifest in Marx's own work. Ironically, in view of the attraction to the praxis school which this document has, the problem centres around Feuerbach's mechanistic materialism, for the Marx of the *Manuscripts* still reflects the philosophical weakness which all mechanistic materialism displays, namely an inability to place the origin of man and his ideas on a firm *historical* footing.

As far as the French materialists of the Enlightenment were concerned, man's origins were "shrouded in mystery": man was a material being, he was a part of nature, but since all material entities moved mechanically, how could it be said that man had *evolved* from the animal world? The problem is insoluble, for men's peculiarities, their *differentiating* features, can only be explained by idealism. The assertion that nature is the foundation of man slithers helplessly into the subjectivist position that nature is only intelligible *through man*, and that therefore, as Feuerbach's anthropological materialism asserts,

> only the human is the true and real, for only the human is the rational; man is the measure of reason. . . .[37]

Truth is only the totality of human life and of the human essence.[38]

[35] Schmidt, op. cit., p. 128.
[36] *Manuscripts*, op. cit., p. 19.
[37] Feuerbach, *Principles of the Philosophy of the Future* (Bobbs Merill, 1966), p. 67.
[38] Ibid., p. 71.

Mechanical materialism, in other words, as I have already noted on a number of occasions, is not consistently materialist at all; and it is precisely because Marx in 1844 has yet to fully emancipate himself from its metaphysical weaknesses, that he still subscribes to some of the circularities and absurdities of the praxis view.

In a passage in which he raises the problem of creation, Marx still rejects questions about the priority of nature to man as having no meaning. He pictures his opponents demanding to know "who begot the first man and nature as a whole?" and protests that this is a question which is perverse and abstract. It seems to assume that man and nature can be postulated as being *non*-existent and this is self-evidently absurd . . .

> if you want to hold on to your abstraction, then be consistent, and if you think of man and nature as *non-existent*, then think of yourself as non-·existent, for you too are surely nature and man.[39]

What is clear from this argument is that Marx still follows Feuerbach in assuming that because man is part of nature, that therefore *nature* can only exist if it is *part* of man! It is no wonder that Schmidt can enthusiastically cite these passages as proof that Marx's atheism was based not on the discoveries of the natural sciences, but rather upon the mysteries of the universe à la Jean-Paul Sartre! There is no doubt that Marx still sees man, not as a concrete material producer, but as some sort of mystically creative being: for socialist man, he says,

> the *entire so-called history of the world* is nothing but the begetting of man through human labour, nothing but the coming-to-be of nature for man,[40]

man has become the being of nature and nature the being of man, a climactic consummation that forges the True Whole. As brilliant as these passages are, they are still in bondage to mechanistic thought, for .the mere assertion of a unity between man and nature is not in itself dialectical. Every philosopher has found some sort of relationship between man and nature: the real question is—*what* relationship? Here Marx's youthful materialism dissolves into abstractness, for the key question of *priority* has yet to be sorted out.

Like the question of creation, the notion of objectification which receives attention in the *Manuscripts* has yet to be placed on an adequately materialist foundation. It is true that through his growing concern with exploitation and the working class, Marx has come to infuse the process of "objectification" with increasing concreteness, but

[39] *Manuscripts*, op. cit., p. 105.   [40] Ibid., p. 106.

lingering "philosophical" echoes still remain. Objectification is not simply the manner in which people produce and reproduce their material life in their daily toil: the concept still possesses the divine, "constitutive" significance that we find in Feuerbach when he speaks of the object as being the creation of the subject's own objective nature.[41] "The object of labour is, therefore," writes Marx,

> the *objectification of man's species life*: for he duplicates himself not only as in consciousness, intellectually, but also actively, in reality, and therefore he contemplates himself in a world that he has created.[42]

and although this process of objectification is identified with *production*, it still conveys mystical, Feuerbachian overtones. It ignores in particular the fact which Marx is to stress from the *Holy Family* onwards, that production cannot "objectify" matter, it can only *change* its objective form, for of course the material world is not the product of human creativity but, in the last analysis, its *source*.

It is thus highly ironical that praxis writers should feverishly reproduce these passages of Marx in order to deliver the ideological *coup de grâce* to those "mechanistic" interpretations by the "orthodox", for all this talk about man "constituting" the world through his labour is *mechanistic* materialism in its most advanced form. To advance the odious cause of "18th-century mechanistic materialism", this is precisely the text the critic of Marx should quote. Indeed, when Petrovic searches for ammunition to sink *dialectical* materialism, he seizes upon Marx's formulation of communism as "naturalism-humanism"—a "synthesis", says Marx, which distinguishes itself both from idealism and materialism by constituting itself "as the truth of both".[43] But this eclecticism, which Marx in 1845 repudiates, derives from Feuerbach who had tried to unite the best of both worlds by simply borrowing a little from each. As he puts it in *The Essence of Christianity*,

> just as man belongs to the essence of nature, this is a point against vulgar materialism, so nature belongs to the essence of man—this against subjective idealism,[44]

but this of course is in no sense a genuine "unity of opposites" and, as Marx is to show in his *Theses on Feuerbach*, can solve nothing. What is lacking is an understanding of the authentically historical or dialectical

[41] Feuerbach's words are cited by the editors of the *Manuscripts*, at p. 73.
[42] *Manuscripts*, op. cit., p. 72.
[43] Ibid., p. 144.
[44] Cited by McLellan, op. cit., p. 112. .

relationship of nature to man, and this means transcending that mechanistic "naturalism-humanism" formulation which Petrovic so reverently quotes.

It is true that Marx sees the reconciliation of man and nature as the theoretical solution to a practical problem for it is, he says in an important passage, *communism* which is the true resolution of the strife between man and nature, essence and existence, freedom and necessity, the species and the individual, and this *political* twist to Feuerbach's "anthropological" humanism is an important advance. But the idea itself of doing away with *abstract* strife is a mystical absurdity which comes straight from Feuerbach, who, like many of the other Young Hegelians, saw in the "new philosophy" the unity of all "antithetical truths".[45] The belief that resolving philosophical riddles would transform mankind was very widespread. *Unite* man and nature, ideals and reality, existence and essence, freedom and necessity and we have the messianic climax to the whole of history. But as Marx himself is later to make clear, what the philosopher poses as a transcendent goal is a scientific fact: ever since human history began, man and nature have *always* been united, indeed, our history would be unintelligible were this *not* the case. As for the antitheses of existence and essence, freedom and necessity, etc., these are merely categorical dichotomies which can have no meaning in the concrete world where of course no development at all would be possible unless essence and existence, the individual and the species were and always had been *dialectically* linked. These metaphysical antitheses are, as I have already argued, real only in so far as they exist as the *illusory* by-products of exploitation and the division of labour: they are no more than the mystifying appearances of a mystified world. But to the Marx of the *Manuscripts* still *emerging* from the chrysalis of idealism, these "appearances" continue to maintain a befuddling stranglehold. No wonder our praxis theorists so enthusiastically applaud them!

If Marx goes beyond Feuerbach in the passage on communism, he does so *not* because he calls for practice as such, but because he calls for practice of a specific political kind. The praxis writers, understandably perhaps, are confused on this point. When they read Marx's call for the resolution of antitheses like subjectivism and objectivism, spiritualism and materialism, etc., through "the practical energy of men", they imagine that this in itself is enough to take Marx well beyond Feuerbach's position, but this is not so. The cry for "praxis" was the rage of the times and it was something which all the Young Hegelians championed. "The doubt that theory will not solve for you," declared Feuerbach, "will be solved by practice."[46] "The question of being is indeed a practical question in which our being participates; it is a question of life and death";[47] the "new philosophy"

> possesses an essentially practical—and indeed in the highest sense, practical tendency without damaging the dignity and independence of theory, indeed, in closest harmony with it.[48]

In other words, the fact that Marx calls for the practical resolution to theoretical problems in the *Manuscripts* shows only that he still endorsed the imagery of the Young Hegelians. If we are looking for evidence in Marx for a development *beyond* this "practice *in abstracto*", then it is the quality of the practice itself we must examine.

For Feuerbach, practice is simply the "practical idealism" of the "new philosophy": whereas Marx in the *Manuscripts* is becoming fed up with these philosophical remedies. The resolution of theoretical antitheses is, he declares, "a real problem of life, which philosophy could not solve precisely because it conceived this problem as *merely* a theoretical one".[49] But although Marx is struggling gallantly against the bonds of this practice *in abstracto*, he is not yet free; for if resolving antitheses is "a real problem of life", then these antitheses should no longer be posed in an *abstractly* theoretical way, for once we *do* examine material reality it becomes clear that these "opposites" are no more than metaphysically conceived dichotomies which *misrepresent* real history. They are mere "appearances" of life's problem: they are not its reality.

This, in my view, is the context in which Marx's subsequent criticisms of Feuerbach (in 1845) should be read. When Marx in his *Theses* reiterates that the proof of theory lies in practice, he was fully aware of the fact that while Feuerbach *believed* his philosophy to be practical, in fact his practice still remained abstract and uncritical. Feuerbach, he says,

> not satisfied with *abstract thinking*, appeals to *sensuous contemplation*; but he does not conceive sensuousness as practical, human sensuous activity.[50]

---

[46] Ibid., p. 110.
[47] *Principles of the Philosophy of the Future*, op. cit., p. 43.
[48] Ibid., pp. 72–73.
[49] Manscripts, op. cit., p. 102.
[50] Thesis 5, addendum to *The German Ideology*, op. cit., p. 652.

Feuerbach may think that he is going beyond abstractions, but his position remains contemplative, in effect if not by design, because (like his modern praxis successors) he cannot understand that practice is that *real movement* which transforms the world. David McLellan cites Marx's criticisms of Feuerbach in the first thesis, and protests that

> this is perhaps not quite just to Feuerbach for it blames him for not doing what he never set out to do. Feuerbach did not underestimate the importance of "practical activity". . . .[51]

But what, in *concrete* terms, did Feuerbach mean by practical activity? He was to say in 1848 that one must not only "believe" in a better life, one must "will" it; but to imagine that there is no more to practice than the pious intentions of the "Will" is itself to accept an abstract illusion. It is to accept appearances for reality.

Engels was to say of the *Theses on Feuerbach* that they contained "the brilliant germ of the new world outlook", and this is indeed true. They are far more scientific than the *Manuscripts*, but they still contain stylistic if not substantive echoes of the Young Hegelian past. There is still the tendency to counterpose theory to practice abstractly, rather than tackle directly and concretely the nature of practice itself. After all, it is clear from the *German Ideology* that the Young Hegelians *are* practical in the sense that Marx and Engels call them "the staunchest conservatives" so that the real question can be more clearly posed: *not* are the writers practical or theoretical, but *rather* is their practice conservative or revolutionary? That, after all, is what *really* matters. Even in the *German Ideology* this is not always clear, as, for example, where Marx and Engels refer to Feuerbach as

> going as far as a theorist possibly can without ceasing to be a theorist and a philosopher . . .[52]

lingering echoes, are they not, of the old jargon of "praxis"?

But if the old style sometimes returns, the content is now unequivocally materialist. It is noteworthy that the *German Ideology* as a critique of the Young Hegelians and Feuerbach is also a critique of the "superseded" standpoints of Marx and Engels. This is strikingly clear in *The German Ideology*'s rejection of any conception of communism as an abstract ideal which harmonises "theoretical antitheses": communism is now explicitly described as "the *real* movement which abolishes the present state of things", it is emphatically *not*

---

[51] McLellan, op. cit., pp. 114–115.   [52] *German Ideology*, op. cit., p. 54.

a *state of affairs* which is to be established, an *ideal* to which reality will have to adjust itself,[53]

and there is no further reference to that rather speculative and misty discussion on "crude communism", "political communism" and "communism as the riddle of history solved" which we find in the *Manuscripts*. Avineri quotes this passage from the *Manuscripts* in order to attack socialism in the Soviet Union ("Communist Russia" he very inaccurately calls it), while Petrovic offers it as "evidence" that Marx couldn't really have meant what he was saying in the *Critique of the Gotha Programme* where of course the development of communism from capitalism is dealt with in a scientific and not in a speculative manner. But Marx did not merely reject abstract notions of communism in 1875: he had already repudiated them a full thirty years earlier. In fact, not very long after writing the *Paris Manuscripts of 1844* themselves.

Once the nature of practice as material production emerges as it does with matter-of-fact lucidity in *The German Ideology*, then the absurdity of treating the "real problems of life" in an abstract way becomes self-evident. Feuerbach's postulated harmony between existence and essence, Marx and Engels complain, always takes refuge in external nature, and in a nature moreover which has not yet been subdued by men. Small wonder that his harmonies show themselves to be fatuous and absurd:

> the "essence" of the freshwater fish is the water of a river. But the latter ceases to be the "essence" of the fish and is no longer a suitable medium of existence as soon as the river is made to serve industry, as soon as it is polluted by dyes and other wasteproducts and navigated by steamboats. . . .[54]

Is the "essence" of the fish in harmony with its "existence" before the impact of man? Marx and Engels have by no means fully worked out an objective dialectics of nature which will explain that, even here, the harmony is only relative and the contradiction absolute, but they are now sceptical, even scathing, about the substitution of abstract unities for real life. If the proletarians are to bring their own "existence" into harmony with their "essence", is Feuerbach aware of the fact that this means a real revolution? The universal "contradiction between the productive forces and the forms of intercourse" which *The German Ideology* draws our attention to,[55] shows just how fragile and temporary

[53] Ibid., p. 47.   [54] Ibid., p. 55.   [55] Ibid., p. 91.

all abstract harmonies must necessarily be. The only immutable is life itself.

It is not surprising that when Marx and Engels come to review the existing state of socialist and communist literature in the *Communist Manifesto*, they have only ridicule and contempt for the German or "True Socialism" of the praxis thinkers, the litterati who transform concrete realities into nonsensical philosophical abstractions, so that the criticism of money is mystically translated into the "Alienation of Humanity" and criticism of the state into "Dethronement of the Category of the General". The French literature which contends with material realities is emasculated into the "Philosophy of Action", "True Socialism", "Philosophical Foundations of Socialism", etc. In the place of a concrete revolution in the interests of a given class, we have a mystical praxis which is to realise "Man in general"

who belongs to no class, has no reality, who exists only in the misty realm of philosophical fantasy.[56]

It is impossible to read these criticisms without realising that they constitute a decisive repudiation not merely of abstract versions of socialism in general, but of the specific Young Hegelian heritage, out of which Marx and Engels had themselves developed. Avineri's attempt to argue that what Marx and Engels are rejecting in 1848 are simply notions of socialism which are not "empirically verifiable" is too silly for words, for the "naturalism-humanism" formulations of the *Manuscripts* suffer from precisely those shortcomings which are here under attack. Besides, what is "empirically verifiable" about the *Manuscripts'* demand for "the real appropriation of the human essence by and for man"?[57] If this is not the projection of socialist demands into "the misty realm of philosophical fantasy", then what, may we ask, *is*?

The early writings of Marx, both the *Manuscripts of 1844* and the works before it, are colourful and often exciting, and it would perhaps be ungenerous for Marxists not to concede that much of the renewed interest in these valuable writings has derived from the theorists of praxis. But this renewed interest is the welcome by-product of an unwelcome trend, for what has motivated praxis investigation into Marx's intellectual development is the desire to *fossilise* it rather than understand its relations to Marx's theory as a whole. The vain hope of discovering a Marx whose work is not fully scientific or consistently

[56] *Communist Manifesto*, op. cit., pp. 83–84.
[57] *Manuscripts*, op. cit., p. 95.

dialectical—a Marx who can serve as textual justification for the theory of praxis.

It cannot be done: for the *Manuscripts* or the *Introduction to the Critique of Hegel's Philosophy of Law* do not, in the last analysis, really strengthen the praxis case: they *weaken* it. For the Marx they claim to have found is so obviously developing "beyond himself", is so patently *dissatisfied* with the idealist heritage in which he himself has been schooled, that his own rapid movement beyond praxis thinking and the scathing critique to which he and Engels proceed to subject it adds still further evidence against the praxis case. For if Marx *himself* has sampled the shallow mysteries of a practice *in abstracto* and thrown them out, is it surprising that his followers should do the same?

Engels for his part followed a very similar road to that of Marx, while Lenin was certainly familiar with much of the earlier writing, if not the 1844 *Manuscripts*. If he was interested, he was not overwhelmed, for he writes in *State and Revolution* that Marx's *mature* writing only really begins in 1847, when with the polemic against Proudhon Marx goes beyond a repudiation of mere ideas about "theory" and "practice" and gets to grips with an analysis of capitalism itself. If there are no mysterious "breaks" in Marx's work, of which some writers speak, there is certainly historical development, and it is this simple point which the ideology of praxis is determined to ignore.

9

PRAXIS AND POSITIVISM

In the first chapter of this book, I briefly sketched in some of the background to the praxis debate, arguing that the cultural climate of our society is being poisoned by a reactionary cynicism and scholastic passivity, whose philosophical basis stems from positivism. For positivism, as Marx pointed out in his doctoral thesis, represents a "turning inward of philosophy",[1] so that in place of a *critical* role for thought which relates itself to the problems of reality, there is a growing mysticism about thought for its own sake. This "turning inward", adds Marx, leads to perversity, indeed, "insanity as such",[2] and I have already touched on some of the reasons why a doctrine which denies reality and rejects reason is a menace to the future of mankind.

Of course, positivism assumes a multiplicity of faces, but my concern here is not with what differentiates one positivist from another, but rather with what differentiates positivism in general from that rationalism and materialism which Marxism alone can consistently defend. Many of the nihilistic theories which are currently fashionable blithely imagine that they have transcended positivism simply because they have outstripped one variety of subjective idealism by another even *more* reactionary, mystical kind. Scepticism has escalated into a veritable *cult* of superficiality, so that the "old fashioned" empiricists, often "instinctively" rational and humane, have become alarmed at the growing subjectivism of the self-styled *avant garde*, and are disagreeably struck by the thought that in continuing to embrace the same philosophy of empiricism they may well be witnessing a future image of themselves.

In this postwar climate of triviality and obscurantism, the growing concern among radicals with the practical consequences of thought and the social ends which it serves is surely welcome, particularly as it is often accompanied by an interest in Marxist theory. But if this concern is *welcome*, its expression through the theory of praxis is not, for the concept of praxis represents an *attack* on Marxism and can do nothing to improve the present climate of thought, for it continues to express many of its worst features.

[1] *Writings of the Young Marx*, op. cit., p. 63. [2] Ibid.

Indeed, nowhere do the critical pretensions of the praxis school appear more transparent than in its *real* attitudes towards positivism. Of course, in appearance the theory of praxis poses as an uncompromising adversary to the positivist outlook, its resolute antithesis, and in fact adopts "positivism" as one of its chosen words of abuse. There is scarcely a single aspect of the Marxist "orthodoxy", from dialectics to reflection theory, from philosophy to determinism, which is not denounced as "positivist", "empiricist", "mechanistic" and so on; but as Marxists we cannot rest content with the frothy surface-appearance of this struggle, but should pause a moment, and then ask: how *real* is the praxis opposition to its apparent *bête noire*? How effectively does praxis theory *in fact* go beyond the foundations of positivist thought?

To answer this question, the simplest thing to do is to return to the themes which I have already explored, and see whether there is any real difference between the position of positivism and the theories of those who consider themselves the deadly enemies of empiricist thought.

(i) *Marxism as a Philosophy*

The basic premise of all positivism is its belief that not merely is knowledge derived through the senses, which of course is true, but that knowledge is derived through the senses in such a way as to cause us to actually *doubt* the objective reality of the outside world. For the process of knowing is seen as something *passive*, a mere act of observation, so that the meaning of the universe and its objective movement are blocked out by a wall of subjectively conceived "experience". David Hume was the most brilliant (and perceptive) exponent of this viewpoint.

Hume asserts the view that "all the laws of nature and all the operations of bodies without exception are known only by experience",[3] and this assertion is an important antidote to the metaphysical belief in *innate* reason. It is, however, more than this. For it not only rejects the idea of innate thinking, it also rejects the idea of reason. For Hume, as a bourgeois thinker, does not challenge thinking as *contemplation*, so that in the place of God's universe (whose metaphysical creation is unprovable), we have a universe beyond the ken of man.

[3] *Enquiries Concerning the Human Understanding and Concerning the Principles of Morals*, ed. Selby-Bigge (Oxford, 1966), p. 29.

The scenes of the universe are continually shifting and one object follows another in an uninterrupted succession, but the power of force, which actuates the whole machine is entirely concealed from us, and never discovers itself in any of the sensible qualities of the body.[4]

To know is merely to *gaze*, so that because our experience is not able to know *everything*, this means that it can know nothing at all. The objects which impress themselves upon our senses remain permanently beyond our ken, and a frightening solipsism is the logical consequence.[5] A promising doctrine of experience, unable to free itself from a passivist theory of knowledge, has therefore disastrous results.

What happens to philosophy? It is no longer a comprehensive world outlook or a universal theory—it is reduced to a set of formal or logical statements, feeding increasingly off its own definitions and premises. "The sciences of quantity and number," declares Hume, "may safely, I think, be pronounced the only proper objects of knowledge and demonstration,"[6] for knowledge and demonstration, contemplatively conceived, can be certain of nothing else.

Now the praxis theorists certainly reject the *formal* limitations which positivism comes increasingly to place upon our knowledge, for man is after all "maker of the world". But what of the *content* of positivist thought? We find Korsch arguing that because Marxism rejects idealism, it therefore rejects all philosophy and

> being a strictly empirical investigation into definite historical forms of society, does not need a philosophical support.[7]

As far as Lefebvre is concerned, philosophising is a thing of the past, for Marxism is about praxis! But if this position *appears* hostile to positivism, in practice its premises are identical. For positivism's treatment of philosophy is itself basically nihilist: experience does not confirm the external reality of the universe, it simply mystifies it, thus showering the poor "observer" with increasingly absurd and self-defeating doubts. Knowable truth *shrinks* to the confines of the doubting mind, so that philosophy as an objective world outlook is done for. In Hume's famous words,

> when we run over libraries, persuaded of these principles, what havoc must we make? If we take in hand any volume; of divinity or school metaphysics,

[4] Ibid., p. 64.

[5] It "has disturbed followers of the empiricist tradition ever since", M. Cornforth, *Marxism and the Linguistic Philosophy* (Lawrence and Wishart, 1965), pp. 47–48.

[6] *Enquiries*, op. cit., p. 163.

[7] Korsch, op. cit., p. 20.

for instance; let us ask, *Does it contain any abstract reasoning concerning quantity or number?* No. *Does it contain any experimental reasoning concerning matter of fact and existence?* No. Commit it then to the flames: for it can contain nothing but sophistry and illusion.[8]

The idea, then, that philosophy as a universal theory is dead is neither new nor revolutionary: it goes back well over two hundred years. The individual may be conceived of as the sceptical analyst whose categories represent his cosmos or as the fiery activist who moulds the world in his own image; but the net result is the same. Objective philosophy withers at the roots and the real world, whether "made", "analysed", "categorised" or "methodologically verified", dissolves into some sort of mystical entity which exists only in the mind. Positivism is catastrophically unable to *build upon* or creatively transform traditional metaphysics: indeed, it is quite uncritical towards its own metaphysical past, for it *accepts* the time-honoured division between an absolute truth and relativist experience, outlined for example in Plato, but instead of embracing the absolute at the expense of the relative, reverses the sequence, and embraces experience at the expense of truth. It simply replaces the metaphysics of the theologian with the metaphysics of the sceptic. And the praxis writers follow positivism along its self-destructive path.

What links the philosophical "specialist", who says more and more about less and less, and Jean-Paul Sartre's praxical notion of man as "the privileged existent" is that both reject the possibility of understanding the world as a whole and therefore neither can understand it in any one of its constituent particulars. For unless we can understand the universal in the particular and the particular in the universal, we can understand nothing at all. The world simply confronts us as a chaos of fragments. "The unsurpassable singularity of the human adventure"[9] may appear revolutionary and exciting, but the truth is that it does not represent the slightest improvement over empiricism's dreary assertions about reality as a series of unrelated "events". It is simply positivism with a "left" face.

Of course the fact that Marxism is a world outlook and thus a philosophy of the universe does not and cannot mean that it asserts an absolute truth *outside* of the historical world. For the truth about the universe, like the universe itself, can only deepen, develop and grow from one historical period to another. Such truth is absolute, for it is perfectly real, but it is also necessarily *relative* for it can only express itself in a partial and historically conditioned fashion. Truth is absolute *and* relative, and unless it is both it is neither. In this, dialectical materialism has at once decisively broken with (and yet creatively built upon) the metaphysics of over two thousand years.

(ii) *Dialectics and Nature*

The attack on materialism launched by the praxis school is not new. George Berkeley in the early 18th century dismissed the idea of matter as a thing-in-itself as simply absurd, for who does not know that the categories of thought, of causality, necessity, time and space, dwell only in the mind? To postulate a logic in nature: this is a categorical outrage!

Jeff Coulter in his critique of Engels fully supports (from a "revolutionary" standpoint of course) the often repeated empiricist attack on the dialectics of nature. The concept of a dialectical logic, Coulter complains,

> confuses propositions in their *relations* to each other with their *subject matter* as such,[10]

but this of course is Kantian idealism, for if *relations* are not intrinsic to their "subject matter" whose objective reality we reflect in our minds, then they can only be introspectively induced, metaphysical postulates applicable *a priori*. The old story ... poor matter is the damsel in distress until Logic, with its shining armour of Categories, comes to the rescue! On this ruling class absurdity, "revolutionary" praxis and conservative positivism speak with one voice.

What appals Coulter, as a good empiricist, is the thought that if nature is dialectical then we will have on our hands the ideological fungus of a "new teleology" and that is unthinkably absurd.

> If contradiction is alleged to exist within some natural phenomena, wherein contradiction has been loosely defined as "conflicting force(s)", a species of teleology underpins it, even animistic assumptions.[11]

Now if by "teleology" is simply meant the intelligible (as opposed to the intelligent) movement of the universe, then Marxism can no more do without "a species of teleology" than any other philosophy, including, as we shall see, praxis itself. Engels made this clear when he stressed that it was the "*old* teleology" (my stress) which had gone to the devil, but he at the same time concluded:

[10] "Marxism and the Engels Paradox", *Socialist Register*, 1971, p. 139.   [11] Ibid.

it is now firmly established that matter in its eternal cycle moves according to laws which at a definite stage—now here, now there—necessarily gave rise to the thinking mind in organic beings.[12]

Marx agreed: it was not enough to simply throw out the teleological tale about "purpose" in the universe: it was necessary to replace a metaphysical with a *scientific* explanation of the movement of things. Hence Marx praises Darwin's *Origin of the Species* not simply because it deals a death-blow for the first time to teleology, but because it also "empirically explains" its "rational meaning".[13] A comment which is extremely important, for note that Marx does not dismiss teleology as mere *nonsense*; it has a *rational* meaning and this must be explained. The often brilliant speculations of the old teleologists can be placed on a much firmer, scientific footing by a dialectical understanding which strips "purpose" of its idealist overtones and can thus get to grips with the *material* development of organic and inorganic life. If Marxism remains "teleological", then that is only because it regards nature as an objective world which develops.

And as we have already seen, it is one thing to snipe at a theory of nature, quite another to actually keep it out. Philosophy, like nature, abhors a vacuum: what is expelled in one form, must return in another, and lurking behind the brave, "anti-metaphysical" front of praxis is a theory which states that nature is not in fact dialectical because it merely goes round in circles. Lenin quotes Mach: "the acceptance of a divine original being is not contradictory to experience",[14] for the point about scepticism is that anything goes. "Teleology" will not disappear from the theoretical scene simply because it encounters one or two implausible empiricist scarecrows. On the contrary, empiricism aids and abets all kinds of mysticism, and the attack on reason and history implicit in the rejection of dialectics in nature simply brings in through the back-door a *metaphysical* "teleology" which postulates a nature whose sole "purpose" is, it seems, to mechanistically chase after its own tail.

The praxis theorists have made absolutely no *substantive* advances in understanding the world since the early empiricists first developed their problematic theory of experience. Coulter complains that a "teleological" conception of historical development denies "the activist-voluntarist notion of revolutionary change",[15] and if by

[12] *Dialectics of Nature*, op. cit., p. 198.
[13] Marx to Lassalle (16.1.1861), *Selected Correspondence*, op. cit., p. 151.
[14] *Materialism and Empirio-Criticism*, op. cit., p. 135.
[15] Coulter, op. cit., p. 140.

voluntarist is meant subjectivist, then of course, it does. But it is worth stressing that only the form of this "activist-voluntarist" notion is new: its content is as old as empiricism itself. The same belief in man's "practico-intellectual appropriation" of the universe, as Schmidt puts it, can be found in Karl Pearson's lucid assertion that "man is the maker of natural law",[16] and it is a subjectivism which is as revolutionary as the scepticism of David Hume himself.

Indeed, just how critical the praxis theorists really are of that positivism which they claim to detest, can be seen in their comments on natural science. Schmidt, for example, declares that Engels' "abstract metaphysical theses"

> have absolutely no connection with the method of natural science itself, which is oriented towards formal logic and is undialectical in the sense that it does not reflect the historical mediation of its objects.[17]

This view of the natural sciences is essentially positivist, and it is one which Marx and Engels explicitly rejected. How absurd it is to say that natural science in its methodology does not reflect the historical mediation of its objects is indicated in the *Manuscripts of 1844*, where Marx stresses the fact (which the Young Hegelians failed to grasp) that

> natural science has invaded and transformed human life all the more *practically* through the medium of industry. . . . *Industry* is the *actual*, historical relation of nature, and therefore of natural science, to man.[18]

Natural science "invades and transforms" human life, and yet has nothing to do with the theory of dialectics! Marx could not have disagreed more. Once we dispel the formalist and positivist illusions about natural science, he argued, then

> in consequence, natural science will lose its abstractly material—or rather its idealistic—tendency and will become the basis of *human* science as it has already become the basis of actual life, albeit in an estranged form. *One* basis for life and another for *science* is *a priori* a lie[19](stress in original).

And yet it is precisely this harmful and abstract division between "one basis for science and another for life" which positivism upholds, and the praxis writers accept. Lukacs in his *History and Class Consciousness* rejects "the methodology of the natural sciences" because

---

[16] Cited by Lenin, *Materialism*, op. cit., p. 146.

[17] Schmidt, op. cit., p. 55.

[18] *Manuscripts*, op. cit., p. 103.

[19] Ibid.

they have, he says, no place for contradiction in their subject matter.[20] But this means that Lukacs quite uncritically assumes that there can only be one methodology of the natural sciences, and that must be positivist. The basis of Revisionism, says Lukacs, is "the methodology of the natural sciences", and this is irony indeed, for it is Lukacs himself who continues to endorse the standpoint of this methodology, namely that nature is something passive, wholly external to man, and without its own dialectical movement. Nature, for the positivist, is the unchanging chaos which we simply contemplate: if there are contradictions between theories, then these arise from formal questions of "logic" and "testing"; they have nothing to do with the actual transformation of nature by man. And praxis, despite its harsh words about "positivist methodology", follows empiricism in its anti-humanist and exploitative illusion that the scientist stands outside nature and feeds parasitically off its fragmented "data". In fact, of course, as Marx makes admirably clear, progress in the *natural* sciences is no more a product of "contemplation" than it is in the social sciences, and this point is firmly underlined by Lenin who shows in *Materialism and Empirio-Criticism* that the "crisis of methodology", which he discusses and debates, has come about because dramatic developments in physics and chemistry, themselves the products of technological change, have thrown traditional materialism into question, and created the pressing need to place the natural sciences on to a dialectical foundation.

The abuse of positivism by the praxis writers is therefore only theoretical: in practice, they follow empiricist critics of Marxism in rejecting the dialectic of nature and supporting the idealist view that the methodology of the natural sciences has nothing to do with the dialectical truth. They continue to separate in a metaphysical way the world of nature and the world of man.

(iii) *The Theory of Reflection*

The theory of reflection receives an early mention in Locke's famous *Essay on Understanding* where Locke asserts that experience is the source of all knowledge and this can only be so because our mind reflects "external sensible objects". But the materialist aspect of Locke's thought was neither sustained nor developed by his empiricist successors; for if, as it was argued, experience is basically an *intellectual*

---

[20] Lukacs, op. cit., p. 10.

activity, then instead of changing reality it simply dissolves it into a mere mental construct, and the theory of reflection peters out. As a result of "experience" the objective world which our minds are supposed to reflect becomes unknowable. Berkeley had no difficulty in transforming Lockean empiricism into outright idealism, and Hume could show with ease that if ideas were simply data of the senses, then even Berkeley's "objective" God was yet another unknowable thing-in-itself.

In his essay on "Truth and Reflection", Petrovic defends his vision of "free, creative beings of praxis" who create rather than reflect reality, on the basis of a philosophy which is, in practice, pure empiricism. It is, he believes, self-evidently absurd that emotions and the will reflect reality:

> are love, hatred, envy, malice only different forms of the reflection of the external objects toward which they are directed?[21]

The proposition strikes Petrovic as foolish precisely because he shares with the empiricists the belief that reflection can only be a *passive* process and is not an activity in its own right, an activity of *conscious* production which necessarily changes the objective world which it reflects. In other words, he assumes a purely mechanistic version of reflection, a version which is neither Marxist nor defensible, and then foists it on to dialectical materialism. The will, by its nature, reflects objective reality because it must *respond* to its pressures. Reflection theory does not eliminate the active nature of the will and emotions, but rather *explains* in rational, material terms the forces which are responsible for their formation. For if, as Petrovic argues, the will and the emotions do not, in fact, reflect reality, then are we to suppose that they form themselves out of absolutely nothing? That they are the timeless impulses of an unchanging Human Nature?

Petrovic, however, remains convinced that when we look to the character of abstract thought, the absurdity of reflection theory becomes even more evident still. For what can abstract or logical propositions be said to reflect?

> A negative existential proposition, for instance, is true if what it denies does not exist. How can such a proposition be interpreted as the reflection of objective reality? The whole system of mathematical propositions is a system of true propositions, which it is difficult to maintain reflect something. And what is reflected by propositions about the past, the future, about possibilities or impossibilities?[22]

[21] *Marx in the Mid-Twentieth Century*, op. cit., p. 195.   [22] Ibid.

The problem arises precisely because, as before, Petrovic accepts a purely empiricist conception of consciousness as something mechanically detached from external reality—a passive contemplation which gazes upon life from the *outside*. As Engels stresses in *Anti-Dühring*, agnosticism is inevitable if we insist on accepting consciousness "quite naturalistically", as "something opposed from the outset to being, to nature";[23] for if we accept this metaphysical dualism, it is not surprising that the theory of reflection becomes impossible to understand. Mathematical propositions are said to inhabit the world of consciousness, and concrete objects the world of the real, as though they had always been eternally apart. Abstract appearances are uncritically swallowed as the truth.

The real question which should be posed, but which of course the empiricist, who is ultimately a theologian at heart, simply ignores, is the *historical* question: how does consciousness arise as a part of human activity, how is the transition from non-knowledge brought about? Once *this* question is posed and answered, then it is comparatively easy to see how the ability to distinguish positive from negative, good from evil, the figure 1 from the figure 100, in short, the ability to *reason*, arises not as a reflection of this or that specific object, but as the result of an *infinity* of reflections on a wide-ranging slice of life's experiences, so that thinking in terms of universal principles becomes possible as a conscious process. Developments in science, mathematics and morals do not spring from *contemplation*; they arise out of man's increasingly creative relations with nature which impress upon him, as the result of rich and varied contact with particulars, growing insight at the level of the general. Mathematics is an extremely practical and concretely based art, as is obvious to anyone who studies its origins: it is only its mystification at the hands of idealist philosophy (itself the product of a perfectly *concrete* exploitation) that endows it with a transcendental appearance, and obscures reality generally with metaphysical juxtapositions between the universal and the particular, the eternal and the transitory, the abstract and the concrete, the ideal and reality. Petrovic's childish objections to the theory of reflection arise, not from the reservations of a practical revolutionary, but merely from this thousand-year-old idealism which, nurtured in an exploitative division of labour, feeds the illusion that consciousness can really be something without being something real.

How tenacious this grip of the past remains on contemporary

---

[23] *Anti-Dühring*, op. cit., p. 55.

thought may be seen in the work of another "revolutionary" positivist, Lesek Kolakowski, whose own "critical" reading of Marx also inclines him to the concept of praxis.

According to Kolakowski in his *Karl Marx and the Classical Definition of the Truth*, traditional empiricism presents cognition as a process of creating concepts which are themselves abstracted from individual observations of the properties of species. The idea, however, that abstract thought can simply derive from the perception of particulars fails to take account of "the basic fact of consciousness",[24] namely the indispensability of general knowledge to the perception of the concrete. And this of course is true. Traditional empiricism with its belief that anything more than the appearances, sense data, must be metaphysical, is notoriously one-sided in its attempts to separate out what in practice form an active unity, induction and deduction, perception and conception, etc. As Hegel understood so well, all objects are "concrete universals", they are *both* similar and different, and they acquire their specific identity only from the particular way they are related to the *universe*, from the way they exist as parts within a wider whole.

But for Kolakowski, the indispensability of general knowledge to the process of cognition points, not to the possibility which opens up of rationally understanding the concrete world, but to the fact that if we need general knowledge in order to think, the objective world is not actually there. Traditional empiricism is to be improved by making its subjective idealism even more explicit, so that even the perceived sense data can be pronounced mere fantasies of the mind. A naïve and fragmented world outlook "advances" into wholesale solipsism. Whereas Hegel tries to transcend empiricism by arguing that "concrete universals" are perfectly real—as real as the unity of identity and difference which exists between parent and child—Kolakowski reaches the opposite conclusion: because thought is universal, this means that it manufactures at its own convenience the fragmented particulars which it is suppose to perceive. Some dialectics! The "indispensability" of the general points to the fact, says Kolakowski, that reality in itself, i.e. outside the mind, must be unknowable. We have no right, he insists, to suppose that "pre-existent reality" bears the qualities of human reality nor do we have the tools to "plumb nature and the kind of distortions it undergoes when it abandons its transcendency to display itself to us".[25] We do not actually deny the existence of this "pre-existent" reality nor do we say that it is unknowable: we merely "reject it as a

[24] *Marxism and Beyond* (Paladin, 1971), p. 66.   [25] Ibid., p. 74.

MARXISM AND THE THEORY OF PRAXIS

possible object of research". It is not *unknowable*, it is just that we have no possible way of finding out what it is! Not only does this revolutionary credo wipe out of existence the sciences of geology, zoology, palaeontology, to name but a few which continue to display a backward concern with a "pre-existent reality", but it invites us to imagine man's social world as his own arbitrary creation.

The world presented in the writings of the young Marx, says Kolakowski, is an artificial world in which linguistic and scientific divisions arise from man's practical needs. Does this mean that because man can only satisfy his practical needs through material production, that these linguistic and scientific divisions are reflections of the objective world? Alas, no. Kolakowski still shares the belief of the exploiter that if someone is "creative", that means that he can do as he likes. Linguistic and scientific divisions are not artificial simply in the sense that they are man-made: they are artificial in the sense that they have no relationship with objective reality. They are mere expressions of arbitrariness. In *this* world, we treat the "sun" and the "moon" as particular sorts of objects not because that is how they are, but simply because that is how it happens to suit us. The point is, however, that any other sort of "arrangement" might equally do:

> in abstract, nothing prevents us from dissecting surrounding material into fragments constructed in a manner completely different from what we are used to. (Thus, speaking more simply, we could build a world where there would be no such objects as "horse", "leaf", "star" and others allegedly devised by nature. Instead there might be, for example, such objects as "half a horse and a piece of river", "my ear and the moon" and other similar products of a surrealist imagination.'[26]

A remarkable admission of the irrationalism and stupidity which follows when the theory of reflection is rejected and in its place is postulated solipsism pure and simple. Kolakowski is not of course the first to make a fool of himself in this way: Hume had warned that the sceptic who failed to mitigate logical empiricism with practical common sense would find himself in a world in which

> all human life must perish, were his principles universally and steadily to prevail. All discourse, all action would immediately cease; and men remain in a total lethargy, till the necessities of nature, unsatisfied, put an end to their miserable existence.[27]

The solipsism is not new: what is new (relatively speaking) is the presentation of this absurdity as a progressive step "beyond Marxism"!

[26] Ibid., pp. 68–69.   [27] *Enquiries*, op. cit., p. 160.

The point needs to be made that since the experience of millions of people under the slavery of fascism, this destructive scepticism is no game. Its nihilism has had the most agonising and pernicious practical consequences, for in a world where everything is deemed arbitrary and artificial, we confront a relativism in the name of which every conceivable social and political abomination can defend itself. For what is fascism but the practical and nightmarish realisation of this "epistemology of the kaleidoscope"? If it is true, as Kolakowski suggests, that

> no division, not even the most fantasic as compared with what we are accustomed to, is theoretically less justified or less "true" than the one we accept in actuality,[28]

then what is to prevent a self-styled *avant garde* from arguing that it is time for a change? After all, who can object, in terms of Kolakowski's argument, if "romantics" divide the world up into supermen and subhumans, Aryans and Jews, masters and slaves. For what can there be to choose between one "product of the surrealist imagination" and another?

Empiricism provides, as I have already commented, an epistemological basis for the darkest reaction and most insance adventurism, for the consequence of its worship of "appearances" and contempt for reflection theory is a rejection of reason and the real world. It is a grim reminder of the gulf between the pious intentions and the possible practice of praxis theory that it should uncritically follow a creed of thought which locks thinking people up in a philosophical strait-jacket so that they come to dunkenly imagine that everything around them is of their own arbitrary making.

(iv) *Historical Materialism and the Relativist Imagination*

The metaphysical dualism which empiricism creates between the general and the particular, between reason and experience, object and subject, manifests itself likewise in the sphere of *morality*, where the dichotomy of the "two worlds" can be seen in the celebrated argument that it is logically impossible to deduce Ought from Is. Facts and values must be kept strictly apart. Moral judgments are mere responses of emotion, personal opinions which, when we enter the domain of science itself, should be kept *private*. Social criticism can thus be

[28] Kolakowski, op. cit., p. 69.

conveniently dismissed as an intellectual blunder, a simple error of scholarship.

Now certainly it *appears* that this positivist dogma meets with a scathing praxical response. Korsch quotes the words of Hilferding (who considered science to be value-free) in order to ridicule the "positivism" of the Second International, while Goldmann actually accuses Marxism of making a positivist distinction between value and fact.[29] And since most praxis theorising has a high moral tone, it seems rather unfair to identify its concepts with positivism at least in this aspect—the rejection by modern empiricism of values in science.

But matters are not so simple. I have already tried to show in the question of dialectics of nature how praxis claims to reject "the methodology of the natural sciences" while uncritically accepting its formulation in positivist terms. The same "uncritical criticism" is evident with regard to science in general. Zivotic, in his critique of natural dialectics, continually contrasts the understanding of *science* in which "the existing state of affairs is raised to the level of the only possible reality"[30] with *dialectics* which critically negates the world in the name of an "authentic generic human essence". Science is restricted to facts, "the existing state of affairs", dialectics to the "value profile of reality", the one is concerned with Is, the other with Ought—a familiar dualism indeed! For this is of course precisely the distinction which positivism itself draws. Positivism, we should remember, does not deny the possibility of all values—it merely rejects the existence of *objective* values, values which reflect the real world, and praxis theory, despite its apparent hostility to positivism, is happy to agree. After all, for its own ethic, the "authentic generic human essence" cannot derive from the existing state of affairs; it is very much, in Marx's words, an ideal "to which reality must adjust", and hence remains firmly entrenched in the fact/value dualism of the positivist dogma. Zivotic, in other words, is as critical of positivism as Kant was of Hume; for Kant accepted the sceptical doctrine of experience, and simply created alongside it a metaphysical *alter ego* which remained essentially apart. The truth is that the theorist is still tied to a positivist outlook whether he is drawn towards a mystical priesthood sermonising over the "authentic generic human essence" or puts in its place the logical scientist whose specialism it is to dabble in appearances. In both cases, the dogma of the "value-judgment" remains intact.

A similar problem appears in Petrovic when he comments on a

[29] Goldmann, op. cit., p. 69.
[30] "The Dialectics of Nature and the Authenticity of Dialectics", *Praxis*, 1967, p. 254.

passage of Marx's drawn from the *Grundrisse* where Marx had referred to the "very exalted view" of production held by ancient and medieval peoples in comparison to the attitudes of the modern bourgeois. Surely, says Petrovic, this is evidence that we cannot regard Marx's historical materialism as a theory which simply concerns itself with economics.

> Not only is this thesis not "economic", it is not really scientific. It might be possible to establish by scientific methods whether one of two views was actually widespread in the ancient, and the other in the modern world. But what scientific methods can establish whether one view is more "exalted" than the other? What kind of observation, experiment, measurement, in other words, what empirical method can establish "exaltedness"?[31]

It is true that empiricism will not get us very far along the road to answering these questions, but where is the serious Marxist who has ever suggested that *science* was a value-free "empirical method"? Certainly it was not Marx, for the whole of *Capital*, as we have already seen, rests upon the anti-empiricist position that capitalism can never be understood from its "appearances"—a position which has of course been branded as "metaphysical" and "Hegelian" by the vulgar who are too timid to look beyond their noses.

The notion of "exalted" is clearly ethical, and it means, Petrovic suggests, "better, higher, more human". But does this mean that "exalted" is simply an arbitrary "value judgment"? Not at all: and Petrovic's own definition of "exalted" shows why. To be "exalted" is to be *more* human, to realise more fully mankind's *infinite* potential for progress, to bring man ever closer to an ideal which by its nature is absolute and infinite, and which unfolds ever more profoundly in the course of history itself. The "mors immortalis" *is* the objective standard which makes the notion of "exalted" scientifically intelligible and perfectly concrete. Our moral principles are not subjectivist inventions: they are reflections of the real world itself.

As for Marx's thesis, Petrovic is so concerned about the empiricist problem of "measuring" morality, that he fails to explain to the reader the real point which Marx intends to get across, and that is this. The "exaltedness" of production in pre-capitalist society is an exploitative *illusion* which capitalism with its blunt and explicit cash-nexus lays bare. In fact, the "nobility" of the ancient and feudal systems is simply the product of backwardness; whereas capitalism, with its barbarism of "the individual", brings man to the brink of a higher and more authentically human society which was inconceivable in early times,

---

[31] Petrovic, op. cit., p. 46.

except as an otherwordly dream. Appearances notwithstanding, and despite the "illusions of the epoch", man is even *less* exalted in ancient times than he is under capitalism, for now he has within his grasp the possibility of eliminating exploitation altogether.

Marx's reference then to this *appearance* of "exaltedness" is not some sort of temporary deviation from science into philosophy: it is a comment which fully accords with real science—a science which is concerned with explaining *historical* reality—even though it contrasts somewhat with "empirical" science whose "methods" are powerless to go beyond fragmented appearances. To juxtapose, as Petrovic does, a scientific conception "empirically proved" with "a philosophical thesis founded on philosophical argument" is simply to express the empiricist dogma at its most unthinking . . . the sorry old tale that values are values and facts are facts, science is science and philosophy is philosophy, and never the twain shall meet!

Positivism by creating a metaphysical barrier between "experience" and our rational understanding veers helplessly into a self-defeatingly relativism which in turn can only lead to intellectual paralysis. Not surprisingly this catastrophic instability affects praxis theory every bit as much as it does the postivist philosophy upon which the praxis concept is "shamefacedly" based. Consider, for example, Lukacs' discussion on historical materialism in his *History and Class Consciousness* where he says:

> A common argument against the validity of historical materialism and one regarded as decisive by bourgeois thought, is that the methods of historical materialism must be applied to itself. For it to be a valid system of thought it must be the case that every so-called ideological formation is a function of economic realities: and (as the ideology of the embattled proletariat) it too, is *a fortiori* just such an ideology, and just such a function of capitalist society.[32]

One such bourgeois thinker was Karl Mannheim, whose objections to historical materialism I briefly touched on earlier. As far as Mannheim was concerned, as he argued in his *Ideology and Utopia*, every social group has its perspective determined by its "situation" and has an outlook relative to its social position. However, by "relative" Mannheim really means simply *relative*, for like all positivists, Mannheim could see no interpenetration between the particular and the general, the absolute and the relative, and hence assumed that if ideas were relative, they could not possibly be true. To find the truth, then, one must find a group which is not a group: a group whose relativism gives them a privileged access into the timeless world of the absolute, in short, a group whose perspective is not itself "situationally determined". But where are such transcendental creatures to be found? Why, of course, among the sect to which Mannheim himself belongs—the "classless" intelligentsia!

Now what is regrettable is that it is not only bourgeois thinkers who take these banal stupidities seriously: it is Lukacs himself. This type of "common argument" floors him. "I believe", he says,

> that this objection can be upheld in part, but to concede it is not to the detriment of the scientific status of historical materialism.[33]

But how can we combat relativism while conceding (at least "in part"!) its objections? Lukacs explains:

> the substantive truths of historical materialism are of the same type as were the truths of classical economics in Marx's view: they are truths within a particular social order and system of production. As such, but only as such, their claim to validity is absolute. But this does not preclude the emergence of societies in which by virtue of their different social structures other categories and other systems of truths prevail.[34]

In other words, we avoid the temptation to "total relativism" by plunging head-first into its midst! For what is the nub of Lukacs' reply? It is that to answer Mannheim's objections we need to remember that Marxism is the "self-knowledge" of capitalist society and therefore is as absolutely true for the proletariat as classical economics was true for the bourgeoisie. But what kind of truth is this? For not only does Lukacs confine Marxism in its scope and relevance to the capitalist epoch (which is absurd), but he reduces a universal science to the status of a "partisan prejudice" or a "pragmatist ideology". For how can we, on the basis of Lukacs' argument, *prove* that historical materialism is the "correct historical method" or that it is Marxism rather than liberalism, fascism, or anarchism which is the "self-knowledge" of capitalist society? It is moreover no answer to this problem simply to say that Marxism is the truth because it is the ideology of the proletariat, for many members of the working class may, and of course do, reject Marxism at any given historical point in time in favour of some other outlook which they believe expresses their best interests. How would we be able to say that they were in fact wrong? Lukacs totally ignores (as does Mannheim) the *objective* interests of the proletariat which

[33] Ibid.   [34] Ibid.

Marxism reflects—an interest which takes mankind a step beyond capitalism—and hence surrenders to a sceptical relativism which, taken to its logical conclusion, wipes out Marxism altogether. Leo Strauss, a reactionary philosopher and right-wing critic of liberalism, has no difficulty in demonstrating the absurdity to which Lukacs' position leads: for if, as he puts it,

> Marxism is only the truth of our time or our society, the prospect of the classless society too is only the truth of our time and society; it may prove to be the delusion that gave the proletariat the power and the spirit to overthrow the capitalist system, whereas in fact the proletariat finds itself afterwards enslaved. . . .[35]

And why not, on Lukacs' terms? For Lukacs rejects the scientific view that the classless society is a material *necessity* that is historically inevitable in some shape or form or timescale, and treats communism simply as an intellectual desire, a utopian dream, a possibility which arises not from the movement of reality, but simply out of consciousness—the *self-knowledge* of capitalism. In this, he is at one with the positivist Mannheim who regards Marxism as one pragmatist truth among many, and perfectly true—for the group which embraces it!

Positivism, with its subjectivist theory of knowledge and history, is hopelessly unable to sort out truth from myth. Its scepticism assures it that "all ideologies are equally bad", while its own "pure science" speaks for the truth. Lacking any other conception of reality, it is understandable that it should end up as the victim of its own. appearances, having ensnared in its trap pragmatists and praxicists who believe that by going round in circles they can somehow change the world.

(v) *Positivism and Necessity*

Determinism, as we have already seen, arouses strong feelings of revulsion in the ranks of the praxis thinkers. Lefebvre, for example, expresses a typical view when he argues that determinism is a philosophical relic of the past and will disappear in that future which the free creativity of praxis alone can create. It is only "official" Marxism with its "empiricist, positivist attitude"—its "technocratic" praxis[36]—which perpetuates man's enslaved subordination to objective laws.

---

[35] *Relativism and the Study of Man*, ed. Schoeck and Wiggins (New York, 1961).
[36] Lefebvre, op. cit., p. 36.

And yet, of course, as I have already commented, this is irony indeed, for positivism does not accept the view that reality is governed by laws. On the contrary, it decisively *rejects* it, and regards the objective world as a chaos of fortuitous events waiting to be "ordered" by the mind of man. It is true that some early positivist thinkers like Comte did speak of *laws* in society, but these laws of motion were themselves seen as the creation of a "scientific" élite, who benevolently imposed them on a chaotic world. They were not pictured as the theoretical reflections of objective laws which exist in reality independently of the human will.

Praxis thinkers, in rejecting determinism as "positivist", ascribe to positivism views which empiricists have always dismissed as "metaphysical", etc. Positivism in fact has always embraced a sceptical creed which, in its essentials, is impossible to distinguish from the "revolutionary creativity" of the praxis school itself.

We see this clearly if we examine for a moment the practical positivism of Eduard Bernstein, the German socialist who developed, towards the end of the 19th century, a revisionist critique of Marx. The praxis writers, whose attack on Marxism comes from the "left", quite correctly charge Bernstein with quietism, positivism, conservatism and mechanism, but they do so in order to prove that *determinism* is basically to blame. It was Bernstein's "fatalistic" belief, they argue, in "eternal laws of nature" which led to this betrayal. But is it true that Bernstein's revisionism derived from a belief in historical laws? Not at all! In fact, precisely the opposite holds. Bernstein's revisionism became evident when he criticised *precisely the same features* of "orthodox" Marxism which the praxis writers themselves reject, and if the form of his critique is somewhat different its ultimate consequences are the same.

We see this not only with regard to determinism, but over the whole range of issues we have already noted. Like the praxis theorists, Bernstein rejected the universality of dialectics on the ground that "the struggle of opposites" was not "the basis of all development", but that "the co-operation of related forces is of great significance as well".[37] Similarly, he considered historical materialism to be far too dogmatic since it allowed insufficient room, he complained, for spiritual and ethical factors. Criticisms which have a familiar ring! Naturally we agree with the praxis theorists: Bernstein was an incorrigibly mechanistic thinker, but he was mechanistic precisely for the same reasons that the praxis version of Marxism is mechanistic, namely

[37] Cited by P. Gay, *The Dilemma of Democratic Socialism* (Collier, 1962), p. 147.

through his rejection of an objective dialectics in the natural and social world.

Indeed, nowhere is this curious unity of right and "left" clearer than on the question which specifically concerns me here: the issue of necessity and determinism. Anyone who believes that Bernstein subscribed to a deterministic outlook ought to read the opening chapter of his *Evolutionary Socialism*, where he *rejects* materialism on the ground that the materialist is

> a Calvinist without God. If he does not believe in a predestination ordained by divinity, yet he believes and must believe that starting from any chosen point of time all further events are, through the whole of existing matter and the directions of force in its parts, determined beforehand.[38]

This too is a familiar criticism, that if matter is believed intelligible, then that can only be because it is *intelligent*! But this is the childish *non-sequitur* of the theologian, for why must matter be endowed with the qualities of consciousness before it can move? Why should we speak of existing matter as "determined beforehand" simply because it moves in a rationally intelligible world where everything must be caused by everything else? Bernstein's protest that a belief in causality is itself teleological derives from the same yearning for subjectivist "critical thought" and "independent activity" which praxis theory displays: materialism is a crude dogma which "interferes" with free thought. It is true that Bernstein's revision of Marxism is blatant and forthright: he proclaims the need to "go back to Kant" in order to refute materialism and warns that "the contempt of the ideal, the magnifying of material factors until they become omnipotent forces of evolution is a self-deception".[39] But if the attack on Marx is more brazen than is fashionable in the praxis school, his revisionism differs not one iota in its content from the idealism of a theory which proclaims that man's freedom can only be found *above* mundane necessity in a metaphysical world where everything created is basically his own. When Lukacs protests that

> a Marxist who cultivates the objectivity of the academic study is just as reprehensible as the man who believes that the victory of the world revolution can be guaranteed by the "laws of nature",[40]

his words could have been those of Bernstein himself. For Bernstein, like Lukacs and the other praxis writers, exalts the independent power

[38] *Evolutionary Socialism* (Schocken Books, 1961), p. 7.
[39] Ibid., p. 223.
[40] Lukacs, op. cit., p. 43.

of the spiritual and the ethical, ridicules the priority of material necessity in historical development, and laments the fact that Marxists tie the ultimate objectives of socialism to the immediate realities of a given situation. Of course, there is an enormous *apparent* difference between the revisionism of the right and the revisionism of the "left": for the one complains, while the other *insists*, that the revolutionary overthrow of capitalism is utopian, so that each accepts the premises of the other, but from an identically opposite standpoint. Both therefore endorse a positivist rejection of that material necessity which dialectically unites fact and value, Is and Ought, the ideals of socialism and the world of concrete reality. Whether the positivism is complacently quiescent, a positivism of the right, or whether it is impotently millenarian, the "left" face, the practical reality and the social consequences are ultimately the same.

We see this ironic "unity of opposites" in Avineri's regret that Marx should have insisted on placing his "utopia" (as Avineri regards it) at the summation of a concrete movement, for like Bernstein, Avineri believes that the movement and the end should remain metaphysically spliced apart. Although Marx's theory of revolution is, he says, based upon universal criteria, its realisation has to depend upon historical circumstances, and

> paradoxically this historicism may be the most disappointing element in Marx's thought.[41]

There is nothing wrong with holding passionately to certain ideals: it is simply a methodological gaffe to believe that they can ever be realised! Where is the positivist who has ever cared to disagree? Conservatism may express itself in rightist form, as a "factual" respect for the *status quo*, but that is not its only shape. It can assume a "leftist" guise which involves, when all is said and done, merely crying for the moon, a cacophony of transcendental "oughts" which leaves the world precisely as it is.

Marxism as a science is irreconcilably opposed to all forms of positivism, whether contemplative or activist, "opportunist" or "ultra-left". It is concerned not simply with decrying one form of this empiricist doctrine while demagogically embracing another: it seeks to expose the foundations of positivism, to tackle the roots of this subjective idealism regardless of the multiplicity of its nuances and forms. As always, Marxism concerns itself with the *reality* of a phenomena and not merely with its multifarious appearances.

[41] Avineri, op. cit., p. 220.

The differences between the praxis concept, which appears revolutionary, and the philosophy of positivism, which is openly conservative, are merely verbal and formal. To judge a theory we must look to its practice, and whether we consider the question of Marxism as a world outlook, as a dialectical theory of nature, as a theory of reflection, as embracing historical materialism or as a deterministic science, what do we find? That on all these pivotal questions praxis and positivism answer with one voice. Sometimes, it is true, the notes soar heavenwards evoking transcendental visions of a self-creating mankind: on other occasions, the tone is sober and earthly, indeed, so timid and feeble as to be positively mole-like. But in each case, the singer is the same; and so too, as I shall now argue, are the social and political consequences which these choruses of mystification have in the outside world.

10

PRAXIS AND POLITICS

> In every new historical phase old mistakes
> reappear momentarily (Marx and Engels)

Since the middle of the 1960s, we have witnessed a considerable upsurge of radical protest against conditions of life under monopoly capitalism, involving, often for the first time, many young people who had not taken part in struggle before. The inexperience and youth of many of the participants have inclined them in the first instance to anarchism, and this of course is not surprising. What is, however, worthy of note is that the attacks on authority, the demand for individual freedoms, the direct action movements which claim to have demolished organisational "hierarchies", have invariably been defended in the name of Marxism, or at least some particular interpretation (usually abstract and "libertarian") of Karl Marx. "Marxisms" have likewise proliferated among small but serious circles of the intellectually "sophisticated" groups whose interests centre on the ideas of the French theorist Louis Althusser, of Jean-Paul Sartre, the Frankfurt school, and so on.

It is in these groups and sects that the ideas of praxis have found a receptive audience. And although any revival of interest in Marxism is naturally welcome, it is significant how, in our present period, this interest has thus far centred around the presentation of Marxism in anarchist terms rather than as a materialist science. A "common intellectual universe", as one writer calls it, has developed, and as a "challenge" to what is seen as the Marxism of the orthodox, it has at its theoretical centre many of the ideas which we have encountered in our critique of praxis.[1]

Now of course, although many of the formulations today are quite new, and "newness" is a quality highly prized by this self-styled theoretical *avant garde*, the ideas themselves, even as revisions of Marxism, are relatively old, and it has been the purpose of this book, in gathering together some of the "leftist" critics of Marxism extending back to the 1920s, to show the underlying unity which exists within the varying formulations of the praxis concept. Indeed, these leftist

[1] See G. Stedman Jones, "The Marxism of the Early Lukacs", *New Left Review* 70, p. 27.

revisions have built their own tradition and lineage, so that it has been possible for publishing houses profitably to translate and revive works critical of "orthodox" Marxism which extend back for at least five decades.

Indeed, the dating of this tradition of leftist criticism is quite significant, for since the October revolution brought into being the world's first socialist State as a confirmation of the teachings of Marx and Engels, it has been all but impossible to present a critique of capitalism without coming to terms with the theory of Marxism. It has been almost obligatory for the serious critic of society to, as it were, wear a "Marxist face", to present his case with a Marxist veneer. But if their Marxist "idiom" is comparatively recent, the ideas themselves are far older, and we see them popping up time and again, in the ideological struggles of Lenin with what he called petty-bourgeois revolutionism, in Plekhanov's criticisms of the anarchists and his fight to establish Marxism on "Russian soil", and of course, they make their appearance in Marx and Engels' attacks on Bakunin and before him, in the polemics with Proudhon and Stirner. In fact, as we have already seen, the debate between Marxism and Praxis extends back to some of Marx and Engels' earliest polemics, most notably those with the Young Hegelians and the "mystic identity of practice and theory"[2] which they preached. For here the true roots of the present school are to be found, and it is no wonder that the praxis theorists often express a strong affinity with the "young Marx", for they continue to embrace ideas which Marx and Engels had thrown overboard by 1845. In fact, the theory of praxis has been decisively discredited for over 125 years. A somewhat unpromising heritage! For the truth is, as I have tried to show, that the praxis theorists propagate a position which was consistently fought by Marx and Engels for the whole of their political lives. The historic battles against anarchism and utopian socialism were battles against ideas no different in essence from the concept of praxis which now, a century and a quarter after it was first vanquished, continues to preen itself as the authentic truth of Karl Marx.

For it was clear to Marx and Engels, and to Lenin after them, that the failure to understand socialism *as a materialist science* could only have the most damaging practical consequences. For unlike Korsch and Lefebvre, Marx and Engels never believed a theory was simply an abstract force confined to men's heads; on the contrary, they knew its practical implications only too well, and it is the cornerstone of their teaching that the unity of theory and practice is not merely some sort of

[2] *The Holy Family*, op. cit., p. 255.

abstract aspiration: it is a concrete fact of life. Scientific theory is crucial precisely because erroneous and metaphysical theories will wreak havoc with the proletarian cause. It is unfortunately, as fascism has so tragically proved, not only progressive ideas which become a "material force" when they seize the minds of the masses.

Let me explore this matter a little more closely, for it goes to the roots of the problem.

(i) *Socialism—a Theoretical Ideal or Practical Reality?*

In their polemics with the Young Hegelians, the *Holy Family* and *The German Ideology*, Marx and Engels frequently stress that communism cannot and must not be conceived of *as an ideal*, in the sense that it stands outside of or above reality. Communism is nothing more than that *real* movement which abolishes the present state of things, and its premises are only abstract in the sense that they are abstract reflections of concrete conditions now in existence. All this might sound disagreeably "positivist" to the praxis critic, but as far as Marx and Engels were concerned, it was the touchstone for a scientific socialism and the essential ingredient in any revolutionary strategy which stood the slightest chance of real success.

This point was reiterated to the Brussels Communist Committee in which Marx and Engels worked in the 1840s, and on no occasion more graphically than at a memorable meeting on March 30th, 1846, where Marx confronted Weitling, one of the founders of German communism, and demanded to know upon what he based his revolutionary activity. Annenkov, who describes the scene, recalls that Weitling, like the praxis theorists of our own time, "seemed to want to keep the discussion on the plane of the commonplaces of liberal rhetoric". He had, Weitling told Marx, succeeded in bringing together hundreds of men and women by invoking the names of Justice, Solidarity and Brotherly Love: he was a tireless champion of the "common good". Just how impressed Marx was by utopian thinking with its millenarian fantasies, abstract harmonies, vague ideals and secular versions of the "promised land" is vividly portrayed in his explosive retort to Weitling. To go, he declared,

> to the workers in Germany without strictly scientific ideas and concrete doctrine would mean an empty and unscrupulous playing with propaganda, which would inevitably involve, on the one hand, the setting up of an inspired apostle, and on the other hand, simply asses who would listen to him with open mouth.[3]

[3] This recollection is cited in Edmund Wilson's *To the Finland Station* (Fontana, 1960), pp. 169–170.

Ignorance, he added, "has never helped anybody yet". Of course, to insist that socialism stands or falls in the last analysis *as a science* is not always easy, and Marx in a letter to Annenkov at the end of 1846 admitted that he had drawn much enmity upon himself, not least from within the German Communist Party, for strongly opposing "sentimental, utopian, mutton-headed socialism". So why did Marx persist? Why did he and Engels continue to fiercely attack the utopians (who, say the philistines, "have their hearts in the right place"), devoting in the *Communist Manifesto* an entire section on the subject? The answer to this question is made absolutely explicit in the polemic with Proudhon in 1847, where Marx charges Proudhon with ignoring the realities of capitalism and substituting in their place unworkable and abstract panaceas for reform. The result? The *real* struggles by *real* workers are either viewed with a "transcendental disdain" or they are actually *opposed* in the name of some utopian ideal which simply re-expresses bourgeois ideals in a topsy-turvy fashion. In other words, the end product of utopian or "idealistic" socialism is not merely impotence, although this is bad enough, it is *conservatism*; and Marx hammers home this point by showing how in practice the conclusions of the bourgeois economists and the utopian reformers are well nigh identical. The economists expect the working class to accept capitalism as it is: the "socialists" demand that workers should wash their hands of the system altogether. The net result is the same! "The socialists," writes Marx, "want the workers to leave the old society alone, the better to be able to enter the new society which they have prepared for them with so much foresight."[4] So what happens? "You will continue none the less to be workers, and the masters will still continue to be the masters, just as before." The promised land turns out to be a recipe for the *status quo*.

Marx and Engels stress this point in the *Communist Manifesto*. The utopians, by erecting socialism into a complete system which the workers must carry out all at once, marching straight into the New Jerusalem, in fact require

> in reality, that the proletariat should remain within the existing bounds of society . . . ,[5]

the New Jerusalem being of course simply the present society in mystical guise.

Utopianism, in other words, fulfils the ideological function of a

[4] *Poverty of Philosophy*, op. cit., p. 144.
[5] *Communist Manifesto*, op. cit., p. 87.

religion in its ultimate defence of things as they are. Lofty notions of "humanist praxis" and authentic "generic essences" turn out to be rather uncritical representations of the world as it is.

Consider the attack of Marx and Engels on utopian thought in relation to the existentialist millenarianism of Jean-Paul Sartre. For what does Sartre see as freedom? Freedom, for Sartre, is nothing as mundane as the right to work, the right to participate in the running of economic and political affairs, oh no, it is something much grander than this! Freedom, declares Sartre, is the unity of Subject and Object, the union of the "signified-signifying" and the "signifying-signified", an ecstatic "self-consciousness" (shades of Bruno Bauer!). And what has this to do with ordinary flesh-and-blood people? Well . . . "by becoming conscious of itself, the Proletariat becomes the subject of history".[6] Isn't that worth striving for?

Sartre's utopianism lacks even the capacity to inspire or exhilarate. At least we can say of Etienne's dream of justice in Zola's *Germinal*, that it is delightful to behold . . .

> as happens in dreams, there grew up a new society in a single day and, shining like a mirage, a great city, in which each citizen lived by his own appointed task and shared in the joys of all.[7]

But what is charming or joyful about Sartre's philosophical mumbo-jumbo? Its conservatism becomes evident when we try to tie down the slogans of "self-consciousness" to something specific or concrete. After all, what does Sartre say, for example, about the socialist societies in the world which are busily engaged in mammoth tasks of reconstruction? The answer is revealing: because, says Sartre, our period is a period in which there are often violent divisions between people and societies, the period has to "make itself without knowing itself". It follows that, because of these divisions, the socialist countries do not yet "know themselves" and History still lacks "one meaning".[8] And this is thoroughly utopian, for by making the achievement of socialism some kind of metaphysical and speculative identity of the Ideal and reality, Sartre, to all intents and purposes, makes it unobtainable. It is an old story: all attempts to historically realise ideals which are timeless are of course tragically destined to fail, so that Sartre comes to the thoroughly *conservative* conclusion that since the socialist countries have not yet achieved "everything", they have not really achieved anything.

---

[6] Sartre, op. cit., p. 89.
[7] *Germinal* (Penguin, 1954), p. 169.
[8] Sartre, op. cit., pp. 89–90.

This "utopian conservatism" is not only evident in Sartre's comments on the socialist countries; it is apparent in his attitude towards society in general. Because they neglect psychoanalysis and other "western disciplines" (as Sartre calls them) which help us to probe the "uniqueness" of the individual, "contemporary Marxists", protests Sartre, have forgotten that "man, alienated, mystified, reified, etc., still remains a man". Reification does not mean that we have been transformed into things, but rather that we are "condemned to live humanly the condition of material things".[9] In other words, "humanity" at one moment out of reach, is at another "realised" already: since the practical likelihood of our "knowing ourselves" in the ecstatic moment of "totalising praxis" is at best rather slight, we may as well accept the fact that we are "condemned" to "live humanly" with life as it is. Man, alienated from a purely abstract essence, had better learn to put up with things as they are, for until the mystical utopia arrives nothing significant can really change. Where is the conservative who would care to disagree?

It is not surprising that since Sartre's utopianism "requires in reality that the proletariat should remain within the existing bounds of society", his analysis of exploitation is based upon conservatism and despair. The basic contradiction in society which exploitation creates, says Sartre, merely provides a framework for events—it does not actually *explain* them. What does? The answer, says Sartre, is *scarcity*! Now of course, if *scarcity* is at the root of our problems, then mankind is really in trouble, for since capitalist crises are caused by an anarchically produced *abundance*, to argue that scarcity is nevertheless ultimately to blame is to convert scarcity into some sort of "human predicament" which nothing can resolve.

Long ago, Engels, in reply to Malthus' "revolting blasphemy against nature and mankind", pointed out that "the productive power at mankind's disposal is immeasurable":[10] the idea that scarcity is the source of our problems is simply a vulgar illusion created by the unemployment and shortages of a capitalist crisis, the distorted reflection of an absurd situation in which, as Engels adds sarcastically,

> the population is only too large where the productive power as a whole is too large.[11]

Scarcity presents itself as the illusion precisely because it has nothing to

[9] Ibid., p. 104.

[10] "Outlines of a Critique of Political Economy" (1844), in *Manuscripts of 1844*, op. cit., p. 182.

[11] Ibid., p. 184.

do with the real problem. But none of this makes any sense to Sartre, who believes that the distinction between appearances and reality does not exist, and so, when confronted between that tragic and inexorable gulf between "existence" and "essence", praxical ideals and concrete reality, it is not surprising that the ultra-revolutionary easily sheds his role as fervent preacher of Perfection and becomes a humbled empiricist unwillingly reconciled to the *status quo*.

The theological bliss of the praxis utopia simply reflects the fact that earthly man remains condemned, as Genesis says, to eat thistles and thorns in a world where scarcities and neuroses, conditioning and "individuality" make his conditions unalterable.

This link between utopianism in theory and conservatism in practice is similarly manifest in the writing of Shlomo Avineri. There is, on the one hand, the Ideal: the "new society" (which Avineri anxiously reminds his reader has nothing to do with the "crude Communism" of the U.S.S.R.) where objective laws have disappeared, where the actual and the potential have become One, where the equilibrium between production and consumption (a thoroughly unscientific idea postulated by Ricardo) has come about. But what is the social reality which lies behind these abstract unities and philosophical "wholes"? Alas, nothing more dramatic than the staid old myths of social democracy. It is Avineri's view, for example (claimed in the name of Marx!), that because the factory legislation and royal commissions on sanitation in Britain "bring the State into direct involvement with some aspects of economic activity",[12] this means that these developments represent "post-capitalist elements", elements which

> introduce into the free market economy aspects of community-oriented considerations and contribute further to social change.[13]

The socialism "all at once" becomes in practice nothing more than the reformist "bit by bit". Avineri is so concerned with that philosophical blitzkrieg which fashions the world in its own creative image, that he fails to observe that there is something of a difference between the social policies of state monopoly capitalism and those of socialism itself. Having denounced Engels for contributing to the conservatism of the German SPD, he proceeds to propagate the illusions of Bernsteinism with its belief that one social system simply "grows" into another. It is no wonder that Avineri is so hostile to Lenin and refers scathingly to what he is pleased to call the "Jacobin tradition of merely political,

---

[12] Avineri, op. cit., p. 14.
[13] Ibid., pp. 159–160.

subjectivist revolutionary action",[14] for Lenin, in stark contrast to the praxical utopians, saw no contradiction between understanding reality and getting things done.

As with Marx and Engels, the ideals for which Lenin fought were those of a concrete world actually coming into being.

Let me explore this matter a little further by considering

(ii) *Praxis Theory and the "Leap" into Communism*

In a rather interesting section of his work, dealing with the "university of capitalism", Avineri points to Marx's argument that in creating a world market capitalism had itself laid the objective basis for world communism. He proceeds then to quote Marx and Engels' comment in *The German Ideology* that

> empirically, communism is only possible as the act of the dominant people "all at once" and simultaneously, which presupposes the universal development of productive forces and the world intercourse bound up with communism.[15]

Now this idea that communism can only be brought about "all at once" on a world scale derives (1) from the fact that *The German Ideology* is by no means wholly free of Marx and Engels' antediluvian Young-Hegelian idiom, and (2) that pre-monopoly capitalism appeared to be "spreading itself" relatively evenly, so that the prospect of a "universal" revolution, at least within the advanced capitalist countries, seemed possible and even likely. But Marx's statement cannot be taken out of its historical context and erected into a timeless dogma. Even in the *Communist Manifesto* we read,

> though not in substance, yet in form, the struggle of the proletariat with the bourgeoisie is at first a national struggle. The proletariat of each country must, of course, first of all settle matters with its own bourgeoisie,[16]

a position which is substantially more concrete than the above-cited comment some two or three years before. In other words, although the struggle for socialism is ultimately international, the forms it takes will differ from country to country.

Avineri seems unable to grasp this. He imagines that because Marxism regards communism as a world system, therefore

[14] Ibid., p. 258.
[15] Cited by Avineri, p. 167.
[16] *Manifesto*, op. cit., p. 59.

socialism in one country, according to Marx, is conceptually and
historically a self-destroying hypothesis,[17]

a statement that is both "conceptually and historically" quite wrong. It
is historically wrong for reasons at which Avineri himself hints,
namely Marx's own realisation that socialism could break out *first* in a
number of different countries, including, Marx believed, within Russia
itself, and it is conceptually wrong, because Marxism as a science
transcends abstract and often arbitrary "hypotheses" and concerns itself
with an analysis which can never be more than the concrete study of a
concrete world. Whether socialism (and by socialism we mean
socialism, not communism) is likely or possible in one country does not
depend upon abstractly conceived "general principles": it depends
upon the specific character of objective reality. Hence even in Marx's
own life-time it was clear that considerable differences existed between
the capitalist countries as to their ripeness for revolution and the
political maturity of their working classes, and this *unevenness* became
for Lenin, as free enterprise passed into monopoly capitalism, "an
absolute law of capitalism".

> Hence, the victory of socialism is possible first in several or even in one
> capitalist country alone. After expropriating the capitalists and organising
> their own socialist production, the victorious proletariat of that country will
> rise *against* the rest of the world—the capitalist world—attracting to its
> cause the oppressed classes of other countries. . . .[18]

Is this a revision of or departure from Marx's own position, as Avineri
appears to suggest? I believe not. There is a clear *continuity* between this
argument of Lenin's and the statement cited above in the *Communist
Manifesto*. Of course, Lenin has significantly *developed* and extended
Marx's theory on this point, but that is only because, like Marx and
Engels, Lenin considered socialism to be a science which continually
deepens its reflections of reality as the concrete world itself continues to
develop.

This point is crucial to grasp if we are to understand that socialism
and communism cannot be built according to abstract principles or
preconceived "hypotheses": it can only be constructed on the basis of
existing realities no matter how "awkward", "tragic" or "unforeseen"
these realities may turn out to be. Even as early as 1843 we find Marx
rejecting the utopian communism of Weitling and Cabet as a
"dogmatic abstraction" and insisting that struggle can only develop

---

[17] Avineri, op. cit., p. 167.
[18] "On a slogan for a United States of Europe", *Collected Works*, 21, p. 342.

"out of the forms *inherent* in existing actuality".[19] The theoretical conclusions of the Communists, Marx and Engels remind us in the *Manifesto*,

> merely express, in general terms, actual relations springing from an existing class struggle, from a historical movement going on under our very eyes.[20]

Communism can never be an ideal to which reality must adjust: it *is* reality coming into being. It is not surprising that both in the years leading up to the revolutions of 1848 and in the years which followed them, Marx and Engels had to struggle fiercely against those who treated communism as a "dogmatic abstraction", as some sort of mystical "act of will" which a transcendental "praxis" could enact as a vision of its own making.

The praxis writers are attracted to what they see as the universality of the socialist struggle: but just as they metaphysically abstract the general from the particular in discussing the theory of reflection or the nature of determinism, so too do they try to splice apart the universal and the specific in their more practical discussions on communism. And yet, of course, at every level of practice, a genuine "universality" is only realisable through the medium of its constituent particulars. The struggle for socialism cannot take place in the abstract. It can only take place in the light of the concrete issues of the time. It cannot ignore the rights of nationalities to self-determination, of women to equality, of peasantry to the land, of the petty bourgeois to protection against the monopolies—for these are struggles which, although not specifically socialist in content, are all vital stages of the revolutionary process and necessary milestones on the path to socialism itself. They convert the struggle for socialism from a dream into a reality, giving this struggle the living tissues from which to mould its strategy and tactics. Only in the world of the abstract do universal revolutions take place "all at once".

This position was fought out by Marx and Engels over and over again in their battles with the "left", who united the universal and the particular by preaching *abstract* internationalism in the name of a dominating or hegemonic national proletariat. Willich, for example, who led with Schapper the "left" faction of the Communist League of 1850, was guilty, declared Marx, of abstract sectarianism and a practical chauvinism, of masking exploitative attitudes with heady talk of an instant "revolutionary will". He exemplified the curious combination

---

[19] *Writings of the Young Marx*, op. cit., p. 213.
[20] *Manifesto*, op. cit., p. 62.

which we often see in "left" politics today, of "proletarian" phrasemongering and a lamentably uncritical attitude to the actual class composition of the "people". Here as elsewhere, Marx thoroughly demolished the essentially *conservative* nature of this mystical belief in the "creative will". As he writes,

> the *will*, rather than the actual conditions, was stressed as the chief factor in the revolution. We tell the workers: if you want to change conditions and make yourselves capable of government, you will have to undergo fifteen, twenty or fifty years of civil war. Now they are told: we must come to power immediately or we might as well go to sleep.[21]

Either communism now or not at all: either the Proletariat instantly "know themselves" or their struggle has failed!

It is scarcely surprising that Marx's stress on the practical and concrete character of the struggle to build socialism has not met with praxis approval, and nowhere is the opposition to Marx's scientific theory of revolution more apparent than in an essay by Gayo Petrovic on "Philosophy and Politics in Socialism". Petrovic takes issue in particular with the *Critique of the Gotha Programme* where Marx emphasises that the building of communism is a process which can only take place in *stages*, and that it is essential to distinguish, for example, between a lower and higher phase, or, as it has become customary to make this distinction, between socialism and communism. The strikingly *anti-utopian* character of Marx's thought could scarcely be expressed more plainly: as he writes in a celebrated passage,

> what we have to deal with here is a communist society not as it has *developed* on its own foundations, but, on the contrary, as it *emerges* from capitalist society; which is thus, in every respect, economically, morally and intellectually, still stamped with the birth marks of the old society from whose womb it emerges.[22]

It is the lower phase of communism (or socialism) which must create the pre-conditions—the *material* premises—for the development to the higher phase; and this means, as Marx points out, that during the first, transitional phase, "bourgeois criteria"—the reward of the individual according to his ability—are inevitable:

> Right can never be higher than the economic structure of society and its cultural development conditioned thereby.[23]

[21] *The Revolutions of 1848* (Penguin, 1973), p. 341.
[22] *Critique of the Gotha Programme* (Progress Publ., 1971), p. 16.
[23] Ibid., p. 17.

The analysis appals Petrovic. To consider the struggle for communism something concrete and real—that is highly dangerous! And why? In the first place, it makes a nonsense of the hallowed visions of praxis theory of a "new society" which has transcended material production and the laws of necessity, and even more worryingly, it allows for the possibility that, in the course of this transition, "inhumanity, unfreedom and violence" will occur, and further be *justified* on the ground that the higher phase of communism or communism proper has yet to arrive. "If Marx could have foreseen such an interpretation of his theory," surmises Petrovic,

> he would perhaps have never formulated it, not even in the passing way in which he did in the *Critique of the Gotha Programme*.[24]

Marx was, however, a student of the real world, and the more deeply he probed into the roots of capitalism and other exploiting societies, the more wary he became of abstractions which serve the naïve or the unscrupulous as benign substitutes for practical realities. Above all, Marx never allowed himself to dogmatise about the form of revolution and class struggle. Revolution was, for Marx, neither a gory bloodbath in which the workers sacrificed themselves unthinkingly for the greater glory of their cause, yet nor was it an agreeably painless "leap" into a world of Abstract Humanity and Brotherly Love. Revolution was the transformation of one social system and its replacement by another, and how bloody or peaceful these transformations were depended upon objective circumstances and the balance of class forces. We have already noted Marx's comments about protracted civil war on the Continent, but this was by no means the only form he considered revolution could take. At the Hague Congress in 1872, Marx declared that "the worker will some day have to win political supremacy in order to organise labour along new lines", and added significantly,

> . . . we have by no means affirmed that this goal would be achieved by identical means.

> We know of the allowances we must make for the institutions, customs and traditions of the various countries; and we do not deny that there are countries such as America, England and I would add Holland, if I knew your institutions better, where the working people may achieve their goal by peaceful means. If that is true, we must also recognise that in most of the continental countries it is force that will have to be the lever of our

revolutions; it is force that we shall some day have to resort to in order to establish a reign of labour.

Marx then neither supported nor opposed "inhumanity, unfreedom and violence" at the level of abstract principle. There could be occasions when violence was essential to the success of revolution and circumstances when it was wholly unnecessary. Consider, for example, Marx's comment to the Central Committee of the Communist League in 1850, when he declares that

> . . . far from opposing so called excesses—instances of popular vengeance against hated individuals or against public buildings with which hateful memories are associated—the workers' parties must not only tolerate these actions but must even give them direction.

But this kind of violence was in no sense a matter of principle: indeed, Marx could even conceive of circumstances in which revolution, as the term is customarily thought of, would not be necessary. In a letter to Hyndman (8/12/1880), Marx wrote:

> if you say you do not share the views of my Party for England I can only reply that that Party considers an English revolution not necessary but—according to historical precedents—*possible*.

> If the unavoidable evolution turns into a revolution, it would not only be the fault of the ruling classes, but also of the working class.

> Every pacific concession of the former has been wrung from them by "pressure from without". Their action has kept pace with that pressure, and if the latter has more and more weakened, it is only because the English working class do not know how to wield their power and use their liberties, both of which they possess legally.[25]

Indeed, in the contemporary situation in Britain today, we see how unrewarding it is to discuss political events in an abstract praxisite manner. Where the working class has been able to display a unity of purpose and organisation as in the struggles of the trade union movement against the Tories' Industrial Relations Act, it has won a number of significant victories without any shedding of blood. Equally, where the trade unions and the left have not been able to

---

[25] These quotations are produced at some length in order to stress the futility of trying to tie Marx down to some abstract position. The comment to the Hague Congress can be found at pp. 84–85, Marx, Engels, Lenin, *Anarchism and Anarcho-Syndicalism* (Progress Publishers, Moscow, 1972); Marx's statement to the Communist League, *Revolutions of 1848*, op. cit.; and the letter to Hyndman in Marx-Engels, *Selected Correspondence* (Lawrence and Wishart, 1955), p. 334.

forge this degree of fighting unity, as in regard to the Irish question and the British government's continuing policies of repression in the north-east of Ireland, there violence has tragically escalated and the dark shadow of civil war now menacingly threatens.

Neither Marx nor Marxism dogmatises about the tactics of revolution nor the methods of struggle which it is appropriate to employ. Of course, if circumstances allow, a peaceful transition to socialism is infinitely preferable to a transition which involves civil war, and Marx recognised this. But what a far cry this is from the Marx in Petrovic's caricature who opposes "inhumanity, unfreedom and violence" in the struggle for socialism solely because they tragically conflict with . . . the abstract principles of praxis! A dogma which substitutes "brotherly love" for "bloodthirsty violence" is still a dogma.

However, Petrovic does not yield the point very easily. Perhaps just somewhere in Marx's writing we can find an alternative to the "stages theory" of the *Critique*? The *Paris Manuscripts*, with its highly speculative and abstract passages on the nature of communism, must be brought to the rescue. According to these *Manuscripts*, says Petrovic, Marx in fact considered socialism to be higher than communism: communism is the negation of private property, and thus still "affirms" man through the abolition of property, while socialism (or better still, humanism) negates the negation and as "positive self-consciousness" requires no mediator at all. Now this argument as summarised by Petrovic is not only obscure, it is not even accurate, for Marx in these passages makes in fact no consistent distinction between communism and socialism at all, and can be found using the terms indifferently to describe "fully developed" naturalism and humanism. But of course, even more significantly, Marx's analysis here is immature and extremely abstract. Communism is still depicted in Young Hegelian style as an *ideal*—a communism whose affirmations and negations operate at the level of *principle*—and the fact that this picture of communism has yet to be based upon a concrete analysis of capitalism itself is made particularly clear in the initial discussion on "crude communism", where we see a purely speculative sketch of what capitalism would look like if everyone was "equally" and "communistically" exploited by everyone else.[26]

In fact, it soon becomes clear that Petrovic is not interested anyway in a serious discussion on the problem of stages in the development to

[26] *Manuscripts*, op. cit., pp. 94–95.

communism, for he proceeds to argue that even if we accept the view that *communism* is the "transitory period" to humanism or socialism,

> this does not mean that it is somewhere in the middle between capitalism and humanism. Communism is communism to the extent to which it is humanism.[27]

In other words, there is no real distinction between communism and humanism at all, and we are back where we started. The truth is that the whole discussion on the question of stages is simply a flimsy window-dressing for the fact that Petrovic cannot really find any justification in Marx's writing for the view that mankind must pass into its praxical utopia without *any* "compromising" periods of transition. His position is of course quite logical, for if we argue as the praxis theorists do that communism is some kind of Ideal Society which has "o'er leapt the banks and shoals of time", then it follows that no transitional periods are necessary before we can arrive there. Like all utopias, praxis humanism turns out to be no more than an immaculate conception which creates itself out of nothing: a mystical "leap" from the World of Estrangement to the World of Man.

It is quite understandable, then, that the scientific idea of communism as the practical development of history which must be built by men and women according to the objective laws of the world around them, is not only "dangerous", "dogmatic", "vulgar", etc., it is positively *annihilating*, for what is likely to survive in this process of these pious aspirations, banal "ideals" and empty utopias upon which praxis so tragically relies? And since communism is, for the praxis theorists, merely a misty utopia, the political means of struggling for its realisation must also be similarly mystified.

I turn to consider briefly a further facet of the practice of praxis,

(iii) Praxis and the Party

It became obvious to Marx and Engels, once they examined the proletariat as a real class in itself and not merely as a conceptual vehicle for abstract ideas, that it is essential for workers to take part in politics: to *organise* themselves for struggle armed with a practical programme and a scientific perspective. The experience of real life, says Engels, the political oppression which is imposed upon them, "force the workers

[27] Petrovic, op. cit., p. 163.

to engage in politics whether they like it or not".[28] To reject politics and the need for a Party organisation can only disarm and demoralise the working class, and hence it is not surprising that a bitter struggle took place within the First International between the political line of Marx and the anarchist conceptions of Bakunin and his faction. Had Bakunin's anarchism prevailed, declared Engels, the International would have been transformed into "a cowardly servile organisation" which would have simply resembled the early Christians in taking the heaven of a future society as their model.[29]

We see clearly in Bakunin's position the link between a metaphysical theory of the "will" and its anarchist consequences. Bakunin, like the praxis writers, blithely substituted "the will" for real economic conditions, and despite his pretensions to materialism, he regarded scientific theory with the deepest suspicion, arguing that "individuals cannot be grasped by thought, by reflection or even by human speech".[30] The deed is all! Spontaneity must rule! Bakunin was himself a disciple of Proudhon, and Lucien Goldmann, in what he calls his "revolutionary-reformist" analysis of contemporary capitalism, acknowledges specific ideological links with this tradition. The fact that anarchism has always led to a nightmare of disorganisation and indiscipline is ignored, for after all, praxis is praxis, whatever the social cost. The working class and the peasantry have paid dearly for the mistakes of anarchism; and Engels' powerful piece on the *Bakuninists at Work*, written in 1873, contains many tragic parallels between the disruptive and divisive activities of the anarchists in the struggles in Spain in the 1870s and in the civil war some 60 years later.

However, the praxis writers appear to have learnt nothing from the past, and the views of sects which were regarded by Marx and Engels as the theoretical symptoms of political immaturity are thoughtlessly reiterated in the name of a "newly discovered" Karl Marx, who in fact spent his entire life fighting them. Marx repeatedly pointed out that the political development of the working class necessarily takes place in a piecemeal and often extremely uneven fashion. It cannot be presumed that the workers will understand the nature of their exploitation or the kind of struggle needed to end it in a blinding flash of inspiration, "all at once" as it were. Hence the necessity arises for a Communist Party which, drawn from "the most advanced and resolute" ranks of the workers, has

[28] Marx, Engels, Lenin, *Anarchism and Anarcho-Syndicalism* (Progress Publ. 1972), p. 51.

[29] Ibid., p. 63.   [30] *God and the State* (New York, 1970), p. 60.

the advantage of clearly understanding the line of march, the conditions, and the ultimate general results of the proletarian movement.[31]

This link between science and the Party was forged explicitly by Lenin in *What is to be done?*, where he argues that socialism as a science cannot arise spontaneously from within the ranks of the workers but must be brought in from the outside. It is no wonder that his views have incurred the wrath of praxis anarchism.

Goldmann refers angrily to the "positivist and objectivising conception of society" which is, he claims, implied in Lenin's famous sentiments, and he proclaims instead that the "idea of the partial identity of subject and object"—the key contribution of Lukacs—is merely the philosophical expression of "the call for a spontaneously revolutionary social force inside society".[32] This of course is correct. If a determinist view of man in the world is cast aside, then it must be assumed instead that the proletariat can somehow or other mystically generate revolutionary activity as the product of its own "nature", for how else is this "spontaneous tendency of the proletariat towards an authentic, non-integrated consciousness" to be explained?

This link between idealist philosophy and political anarchism is even more clearly portrayed in a recent interview with Sartre on the subject of "Masses, Spontaneity and Party" and a New Left group in Italy. The "mass" by itself, Sartre concedes, does not possess innate spontaneity, so that there is a role to be played by a revolutionary Party. But what kind of role? A role in which a coherent strategy must be worked out by a Party directing its struggles towards *political* ends, so that specific demands are tied to the ultimate goal of transforming capitalism altogether?

Sartre has unfortunately lost none of his anarchist fear that organisation *by its very nature* tends towards ossification and bureaucratisation, regardless of what it is trying to do or how it is trying to do it. Without a Party, says Sartre, the working class is "serialised", by which he seems to mean: it lacks the solidarity of class consciousness. The Party's task, then, is to liberate the working class from this "seriality", so that, in a particular strike or struggle, it manifests itself as a *fused* group, a situation which Sartre defines as one in which individuals establish "relations of reciprocity" and enjoy a "wild freedom"—"a definite consciousness of their class position".[33]

[31] *Communist Manifesto*, op. cit., pp. 61–62.
[32] Goldmann, op. cit., p. 70.
[33] "Masses, Spontaneity, Party", *Socialist Register*, 1970, p. 234.

How then does the Party stand in relation to the "fused group" which it is supposed to bring about?

It is here our problems begin. According to Sartre, every Party (by its nature) has an inherently institutionalised structure, which means that it inevitably places its own theories and perspectives between itself and the real world. Now of course it is always *possible* that a Party will indeed hold on to a particular perspective or programme even when the material conditions for which they were once appropriate have altered; but to claim that this tendency to dogmatism is absolutely *inevitable* is simply absurd, particularly as Sartre considers that it is precisely a Party's insistence upon a *scientific* outlook which distances it from objective reality. As before, Sartre's answer to one dogma is to replace it with another. The Party is now caricatured as "a closed static system" which is "always behind in relation to the fused mass, even when it tries to guide that mass".[34] An example? The May events of 1968 in France in which, says Sartre, the fused groups of students represented "a *truer* kind of thought" because here there was no institution interposed between experience and the reflection upon this experience.

Now this analysis is in fact, for all its rhetorical flourishes, inane in the extreme. What sense does it make to picture the "fused groups" as representing mercurial flashes of lightning militancy, spontaneously defying all institutionalisation? Were the students in France during the fierce battles with the riot police in 1968 "uninstitutionalised"? Sartre seems to childishly accept the appearances as the reality. Surely a little serious thought reveals that even the most militant anarchist outburst follows in *reality* some specific social pattern which displays its own regularities, rules and constraints. Even the most absolute spontaneity is only possible as a form of *organised* behaviour, opposing one set of institutional forms with another. It is of course true that there are important differences between a Marxist political Party and a "fused group". The Communist Party is conscious of where it is going, of what it is trying to achieve and of how a particular tactic fits into its general strategy. The "fused group", on the other hand, blunders blindly, and at times even dangerously, but its anarchic appearances should not be allowed to conceal the underlying institutional links which exist, of necessity, in order to give it reality as a social phenomenon. Sartre seems to imagine that only political parties "reflect" upon experience, but even the fused group needs to reflect

[34] Ibid.

upon its goals and direction, if only to enable it to go round in circles!

We meet once again, that is to say, the same shallow formalism which we find in praxis theory when we consider its extravagant claims to have abolished philosophy, universals, schemas, world outlooks and the like. The students who fling themselves against the police may *imagine* that they are enjoying a "wild freedom"; but anyone who takes the trouble to investigate the material realities of their social existence will be able to readily see the connection between a "wild freedom" and the *institutionalised* atomism of a college life which nourishes and nurtures these anarchist illusions. The real question, then, is not whether the Party "lags behind" the fused group, but rather the question of which of *two* institutions best meets the interests of the working people and enables them to fight to protect and extend their political and economic rights. And this question cannot be answered by abstract formulas and banal formalism, but only by investigating a world which praxis prefers to despise—the world of concrete reality.

Sartre offers no serious examination of the objective circumstances surrounding the French struggles of 1968, but why should he bother? The loyalty of the armed forces, the unity of the left, its popular standing in the country at large, the democratic quality of the existing constitutional channels for change—what do these "empirical" factors matter in comparison with the "relations of reciprocity" which exist in the "wild freedom" of the fused group? A brilliant opportunity to "storm heaven" has been lost and the French Communist Party (the PCF), predictably described as "a brake on any revolutionary movement in France",[35] is of course to blame.[36]

Sartre's almost textbook ultra-leftism graphically manifests the disastrous practical consequences to which praxis ideology can lead, for unfortunately it is by no means impossible for Communist parties or parties purporting to be communist, to be infected by the very infantile leftism which Sartre ascribes to the "fused group". The result: hazardous adventures likely to end in catastrophic failure. Engels himself warned the parties of the Second International that adventurism and voluntarism—and what else is praxis thinking?—could "ruin even the strongest party with millions in its ranks, to the well merited applause of the whole hostile world".[37] And there is little doubt that a

[35] Ibid., p. 240.
[36] For an extremely valuable account of the May events, see Jack Woddis' *New Theories of Revolution* (Lawrence and Wishart, 1972), pp. 346–376.
[37] Marx-Engels-Lenin, *Anarchism and Anarcho-Syndicalism*, op. cit., p. 19.

suicidal attempt by the PCF in 1968 to overthrow the state would have suited very well those of the mass media (and the interests they represent), who saw fit to demagogically caricature the French party as the saviour of De Gaulle. But Sartre of course knows only his blinkered world of "principles". Recently he went on record as stating that "true action", if it is to be authentically revolutionary, must be neither legal nor constitutional. It must have nothing to do with the electoral system. It can, it seems, only be authentically praxical if it is guaranteed to fail.

"Only from below and never from above" is, as Lenin frequently stressed, simply an anarchist dogma which metaphysically separates democracy and centralism, liberty and authority, freedom and discipline. Naturally it is not always easy for a party to forge the correct dialectical unity of these "opposites": a party may err on the side of "leftism" or it may infringe democratic norms. But the question is a complex one: it requires a careful examination of the concrete circumstances prevailing at any given time and cannot simply be solved by glib chatter about the Party as a "closed static system" *vis-à-vis* the so-called "fused group". The argument that every seriously organised Marxist party must, of necessity, be a "brake" on the revolutionary movement is a recipe for cynicism and impotence, and further underlines the remoteness of theoretical "praxis" from the real world.

Indeed, the critical weaknesses of praxis arguments on the subject of the Party stem from its radical inability to understand the nature of authority in general. In particular, it is important to devote some attention to examining the question of

(iv) Praxis and the Nature of the State

The key to understanding Marx's theory of the State is the concept of the *dictatorship of the proletariat*, the concept which emphasises the great divide between Marxism and anarchism, scientific politics and mere utopia. Curiously enough, the praxis writers, interpreters of the "true Marx", steer well clear of Marx's writings on this subject, with the exception of Sartre who bluntly rejects the dictatorship of proletariat and Avineri who contents himself with the observation that it was not actually Marx who referred to the Paris Commune as a dictatorship of the proletariat, but Engels.

The importance of this pivotal political concept to his theory was made clear by Marx in 1852 when he stated in a letter to Weydemeyer that while the existence of classes was known to historians centuries before,

> what I did that was new was to prove: (1) that the *existence of classes* is only bound up with *particular historical phases in the development of production*, (2) that the class struggle necessarily leads to the *dictatorship of the proletariat*, (3) that this dictatorship itself only constitutes the transition of the *abolition of all classes* and to a *classless society*.[38]

The class struggle, in other words, is not simply an economic struggle between the propertied and propertyless, it is a *political* struggle directed at the State. Indeed, it is precisely because the struggle for socialism is a real historical struggle and not some kind of imaginary "leap" into utopia, that the question of politics comes to the fore. "Political power", declares Marx in the *Poverty of Philosophy*, "is precisely the official expression of class antagonism in bourgeois society",[39] for politics is of course the embodiment of class struggle.

This means, then, that not only must the working class fight politically, but in order to preserve their gains they must also *rule* politically, the first task of the revolution being, as the *Manifesto* says, to raise "the proletariat to the position of the ruling class, to win the battle for democracy".[40] This profoundly significant comment not only tells us something important about the nature of politics: it also tells us something important about the nature of democracy. That democracy is not some sort of misty abstraction in which "everybody rules", for then, of course, nobody rules. It is class rule, and in the *Manifesto* Marx and Engels see the need clearly for the proletariat as ruling class to centralise all the instruments of production in its hands—a process which cannot be effected "except by means of *despotic* inroads on the rights of property" (stress mine).

There are, then, as Lenin stresses in his *State and Revolution*, two processes at work. The first is to conquer political power, and this can only be done by breaking the grip of the old ruling classes and destroying their State or, more concretely, the bureaucratic-military machine, the heart of the repressive State system. The second, to *consolidate* political power, and that is only possible if in place of the capitalist State, there is a socialist one. In other words, Marx's position on the State differs sharply from both the social democratic view and the anarchist view. The social democrat naïvely imagines that the State is "neutral" and "above classes" and can simply be taken over by the

[38] *Selected Correspondence*, op. cit., p. 86.
[39] Op. cit., p. 147.
[40] *Communist Manifesto*, op. cit., p. 74.

workers, while the anarchist, although he speaks loudly about abolishing the bourgeois State, cannot see the need to put anything in its place. Both tendencies, from their "identically opposite" positions, reject the dictatorship of the proletariat and both embrace an abstract and petty-bourgeois conception of democracy, which is, when all is said and done, merely the "left" face of the capitalist class. The social democrat fails to see that, under socialism, the State must be drastically changed; the anarchist, on the other hand, is unable to understand that its ultimate disappearance can only take place with the disappearance of classes. The State, even the socialist State, cannot be conjured out of existence simply because the praxical revolutionary has an "ethical distaste" for dictatorship or coercion. It must, in the famous phrase, *wither* away.

The praxis writers however accept none of this. Just as they reject the necessity for an epoch of *transition* which runs from capitalism to communism, so too will they have nothing to do with the political form of this transition, what Marx, in the *Critique of the Gotha Programme*, calls "the revolutionary dictatorship of the proletariat".[41] Petrovic, for example, believes that it is possible to adopt any definition of politics one likes, and the definition which he "chooses" (in the supermarket of subjectivism anything goes) is that politics embraces

> every activity of administering social life, whether this is done through the State or through a stateless form,[42]

and this of course is liberalism pure and simple. What has happened to the real State—the State which is and always has been the institutionalised expression of *irreconcilable* class struggle?—why, the disagreeable reality has been glibly supplanted by an anaemic abstraction which means all things to all men! The fact that the State necessarily involves a *dictatorship* of one section of the people over another, the use of violence, coercion, police, prisons, army and navy, either for progressive or for reactionary ends, does not, as far as Petrovic is concerned, set the State apart from all other activities of "administering social life". The inference is clear. Whereas Marxists wish to relegate the State to the museum of class history *as soon as this is historically possible*, for as long as this barbarous relic remains, "human history" proper has yet to begin, Petrovic, on the other hand, seems perfectly content to see this cruel institution stay. His dreams of abstract

[41] Op. cit., p. 26.
[42] Petrovic, op. cit., p. 165.

"freedom" and "self-creativity" are not only utopian, they are fundamentally *uncritical* of the real world.

Like every liberal, Petrovic abstracts the *content* from politics. Political acts, he states piously, should not be "prescribed by philosophy or by a philosophical forum. These should come about by a democratic, free decision of all those interested";[43] but this is merely naïve. For in politics, as in philosophy as we have already seen, nature abhors a vacuum, and politics "without philosophy" is like trade unions "without politics": it is of necessity the politics of the capitalist *status quo*. No wonder Marx grew angry with the whimpering preachers of "Brotherly Love" and "Abstract Democracy", while Engels in his Preface to the English edition of *The Condition of the Working Class in England*, referred bitterly to

> people who from the "impartiality" of their superior standpoint, preach to the workers a Socialism soaring high above their class interests and class struggles and tending to reconcile in a higher humanity the interests of both the contending classes. . . .[44]

Such people are, he said in disgust,

> either neophytes, who have still to learn a great deal, or they are the worst enemies of the workers—wolves in sheep's clothing.

For what are the practical consequences of abstract ideals which are simply, when all is said and done, bourgeois concepts turned inside out?

Engels noted that while Bakunin's faction wore the *mask* of autonomy, anarchy and anti-authoritarianism, its reality was somewhat different. In the name of abstract freedom, Bakunin practises, said Engels, "absolute authoritarianism",

> treating the working masses as a flock of sheep blindly following a few initiated leaders.[45]

A betrayal of anarchist principles? In theory, yes, but in practice, a "betrayal" which is as predictable as the setting of the sun. For subjectivist politics—the belief that the will can mould conditions as it sees fit—is necessarily the politics of an élite, for why should the Talented Individual respect the views of his followers when all creativity springs from the genius of the mind? After all, are not the

[43] Ibid., p. 166.

[44] *Condition of the Working Class in England* (Lawrence and Wishart, 1962), p. 23.

[45] *Anarchism and Anarcho-Syndicalism*, op. cit., p. 78.

masses themselves simply part and parcel of that external world which "creative praxis" can make and unmake in its own utopian image?

A democracy *without* materialism is a democracy without progressive content; it is democracy in which the appearances are preserved while the reality erodes, in which one civil liberty after another is attacked (is this not the situation in Britain today?), leaving only the façade behind. Abstractions in politics, their pious proclamations notwithstanding, are extremely dangerous, for in the concrete world these abstractions vanish like snow in the sun. A serious crisis, and a democracy of forms can easily somersault into "absolute authoritarianism". It has happened before!

In short, the praxis writers in embracing subjectivism and irrationalism are playing with fire. At best, their "libertarian" abstractions mislead and confuse; at worst, they can turn into the grim reality of the politics of "genius", of a mindless *avant garde*, of "praxical" leaders who embark upon monstrous adventures to refashion the world afresh in the name of some surrealist or mystical idea.

Petrovic may consider it "a formal compliment" when Heidigger, philosopher royal of the Third Reich, states that the Marxist conception of history is superior to all other conceptions, but who was Heidigger's "Marx"? A nihilist subjectivist in his own irrationalist image! Schmidt likewise seems gratified by Heidigger's "support". He quotes Heidigger's so-called defence of Marxism as

a metaphysical determination according to which everything existent appears as the material of labour,[46]

but this subjectivist caricature has no more in common with scientific socialism than . . . the doctrine of praxis! Let it suffice to point out that irrationalist theories about man and even "freedom" can have, and indeed *have had*,[47] practical consequences of a most pernicious kind. There is nothing particularly progressive or humanitarian about libertarian abstractions in our time: they act simply as a smokescreen behind which those who deny the class struggle in theory can practice

[46] Schmidt, op. cit., pp. 227–228.
[47] Anyone who finds *avant garde* mysticism appealing ought to acquaint themselves with some of the doctrines of Italian fascism. Here is Giana of *Mistica Fascista*: "we are mystics because we are mad and absurd. Yes, absurd, because history itself is an absurdity, that is mystical, the absurdity of the spirit and the will which bends and conquers the merely material". Is there not in this ugly diatribe against reason an uncomfortable "praxis" ring?

it with a reactionary vengeance in that real world which praxis idealism blithely imagines it can conjure out of existence.

The problem is that good intentions on their own are not enough, and abstract formulas may have consequences which appal their creators. Luther never intended the German peasants to use his theological protest against the "earthly" institutions of feudalism, any more than the puritans envisaged that St. Paul's dictum, "he who does not work, neither shall he eat", would become the basis of socialist morality. The praxis writers *see themselves* as the champions of humanity, but where does their abstract theory lead them?

Consider Kenneth Megill's search for a "democratic Marxism". For what does Megill mean by "democracy"? Something concrete ... a dictatorship of the proletariat and its allies? A government of the working people against the monopolies? No, unfortunately, by democracy Megill means something *abstract*, apparently above classes. "Democracy today, as always," he says, "means a rule by the people,"[48] and his chapter on the subject is prefaced with a motto from Aristotle which refers to

a constitution in which the free-born and poor control the government.

The quotation from Aristotle graphically illuminates the weaknesses of his praxical "democracy". For Aristotle, of course, meant precisely what he said: democracy is the rule by the *free-born* because it is a dictatorship *over* the slaves. The benevolent abstraction conceals the real content. This is even more true with bourgeois democracy in which even the slaves are "free" and have "rights": the apparent universality masks the exploitation of one class by another.

It is for this reason that Lenin severely castigated "philistine phrasemongering about liberty and equality in general", because, despite its intentions, these abstract concepts do not take us *one iota* beyond the order of capitalism. They are the mystified reflections of a mystified world.

Indeed, not only does Megill's abstract democracy amount to a defence of capitalism in practice, but it also leads him into an attack on the existing socialist societies which naturally, as real societies with real problems, far fall short of the praxis democratic ideal. Megill's anarchist "democracy" can see no distinction between "the political order established by the United States and the Soviet Union": both fall short of the abstract "rule by the people" and both must go! A "new democratic coalition"

[48] Megill, *The New Democratic Theory*, op. cit., p. 65.

must be forged out of forces which are a part of the effective reality of the twentieth century,[49]

a "third road" found which "transcends" the existing class struggles between the imperialist world and the socialist countries.

The socialist countries are, it goes without saying, not utopias, nor are they above criticism: one can always admire and respect without actually having to worship. But there is criticism and criticism, and merely to observe, as Megill does, that in the East European countries there are restrictions on the right to "conduct research freely, to organise freely and to publish freely"[50] is not necessarily helpful or constructive. The real question is not whether freedoms are restricted (for they are restricted in all class societies which are dictatorships of one sort or another), but whether, given the specific stage of development a socialist society is at, these restrictions are politically justified. And this is a concrete question which cannot be solved by vague appeals to democracy in the abstract. In the *British Road to Socialism*, which is the Communist Party's programme for a Socialist Britain, the *maximum* freedom is urged in order to develop a socialist democracy, but this freedom is in no way abstract or unqualified. The Party's section dealing with civil liberties, for example, states that centuries-old civil liberties would be consolidated and extended to include

> freedom to think, work, travel, speak, dissent, act and believe, *subject only to those limitations required in any ordered and just society to protect citizens from interference and exploitation by others, and to safeguard the state*[51] (stress mine).

How "restrictive" these limitations are is a concrete question, to be decided in the light of given circumstances. Of course, a socialist society may be mistaken either because its restrictions are too severe for the circumstances or indeed too lax; but to criticise it (along it seems with every other existing society) for having these restrictions at all is simply childishly utopian. And it may in fact be worse. For we cannot ignore the fact that just as under capitalism there are forces working for progress, so under socialism, and of course in existing socialist societies, there are forces of reaction, and it is precisely in this area that the abstractions of praxis become dangerously ambiguous. Sartre, for example, speaks of praxis as the force which negates the objective situation in which one finds oneself and which is thereby liberating. In a People's Democracy, he adds,

[49] Ibid., p. 66.   [50] Ibid., p. 92.
[51] *Programme of the CPGB* (October 1968, 3rd rev. edn.), p. 54.

this may be, for instance, by working a double shift or becoming an "activist" or by secretly resisting the raising of work quotas. In a capitalist society it may be by joining a union, by voting to go on strike etc.[52]

Like "democracy", praxis remains abstract and vague: it embraces all, from the struggle against capitalism (or at least its authoritarian "symptoms") to outright sabotage in a socialist factory. In fact, *what* may we ask is *not*, in the last analysis, praxis, particularly if its participants believe that it is a revolutionary act-in-itself simply to negate an objective situation?

For all its leftist phraseology, the theory of praxis is surprisingly uncritical. Its philosophy is positivist, its politics are anarchist, and its economics, as I shall now argue, are characteristically naïve and superficial in their relation to the capitalist system.

(v) *Praxis and "Workers' Control"*

According to Megill, "the primary democratic demand" is "that the worker has control over his working situation. Until this demand can be met, there is still revolutionary potential in the working class."[53] Neither individualism nor collectivism suits the theory of praxis: only a "workers' democracy" will do.

Now the demand for workers' control is both a legitimate and important demand, and no socialist society will succeed in its policies unless machinery exists for close co-operation between the workers, managers, planners and politicians. Unfortunately some of the praxis writers do not content themselves simply with a demand for consultation and co-operation: they postulate workers' control *in opposition* to Party leadership, to the need for a plan, and indeed, to the entire apparatus of the workers' State.

In other words, praxis rests its arguments not on the concrete problems of ending the anarchy of the market and the introduction of planned production, but upon purely doctrinaire and abstract assumptions of the "spontaneity" and "self-government" of praxical man who must, if he is free, be able to do as he likes. Indeed, praxis theory seems unaware of the importance of economic planning at all.

It is obvious to anyone who has troubled himself to look at capitalism *concretely* that the system's chronic tendency to unevenness of development, inflation, unemployment and crisis cannot be ended until production is co-ordinated in the light of a central plan, so that State-

---

[52] *Search for a Method*, op. cit., p. 93.
[53] Megill, op. cit., p. 73.

regulated or owned factories and farms can develop *harmoniously*. The market, "left to itself", has long ceased to serve the cause of social progress, and indeed, even under capitalism, we find State intervention increasing in order to try to impose a measure of order upon anarchy in the long-term interests of the monopolies themselves. State control over wages, the rationalisation of sectors of the economy where capital is unproductively tied up, incentives to invest in economically backward areas, these are simply a few of the ways in which contemporary State monopoly capitalism tries to "plan" the economy in the interest of profits. In other words, if even capitalist society is forced to increasingly make "gestures" in the direction of planning, it is utopian to imagine that under socialism the worker can "spontaneously" control the means of production. At the very time when capitalist economists have come to increasingly realise that unfettered "spontaneity" and "self-interest" brings only chaos and dislocation, the praxis writers philosophically glorify the "independent" and "self-determining" activities of what are, in the last analysis, simply abstract individuals in the capitalist market place! No wonder the menacing spectre of the "bureaucracy" eternally threatens, for the "invisible hand" doctrine, in which the praxis champions of autonomy still appear to believe, offers only an ironic parody of the real workings of the State monopoly capitalist economy. In this sense, the praxis yearning for a "self-determining freedom" tragically reflects a freely competitive capitalism which exists today, if at all, only in the market place of abstract ideas. For this is the curiously reactionary and romantic nature of syndicalism and anarchism: the pathetic attempt to build a socialist economy according to the principles of capitalist thought.

For it is not difficult to see where the attacks on determinism and materialism lead: a rejection of *planning* with its co-ordinating criteria in the light of which production must be determined, and a rejection of those objective constraints, those economic laws, which of course it is the task of the planners to control. Since praxical anarchism shuns all universals, it is unable to see the economy *as a whole* with its balance of heavy to light industry, producer to consumer goods, agriculture to industry, commodity production[54] to State production, and the distribution of industry throughout the regions. Instead, all it sees are

---

[54] Commodity production of course is simply the production of goods for a market. It is possible within slave society, feudal society and indeed under socialism. It is only under *capitalism*, however, that commodity production *predominates* and where the worker himself becomes a commodity.

individual factories and particular co-operatives, which must, it insists, "govern themselves".

Now of course, the process of planning is not something static or without direction. After all, planning under socialism is a preparation for planning under communism, and it is entirely correct that communist or workers' parties should increasingly *prepare* the masses of people for exercising greater and greater control over their economic life, as the decision-making for central planning can be more widely spread. But in economics as in politics, the unity of democracy and centralism is not a static, abstract *ideal*, it is a living reality which continually adjusts itself to the concrete circumstances at hand. It is no wonder that Lenin ridiculed the doctrinaire demands of the "workers' opposition" in the early years of the U.S.S.R. for some kind of "instant" industrial democracy in which, according to the time-honoured principle of "always from below, never from above", the All-Russia Congress of Producers was to elect a central body of delegates entrusted with the charge of running the national economy—and this, as Lenin pointed out, in a nation consisting mainly of peasants and small-scale commodity producers. Industrial democracy like political democracy is nonsensical in the abstract, and the reference by Engels to the need for "an association of producers" assumes for its context a classless communist society: a distant cry indeed from the then politically encircled and economically backward Soviet Republics!

The truth is that both a democratically centralised *Party* and a *State* which is the dictatorship of the proletariat are necessary because a transition from capitalism to communism is necessary: without the guidance of the Party and the machinery of the State, economic planning and therefore socialism itself remain utopian dreams. Lenin was extremely firm on this point. Syndicalism with its fetishistic formulas of "industry democracy" in the abstract,

> hands over to the mass of non-Party workers, who are compartmentalised in the industries, the management of their industries ("the chief administrations and central boards"), thereby making the Party superfluous, and failing to carry on a sustained campaign either in training the masses or in *actually* concentrating in *their* hands the management of *the whole national economy*.[55]

In other words, the need for "workers' control" must not be propagated as an abstract thing-in-itself, but as a specific demand

[55] *Anarchism and Anarcho-Syndicalism*, op. cit., p. 319.

which is progressive in circumstances which *strengthen* the power of the trade unions, the solidarity of the working class as a whole, and ultimately the building of socialism. In that sense, workers' control is a *formal* demand, which does not, on its own, automatically change the *character* of the economic system under which it operates. Indeed, we find Lenin in 1917 urging the introduction of workers' control *over* the capitalists,[56] in other words, as an important measure to strengthen the working class even *before* the introduction of socialist relations of production. Workers' control is therefore no substitute for socialism: it can be fought for (and to an extent realised) even under capitalism. Moreover, as an abstract demand, it is not automatically progressive in its consequences. It is progressive only if it strengthens and unites rather than divides and weakens the economic and political power of the working class *as a whole*. A workers' control which operates anarchically in opposition to economic planning could paradoxically play a part in strengthening capitalism, not socialism, if, for example, syndicalist-minded workers tried to consolidate a privileged position in the economy in opposition to less advantaged sectors, so that instead of harmonious development the gap between town and country, region and region, white-collar and manual could *widen* rather than narrow, and the anarchy of the market be given a fresh lease of life.

Indeed, this is even conceded by praxis writers themselves. Goldmann, who presents his reader with a picture of "self-management" by white-collar workers and technicians in which "the dialectic of spontaneity and hierarchy can now be reversed in favour of the former",[57] points out that under these circumstances the formation of what could be called a new bourgeoisie would be quite possible . . .

> the democracy of producers—which socialist thought equated with real economic democracy for society as a whole—could in its turn become the domination of a privileged group (that of all the producers taken together) over a more and more numerous section of society, which technological change and automation would have eliminated from the process of production.[58]

What a revealing glimpse into the utter bankruptcy of praxis thought! With the so-called "dialectic of spontaneity" in control, not only is unevenness liable to *intensify* rather than diminish, but not even full employment can be planned for. It appears that stripped of its

[56] *Collected Works*, vol. 26, p. 107.
[57] Goldmann, op. cit., p. 83.
[58] Ibid.

ideological mystique, the praxical "dialectic of spontaneity" is nothing more than a leftist version of the "invisible hand" which will, one hopes and prays, somehow or other miraculously harmonise the interests of the individual with those of society at large. No wonder the domination of a "privileged group" is a real possibility in the praxis utopia, for all the *essentials* of capitalism, unchecked commodity production, the profit motive, the private or syndicalist ownership of the means of production, still remain intact.

This point was specifically made in a recent discussion on the subject of workers' control by Bert Ramelson, the National Industrial Organiser of the Communist Party of Great Britain, when he warned that an *anarchist* conception of workers' control would exclude the real possibility of a planned economy and therefore seriously impede the advance to socialism. For if, argued Ramelson, workers' control is to mean the right of workers to determine *every* aspect of the process of production as well as marketing processes, pricing and so on,

> I do not see how it is possible for socialist planning to take place. The anarchy of the market is recreated, but instead of being determined by individuals who owned the particular plant under capitalism, it is by groups of individuals, the workers in that particular plant, who determine the whole process unrelated to what may be the needs of society as a whole.[59]

And it is not surprising that in Yugoslavia, in which praxis theories have been widely propagated and appear to have been influential, that "very serious economic problems and difficulties" have arisen, including among other things, a significant measure of unemployment, migrant labour and social demoralisation. And no wonder! For the "spontaneity" and "self-government in the abstract", which praxis theory so highly prizes, are simply ideological (and hence topsy-turvy) reflections of bourgeois society, and hence are unlikely to assist much in the building of socialism.

The link between praxis as a mystical philosophy and praxis as a programme of anarchism or anarcho-syndicalism is well indicated in a passage drawn from Lukacs' *History and Class Consciousness* where he declares that the workers' council must become "the organ of the State", and is "a sign that the class-consciousness of the proletariat is on the verge of overcoming the bourgeois outlook of its leaders": "the workers' council", he adds, "spells the political and economic defeat of reification", and during its struggle for control, its mission is two-fold:

---

[59] Discussion with Ernie Roberts, *Comment*, 30.6.1973, p. 201.

on the one hand, it must overcome the fragmentation of the proletariat in
time and space, and on the other, it has to bring economics and politics
together into the true synthesis of proletarian praxis. In this way it will help
to reconcile the dialectical conflict between immediate interests and ultimate
goal.[60]

This is archetypal Young Hegelian millenarianism! And it shows no
understanding of the real problems of building a socialist economy.
What can the bringing of economics and politics into the "true
synthesis of proletarian praxis" possibly mean, when only in the
metaphysical world of mechanistic abstractions have economics and
politics ever been apart? They are "synthesised" under capitalism, they
are "synthesised" under socialism, indeed, they are "synthesised" in
slave society: what, of course, is relevant is how and in whose *class
interests* this synthesis occurs. And to find this out requires rather more
than an arid formalism masquerading as a philosophically "profound
truth". The "synthesis" by itself will not get us very far.

Nor, for that matter, will workers' councils *by themselves*, as some
sort of magical all-in-all, help "to reconcile the dialectical conflict
between immediate interests and ultimate goal", if by this is meant to
plan a socialist economy. For it is a dangerous and sectarian blunder to
imagine that workers' councils, which represent all the workers at a
point of production, are a *substitute* for the leading role of a Communist
Party and its political allies which must tackle the problems of planning
the society *as a whole*. The real and complex problems of constructing
socialist forms of production in town and countryside on the basis of
the capitalist society of the past will assuredly not be solved by the cry
for "workers' control", and in fact, as Lukacs' own Hungary showed
so tragically in the counter-revolution of 1956, it is by no means
impossible for "workers' councils" to be demagogically used as an
attack on the institutions of socialism. A sobering thought.

The problem, then, with praxis theorists in this sphere as in others, is
that as far as they are concerned Marxism is not a science, it is a utopia:
it is not a reasoned outlook which guides the proletariat, its Party and
its allies in the construction of socialism, but a transcendental "leap"
into libertarian "perfection". Lenin devoted many long hours of
polemical struggle to fighting this abstract trend, and his comments
have not dated at all when he says that

the majority of these so-called socialists who have "read in books" about
socialism but who have never seriously thought over the matter, are unable

[60] *History and Class Consciousness*, op. cit., p. 80.

to consider that by "leap" the teachers of socialism meant turning points on a world historical scale, and that leaps of this kind extend over decades and even over longer periods.[61]

Why, he might well have had Gayo Petrovic or George Lukacs in mind!

To build socialism, Lenin says in *The Immediate Tasks of the Soviet Government*, it is essential to work with the real world in all its objective *particularity*.

It is not enough to be a revolutionary and an adherent of socialism or a Communist in general. You must be able at each particular moment to find the particular link in the chain which you must grasp with all your might in order to hold the whole chain and to prepare firmly for the transition to the next link;[62]

but how can this be possible if we reject, as the praxis theorists do, a belief in the independent objectivity of the external world, and are invited to surrender instead to the "illusion of the epoch"? Can we seriously set about looking for the "next link in the chain" if we fancifully assume that the laws of reality are of our own making? How can we hope to embark upon so dangerous and difficult a task as that of transforming capitalism into socialism, if we think that "ideas create the world" and that we have a "free will" which enables us to do as we please?

Both in this section on "workers' control", and in the chapter as a whole, I have tried to draw out some of the economic and political consequences which can flow from the praxis doctrine. These consequences are not, of course, necessarily intended nor foreseen by those who hold them; but it is worth making the point that sincerity is scarcely enough for those who stubbornly insist on taking the primrose path to the everlasting bonfire. We are not the first, says Cordelia in *King Lear*, who have with best intentions incurred the worst. Utopian dreams can only cultivate cynicism and despair, and there is perhaps more than one "well-meaning radical" who has ended his career in the ranks of the extreme Right.

For how can any protest movement hope for success if it arms itself with a doctrine which virtually ensures that it has lost the battle before it has begun? The praxis doctrine is a recipe for defeat and disaster, nor, as we have already seen, are its ideas in essence new. They are in fact merely reformulations of viewpoints which have long been dis-

[61] *Collected Works*, vol. 27, p. 273.   [62] Ibid., p. 274.

credited in socialist movements throughout the world, and they have been adopted by theorists and sects whose practical contribution to the construction of socialism has, at best, been problematic, and at worst, downright destructive.

And why should we be surprised? The very concept of praxis itself, this voluntarist, subjectivist and utopian theory of human activity, is merely an *uncritical* product of that very system of capitalism which all socialists wish to see radically replaced. Praxis thinking does not reflect capitalism as it is really is, but merely the illusions of "spontaneity" and "creativity" which this system has about itself.

Marx was familiar with praxis ideas. Although he later criticised them, as a young man he fell partially under their spell, as many Marxists do today at some time or another in their development, particularly when the *conservative* face of positivism is the one which currently predominates in our cultural life. "Leftism" is always tempting; but resist its temptations we must, for good intentions and heroic gestures notwithstanding, the simple truth is that the cause of socialism cannot possibly triumph unless Marxism is understood and applied *as a materialist science*.

To do this is never easy. "There is," Marx warned, "no royal road to science, and only those who do not dread the fatiguing climb of its steep paths have a chance of gaining its luminous summits."[63] There are no short-cuts, and no abstract dogmas *à la* praxis which can act as a substitute for these steep paths to the luminous summits. We must continuously examine the real world and continually return to it: heady abstractions, no matter how messianic or "impressive", simply will not do.

[65] *Capital*, I, op. cit., p. 21.

INDEX